H·O·C·K·E·Y
HALL OF
FAME

THE OFFICIAL HISTORY OF THE GAME AND ITS GREATEST STARS

H·O·C·K·E·Y
HALL OF
FAME

Dan Diamond / Joseph Romain

A Doubleday Book
Doubleday
New York Toronto London Sydney Auckland

Design, Typesetting & Assembly: First Image

Canadian Cataloguing in Publication Data

Diamond, Dan
 The Hockey Hall of Fame

ISBN 0-385-25188-2

1. Hockey Hall of Fame. 2. Hockey - Canada -
Biography. 3. Hockey - United States - Biography.
4. Hockey - Canada - History. 5.Hockey - United States -
History. I. Title.

GV848.5.AID52 1988 796.96'2'0922 C88-094116-2

Library of Congress Cataloging-in-Publication Data

Diamond, Dan.
 Hockey hall of fame: the official history of the game and its
greatest stars / Dan Diamond and Joseph Romain. — 1st. ed.
  p. cm.
 ISBN: 0-385-24830-X:
 1. Hockey — History. 2. National Hockey League. 3. Hockey
players — United States — Biography. 4. Hockey players — Canada
— Biography. I. Romain, Joseph. II. Title.
GV846.5.D53 1988
796.96'2'09—dc19
88-18760
CIP

Published in Canada by
Doubleday Canada Limited
105 Bond Street
Toronto, Ontario
M5B 1Y3

Published in the United States by
Doubleday, a division of Bantam Doubleday
Dell Publishing Group, Inc.
666 Fifth Avenue
New York, N.Y.
10103

"Doubleday" and the portrayal of an anchor with a colophon are
trademarks of Doubleday, a division of Bantam Doubleday Dell
Publishing Group, Inc.

Printed and bound in Canada by John Deyell Company

Contents

Message *from Scotty Morrison*, President
Hockey Hall of Fame and Museum

It is with great pleasure that I welcome you to this printed version of the Hockey Hall of Fame. This book, which is the Hall of Fame's official publication, features a complete history of the game along with profiles of its greatest stars from more than a century of competition.

As a young player growing up in Montreal, I was fortunate to play junior hockey with the Montreal Canadiens' chain. Bernie Geoffrion was a teammate and we played against teams led by Dickie Moore and Jean Beliveau. It was also a special thrill watching greats like Maurice Richard, Toe Blake, Elmer Lach and Butch Bouchard. All of these players made significant contributions to the history of the National Hockey League and, today, all are members of the Hockey Hall of Fame.

The Hockey Hall of Fame is more than bricks and mortar. It is a shrine which rewards the outstanding achievements of the very best builders, players, referees and linesmen. The members of the Hall share great skills, integrity and love for the game of hockey.

The Hockey Hall of Fame — and this book — tells the entire story of hockey, from the origins of the sport, through its growth, golden eras and modern times. Hockey fans from all over the world and of every age enjoy what they see in the Hall, from the Stanley Cup trophy, through our international hockey exhibits, video and film theatre and special display of goaltenders' masks. Much of the credit for this goes to Curator Lefty Reid who, for the past 20 years, has worked diligently to assemble the outstanding collection of artifacts.

From Wayne Gretzky and Mario Lemieux to Fred "Cyclone" Taylor and "Bullet" Joe Simpson, the current and the historic connect in the Hockey Hall of Fame. Enjoy!

SCOTTY MORRISON

Introduction

The documentary jumps abruptly to an unidentified setting. The ambient haze and echo suggest an arena out of season, perhaps a community hall. Three people are in the frame, one of them the prepossessing figure of Jean Beliveau. He wears a stylish suit and tie and is flanked not by hockey players or executives, as one might expect, but by two aging women, adoring pensioners with apricot-colored hair. They gaze up at him, *way* up, with the rapt attention of supplicants. He says something to one of them in French, then turns to the other and, in a rich fatherly voice, says in English, "It's the heart that counts."

One woman squints at him through bottle-thick glasses and whispers, "That's what they tell me every time."

It's the heart that counts.

Les Canadiens, is one of a group of films that plays regularly in the little open-concept theatre at the Hockey Hall of Fame in Toronto. In 45 minutes, the piece documents the past and present of the most successful franchise in the history of professional sport. As far as Beliveau's *bon mot* is concerned, it might be assumed that he was speaking in the context of his own remarkable career — or of the fabled exploits of the Montreal Canadiens, with whom he starred for 18 years. Or for hockey players or athletes at large. The location of the theatre notwithstanding, he might just as easily have been uttering the unofficial motto of the Hall of Fame itself. Skill alone has never been a sufficient standard for election to the Hall. Impressive talents flash across the hockey galaxy with regularity, and disappear. But the greats of the game — the Clancys, Morenzes, Conachers, Richards and Howes, the Sawchuks, Hulls and Clarkes — have always amplified their skills with a will and endurance abundantly implied by Beliveau's simple statement: It's the heart that counts . . . That's what they tell me every time.

One of the more pleasant rewards of strolling among the displays at the Hockey Hall of Fame is to see the game and its heroes so convincingly humanized by the collected artifacts: the faded jerseys, the battered skates, the sweat-stained gear. The players, more often than not perceived as tribal gods or matinee idols, are brought up close in a way we seldom see them from our distant seats in the arena or on the limited field of the television screen.

The past, too, is brought in close. Here is Aurel Joliat's blue peaked cap, faded and frayed along the brim. It is the cap he wore when he flanked the great Morenz during the 1920s and wore again on that festive night in 1985, when, at the age of 84, he joined other Canadiens stars of the past in a ceremonial skate before 19,000 fans at the Montreal Forum. The public appearance was Aurel's last before his death later that year. A placard near his cap declares that he suffered six shoulder separations, three broken ribs, and "routine injuries such as five nose fractures" on his way to immortality.

Nearby, King Clancy's Toronto Maple Leaf sweater, made of uncomfortable looking wool, is preserved from the early 1930s. The sweater is moth-eaten and faded, but not nearly as deteriorated as Lionel Conacher's 1934 all-star jersey. The latter, with its yellow and black cresting, is air-conditioned to the point that you could pass a fist through at least two of its unintended vents. Other sweaters, some as recent as the 1950s, are darned and patched — silent testimony to an era less affluent than the present.

Over here is a tiny pair of skates, surely no more than five inches long, worn by Wayne Gretzky as he practiced his infant skills on the Nith River near the family farm in Canning, Ontario. Above them hangs a baby photo of little Wayne in a white flannel nightshirt, his walnut-sized fists uncharacteristically clenched. The only other baby photo on display is one of King Clancy, taken in 1903, showing the infant defenceman in a white frock, his dark eyes already alive with the high spirits that would define his personality for decades to come. The all-too-quick passage from cradle to old age is realized with a turn of the head, as the eye comes to rest on a modern Maple Leaf jersey presented to Clancy on his 80th birthday in 1983.

Over here is a brutalized puck, the only one known to have remained in play for an entire NHL game (Los Angeles vs. Minnesota, November 10, 1979); and the stick with which Darryl Sittler achieved his record-setting 10-point night in 1976; and a remarkably slender-shafted stick once used by Bernie "Boom Boom" Geoffrion. An untaped stick wielded by Howie Morenz in his fateful last game in 1937 is displayed beside a life-sized photo mural of the Montreal Canadiens' dressing room, circa 1984.

Here are Bill Gadsby's boat-sized skates, with a crudely painted "4" on the heel. And a stick with a fiercely hooked blade used by the prince of the slap-shooters, Bobby Hull.

There must be half a ton of sterling in the Hall — cups, plaques, sculptures, trophies; from professional leagues, amateur leagues, defunct leagues; for gentlemanly play, enthusiastic play, heavy-hitting

defensive play; for scoring goals and for preventing them. Cups for the best and cups for the second best. Towards the west end of the Hall is the granddaddy of all North American sports trophies, the Stanley Cup — the *real* Stanley Cup as the sign says — bearing the names of well over a thousand players from Cup-winning teams. (The "k" in Peter Stemkowski's name was engraved backwards when the Leafs won the Cup in 1967, and a name from one of the recent Edmonton Oiler championship teams has been obliterated by a row of stamped X's.) The magnificently corpulent bases that have supported the Cup since 1948 make previous bases — the slim-jim version of the '30s and the knee-high '20s version, both often seen in photos — seem puny and inadequate by comparison.

Not far off stands the Avco Cup, late of the WHA, and above it is a display of WHA jerseys from cities such as Phoenix and Indianapolis, where big-league hockey reared its head for a moment during the 1970s then scuttled from sight.

What about oddball items, rummage, knick-knacks? Surely the most unusual artifact in the Hall is a gold-painted casting of Wayne Gretzky's feet, presented by Wayne to his father Walter when Wayne scored his record 50 goals in 39 games in 1981. Only the Mercurial wings are missing. Down the aisle is a square of cardboard on which 108 Coke bottle caps are mounted, each of them bearing a photographic likeness of an NHL player from the early 1960s. The faces, disembodied at chin-level, stare out from their metallic backgrounds, suggestive of Marley's ghost as it appeared on Scrooge's door knocker. Elsewhere is a puck carried into outer space by Canada's first astronaut, Marc Garneau.

Of course there are the Hall of Famers themselves, or at least their portraits — ennobling black and white drawings, some executed in almost photographic detail, others in slightly bolder shading and strokes.

Inasmuch as the Hall of Fame humanizes the players, it also romanticizes them, imbues their portraits and belongings with an almost sacramental glow. As well it might. After all, the images and objects are the symbols and trappings of greatness. But they are merely that: symbols and trappings, forever hinting at something beyond their physical existence. Certainly for the players whose portraits appear on the walls, the Hall of Fame is less a physical reality than a measure of recognition unanchored in time or place. For the fans, too, it is something more than a collection of artifacts or a pantheon of legendary players. It is a state of recollection that encompasses many places, many faces and times; a playoff or season, or the smaller memory of an autograph, a newspaper headline, a souvenir puck; a childhood visit to Madison Square Garden or the Montreal Forum or the Detroit Olympia. It is an ongoing fable peopled by players named Morenz, Richard, Conacher, Esposito and Orr. It exists partly in reality, partly in the notions and fantasies that our imaginations construct around the game and its heroes.

On a more functional level, it is a well-ordered history lesson. In fact, one of the recent additions to the Hall might well be called evolution corner — a series of displays chronicling the birth and development of the North American game. Hockey's beginnings and early years are represented by a display of sticks and skates that by today's standards are almost laughably frail. Some of the stick blades are barely bigger than pallet knives. The only pieces of gear that are heavier (by far) than today's equivalents are the sweaters, which of course were worn outdoors. They belonged to teams that only a centenarian could possible remember: the Ottawa Silver Seven, the Quebec Bulldogs, the Montreal Victorias.

The emergence of the NHL as the dominant North American league in 1926 raised the curtain on a new phase in the history of the sport — a phase that saw the NHL expand to ten teams and ride the radio waves to unimagined popularity. Some of the team names are pretty remote to the modern fan — the St. Louis Eagles, the Montreal Maroons, the Pittsburgh Pirates — but the names of the predominant players of the day have a decidedly familiar ring: Dit Clapper, Nels Stewart, Joe Primeau, Ace Bailey, and of course the unforgettables such as Morenz, Clancy, Conacher and Shore. It was an era that saw the rise of hockey's greatest ambassador, a round-faced, shrill-voiced broadcaster named Foster Hewitt, who not only popularized the early NHL, but simultaneously made a legendary figure of himself through his Saturday night broadcasts from Maple Leaf Gardens. Former NHL coach and manager Punch Imlach once said that Hewitt "did more for the game than any man alive."

The end of the war introduced the period nostalgically remembered as the Golden Age of hockey. By this time the NHL had been reduced to six teams — the "original six" as they are usually, but inaccurately, called. Thanks to the vastly increased media coverage in the 1950s and '60s, many of the 108 players who staffed the six teams became as recognizeable as movie stars. Records that had stood for years fell to Howe, Richard, Mahovlich, Geoffrion, Hull, Mikita — television heroes all.

It is difficult to believe that 21 years have passed since the six became twelve, ushering in the expansion era in 1967. Nine more teams have since been added, and already expansion has produced its share of great Stanley Cup champions:

the Flyers, the Islanders, the Oilers. In fact, of the five teams that have won the Cup since 1967, only two, the Canadiens and the Bruins, were around before expansion. Expansion has also produced a bright new galaxy of individual stars: Gretzky, Lemieux, Lafleur, Bossy, Perreault, Clarke, Stastny, Sittler, Dryden, not one of whom ever played a game in the old six-team league. Three post-expansion players — Ken Dryden, Bobby Clarke and Guy Lafleur — are already members of the Hall of Fame.

How does a player *get* to the Hall?

The simplest answer is that he is elected by the Player Selection Committee, an eleven-man group made up of former players, media veterans and hockey executives. The committee is currently headed by former Hockey Night In Canada broadcaster Danny Gallivan. Three players are elected yearly, each of whom must have been out of active hockey for a minimum of three years. As well, starting this year one veteran player who has been retired for more than 25 seasons can be selected. In addition, members can be elected in the Builder or Referee/Linesman categories.

In many ways, the decorum of the Hall belies the long, sacrificing struggle enacted by a player en route to his induction. Indeed, the technical process of election is the last and least of the ramparts that a Hall of Famer has to scale.

For most players the process begins many years earlier with the acquisition of a small pair of skates, perhaps delivered by Santa Claus, perhaps bought secondhand at the local skate exchange. From the first donning of the skates, the trail leads across frozen sidewalks or fields to an outdoor rink or pond — or down snow-packed roads to the local arena. Parents get involved, perhaps only as chauffeurs and onlookers, perhaps more actively, exhorting their youngsters from

the bleachers, or becoming mentors and coaches. It is verging on legend how Walter Gretzky would take young Wayne out on the backyard rink every evening of the winter and have him practice turns and stops and shooting drills.

"Peewees" grow into "Midgets" as discipline and training enter the picture, which can mean six- or seven-month schedules, daily practices and year-round conditioning programs.

For those with the talent and the willingness to take their chances beyond the amateur levels, there may be a place in professional hockey, perhaps even in the NHL. But of the million-odd youngsters playing hockey in a given year in Canada and the United States only a handful ever make it to the top. Among those who do, the competition to keep a big-league job is so fierce that the average NHL career is only two and a half years long.

Through superior talent and endurance — "heart" as Jean Beliveau described it — a few dozen players in any decade beat the odds and extend their careers to 10, 15 or sometimes even 20 years. Of the 1,230 players who have retired from the NHL since 1950, just 22 were active for more than 20 seasons (the remarkable Gordie Howe played 32 years in the big leagues, and is the only player in the history of the game whose career has touched five decades).

It is invariably true that for the most talented and spirited players the end of a career approaches too soon. The reflexes lose their edge, the body checks become more devastating, the bruises take longer to heal; goal production drops.

One day it is over, but for a very few of the best — less than half of one percent of the players who ever make it to the NHL — there is a permanent place, a measure of immortality, in the Hockey Hall of Fame.

—**Charles Wilkins**

First Formations

1880-1925

First Formations *(clockwise from top left)*
The Ottawa Senators won the Stanley Cup in 1922-23 and proclaimed this fact on their *sweaters* the following season. As NHL champions, the Senators claimed the *O'Brien Trophy*, first awarded in 1910 to the champion of the NHL's predecessor, the National Hockey Association. Art Ross, a member of the champion Kenora Thistles club of 1906-07, received this small *silver cup* from the citizens of the town. Before the days of the whistle, hockey referees used *handbells* to stop play. This example was owned by Hall of Fame goaltender Percy LeSueur, who also served as an on-ice official. The Toronto Blueshirts defeated Victoria 13-8 in a three-game total-goals series to win the Stanley Cup in 1914. The result was carved on this *puck*. The Toronto Wellingtons marked their 1900 Ontario Hockey Association Senior Championship by adding an engraved *silver shield* to the puck used in the final game. The Portage Lakers branded this *stick* when they proclaimed themselves champions of the world in 1904. Portage played in hockey's first pro circuit, the International League in northern Michigan, and, though they were never allowed to play for the Stanley Cup, boasted some of the top players in the game. These *skates* belonged to Cecil Blatchford, a forward who won four consecutive Stanley Cups with the Montreal Wanderers from 1906 to 1910. The *Stanley Cup* trophy began life as this simple bowl first awarded in 1893.

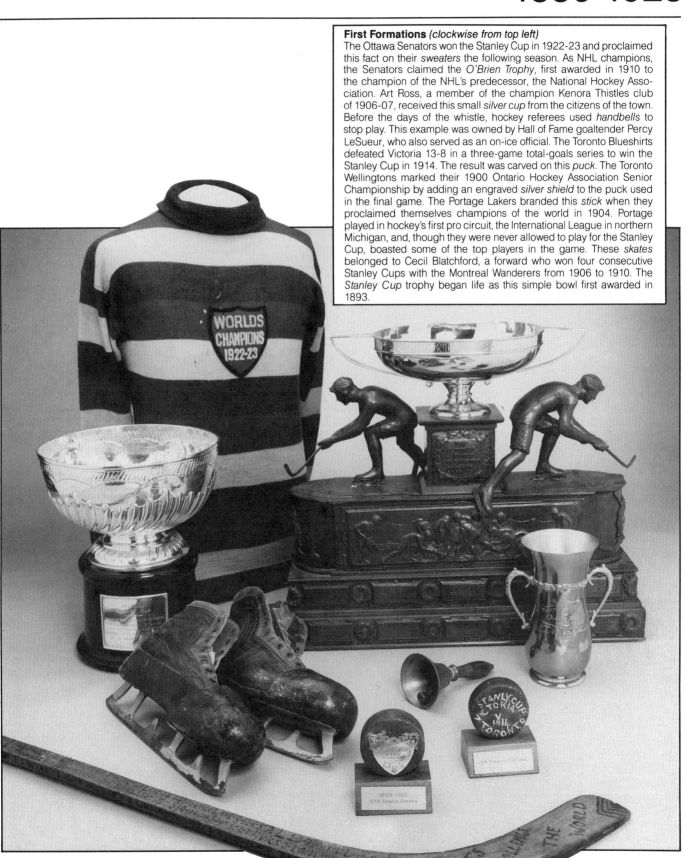

Students of the history of hockey have tracked its origins as far back as the imagination will allow. It has been argued that the image of two figures holding sticks in a "face off" position carved into early Egyptian or Mesopotamian pottery offers proof of a very early emergence of the game. Accepting this as anything more than evidence that stick and ball games are very old really stretches notions of proof and evidence.

The best available evidence suggests that ice hockey emerged out of various earlier games in Montreal in the middle 1870s, when a set of rules was applied to the notion of skating and moving a ball or puck about the ice surface in such a way as to score on an opponent. It became very much what it is today over the next ten years. Credit for the formulation of the original rules goes to J.G.H. Creighton, though recent evidence suggests that he did little more than organize an on-ice version of British field hockey.

Creighton hailed from Halifax, Nova Scotia, where in the second half of the nineteenth century soldiers and civilians spent leisure hours in huge games of shinny on the frozen waters. Homesick for this kind of entertainment, Creighton gathered together fellow students and worked up games of "ice lacrosse" at the local arena. After a period of trial and error, Creighton and his colleagues came up with a set of rules that proved entertaining and physically gratifying. How much like our game these rules were is a point of contention, but the direct line between the games played at the Victoria rink in 1875 and the current game is beyond dispute.

The earliest reported hockey game was played on March 3, 1875. According to the Montreal *Gazette*, Creighton captained one of the nine-man sides, while skating

CONTINUED ON PAGE 16

John James Adams was one of the most successful executives in the history of the NHL. He was an outstanding player before joining the Detroit organization in 1927 as manager-coach. Born June 14, 1895, in Fort William, Ontario, Adams played in the Northern Michigan Senior League at the age of 16. After amateur stints in Peterborough and Sarnia, Ontario, he turned pro in 1918, joining the Toronto Arenas, Stanley Cup winners in 1918.

Adams was 24 when he joined Vancouver and went on to win the scoring title in the Pacific Coast League with 24 goals and 18 assists in 24 games. He later played for the Toronto St. Pats and for Ottawa's Stanley Cup winners of 1927.

As coach and manager of the Red Wings, Adams sold hockey in Detroit. He was an innovator, developing the hockey farm system and building winning teams. His Detroit clubs won 12 regular season championships including a string of seven straight and seven Stanley Cups. Only seven times in 35 years under Adams did the Wings miss the playoffs. His greatest personal satisfaction came from the development of Gordie Howe, the top scorer in NHL history.

Following his departure from the Wings in 1962, Adams was named president of the Central Pro League. He died at his desk on May 1, 1968. Elected 1959.

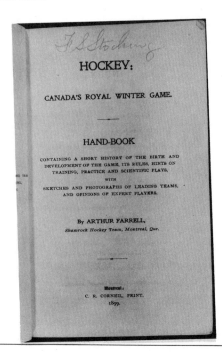

S̲ir Montagu Allan, Montreal sportsman and financier, donated the Allan Cup in 1908, for senior amateur competition in Canada. By then the Stanley Cup had changed from an amateur to a professional trophy, and William Northey of Montreal prevailed upon Sir Montagu to donate the trophy, which was valued between $300 and $500 at that time.

A board of Trustees governed all challenges for the trophy until 1928, when it was donated outright to the Canadian Amateur Hockey Association. Sir Montagu was born in 1860 in Montreal and died in September, 1951. Elected 1945.

D̲onald H. (Dan) Bain, an extraordinary sportsman, is often referred to as Manitoba's all-time greatest athlete.

Though born in Belleville, Ontario, in 1874, he moved with his family to Winnipeg at the age of six and spent the rest of his life there. Bain was a great leader on the ice, played center and captained the Winnipeg Victorias in four Stanley Cup challenge rounds. He never played professional hockey but was a member of two Stanley Cup champions with the Winnipeg Victorias of 1895-96 and 1900-01. They defeated the Montreal Victorias for their initial Cup triumph and the Montreal Shamrocks for their second.

Dan Bain's talents as an athlete enabled him to win championship honors in various sports over a span of more than 35 years. He won the Manitoba three-mile roller skating title first, and at 17 was the champion gymnast of Winnipeg. He was the one-mile bicycle racing champion for three years, from 1894 to 1896. By 1903, when he had retired from active hockey competition, he turned to rifle shooting and captured the Canadian trap-shooting title. There seemed to be no sport that Dan Bain could not master. Over ensuing years, right up to 1930, he continued to add to his laurels, winning championships in speed skating, roller skating, snowshoeing, lacrosse and golf.

Undoubtedly an outstanding athlete in any era, Dan Bain died at the age of 88 on August 15, 1962. Elected 1945.

◁ "Canada's Royal Winter Game" was the subtitle of the earliest known book on hockey. Published in Montreal in 1899, the author was Hall of Famer Arthur Farrell, a slick scoring forward for the Montreal Shamrocks.

The name of **Hobey Baker** is almost legend in United States college hockey history. He was born Hobart Amery Hare Baker — but everyone called him Hobey — in Wissahickon, Pennsylvania, in January, 1892. Somewhere, very early in life, Hobey learned the arts of effortless skating and stickhandling. He was a master craftsman with a stick; it was often said that once the puck touched his stick, he never had to look down again. He entered Princeton University in 1910, proficient not only in hockey but in football, golf, track, swimming and gymnastics.

In his senior year, he captained the football team and dropkicked a 43-yard field goal to tie a game with Yale. He also captained the hockey team in his final two years. A rover, he was a one-man team called "Baker and six other players."

After graduation in 1914, Hobey joined the St. Nicholas hockey team. After they won the Ross Cup from the Montreal Stars, a Montreal newspaper reported: "Uncle Sam had the cheek to develop a first-class hockey player . . . who wasn't born in Montreal." Baker joined the Lafayette Escadrille, a flying unit, during World War I and here, too, performed admirably. He survived the war but crashed while testing a new plane and was killed.

Princeton's ice arena today is named after Hobey Baker and St. Paul's School competes for a sacred trophy — Hobey's stick. Elected 1945.

This is the first known photo of a hockey team playing in an indoor rink. This Quebec City team won the province's intermediate championship in 1893, the year in which this photo was taken.

Clint Benedict spent 17 years ▷ in the NHL and is considered one of the great goaltenders of all time. Born in Ottawa on September 26, 1894, he played on four Stanley Cup-winning teams — three with the Ottawa Senators and one with the Montreal Maroons — as well as playing for Ottawa in the 1915 Cup final, which was won by Vancouver.

Benedict also helped remove a rule that prohibited goaltenders stopping play by falling on the puck. Benedict pointed out, "If you did it a bit sneaky and made it look accidental, you could fall on the puck without being penalized." Other netminders copied him and eventually it became part of the game.

In Stanley Cup play, Benedict had 16 shutouts and an average of 2.16 goals-against per game. He died November 12, 1976, in Ottawa. Elected 1965.

Both a rover and center, **Russel (Dubbie) Bowie** was an outstanding product of the seven-man era in hockey. Born in Montreal, on August 24, 1880, Bowie remained a rigid amateur throughout his playing days while rejecting several offers of professional contracts. This great stickhandler once turned down a grand piano offered to him by the Montreal Wanderers in return for his services on the ice.

Bowie, whose style was something like that of the great Nels Stewart, collected a total of 234 goals in 80 games over a ten-year period with the Montreal Victorias. A wizard with a stick, he played his entire career with this team from 1898 to 1908, when a broken collarbone brought his playing days to an end. A slim 112 pounds when he joined the Vics at age 17, he played on his first Stanley Cup championship team the same year. In the 1907 season, Bowie scored a total of 38 goals in ten games and is one of the few players ever to score ten goals in a single game. When Bowie retired from the game he had an average of nearly three goals per game.

Following his retirement he went on to become an outstanding referee. Russel Bowie died April 8, 1959, in Montreal, at the age of 79. Elected 1945.

◁ **O**ne of the immortal "Little Men of Iron," **Richard (Dickie) Boon** was born January 10, 1878, in Belleville, Ontario. Boon started his illustrious career with Montreal South in 1895 and played for the Montreal Monarch Hockey Club in 1897 before moving up to the AAA juniors. By the 1901-02 season, he was with the Montreal AAA's senior club, which successfully challenged the Winnipeg Victorias for the Stanley Cup in 1902.

The outstanding ability of this team won its players the collective nickname of the "Little Men of Iron" after their 2-1 victory. In 1903, Dickie became manager of the Montreal Wanderers, a post he held until the Westmount Arena was destroyed by fire in 1918. Boon finished his playing career with the Wanderers in 1905, then became their director and coach. During his time with the team they won three Stanley Cup challenges.

Boon lived in Outremont, Quebec, until his death on May 3, 1961 at the age of 83. Elected 1952.

champion Fred Torrance captained the other. The events of the day ended in a brawl (which included players and spectators) and the final game was canceled.

There is another story of how and when the game of hockey came into being. Some historians claim that the game played in 1875 was little more than shinny, and could not be called an organized sport. Instead, W.F. Robertson, "Chick" Murray and Dick Smith are credited with codifying the game.

The claim is that Robertson envisioned an ice game that would keep the McGill football team in shape during the off-season. He encountered Murray on campus, and the two of them were joined by Smith in their rooms, where they drafted the rules using rugby as the model. This momentous day was November 9, 1879.

There is very likely some truth here, but how do you accept the veracity of this claim while acknowledging the published accounts from three years earlier? Bill Fitsell, a leading authority on the early development of the game, puts it down to "creative thought expressed years after the fact," and thereby writes off the claim. But it is this author's position that the exact story will never be known.

Ice hockey became an event at the Montreal Winter Carnival in 1883. A challenge for the "world championship" of ice hockey was issued by the carnival committee, and teams from Toronto, Ottawa, Quebec and three from Montreal competed in the world's first ice hockey tournament.

In 1886, representatives of teams from Montreal, Toronto, Kingston, Quebec City and Ottawa gathered to clear up some ambiguities in the rules of play. They came up with what would become known as the "Montreal Rules," and also established a body to mediate disputed rules,

CONTINUED ON PAGE 20

The NHL record for scoring in consecutive games belongs to Harry L. (Punch) Broadbent, who scored one or more goals in 16 straight games during the 1921-22 season. Punch Broadbent was an excellent rightwinger, an artist with the puck and with his elbows. He once led the NHL in both scoring and penalty minutes.

Born in Ottawa in 1892, Broadbent played most of his career in that city. He played amateur with New Edinburgh and the Ottawa Cliffsides and was called up to play pro hockey at the age of 16, although used sparingly. He joined Ottawa of the National Hockey Association in 1912-13 and scored 21 goals. Two seasons later, he scored 24 goals but left to serve with the Canadian armed forces in World War I where he was awarded the Military Medal. In 1919, he rejoined Ottawa and stayed five seasons with their NHL club until sold to the Montreal Maroons in an attempt by the NHL to balance the league. In 1921-22, he led the league with 32 goals.

He came back to Ottawa for the 1927-28 season, then went to the New York Americans in 1928-29. He was on four Stanley Cup winners — three at Ottawa and one with the Maroons. He died March 6, 1971. Elected 1962.

The women of the late 1800s may have shed ▷ their inhibitions, but they didn't shed their long coats or bonnets when they lined up alongside the men for outdoor hockey. This game, circa 1885, was played on a frozen Saskatchewan slough. Note the tree branches being used for sticks.

George V. Brown was a hockey pioneer in the United States. In 1910, when the old Boston Arena was built, he organized the Boston Athletic Association hockey team to play in top amateur hockey competition in the Eastern U.S. When the first Boston Arena was destroyed by fire in 1918, he formed a corporation to construct a new arena, served as manager of the building and continued to operate the BAA team. When the Bruins moved into the new Boston Garden in 1928, he helped form the Canadian-American League and entered a team. This was the forerunner of the American Hockey League.

He became general manager of both the Arena and Boston Garden in 1934, positions he held at the time of his death in 1937. Elected 1961.

His name was **Harold Hugh Cameron** but almost everyone called him Harry. Over a 14-year span in three major hockey leagues, Cameron scored 171 goals in 312 games.

He was born February 6, 1890, in Pembroke, Ontario, and went on to play pro with the Toronto Blueshirts and the Montreal Wanderers of the National Hockey Association; Toronto, Ottawa and the Canadiens of the NHL; and Saskatoon of the Western Canada League. He is best remembered for his ability to curve his shots. Cameron is believed to be one of the first to do this without modifying his stick.

Harry Cameron played on three Stanley Cup champions based in Toronto. He was a member of the Torontos of 1914, the Arenas of 1918 and the St. Pats of 1922.

Harry Cameron died October 20, 1953, in Vancouver. Elected 1962.

Astrong silent Scot, **Frank Calder** proved a perfect choice as president when the National Hockey League was formed in 1917.

Through the hectic formative days of the NHL, through many rule changes and disputes, Calder sat at the head of the league, an unruffled, firm executive. Under his astute guidance the NHL reached the stature that it now enjoys. Calder was a keen follower of many sports, and his knowledge of athletics enabled him to adjudicate player and team grievances.

From 1936-37 until his death in 1943, Calder purchased a trophy each year that was given to the league's outstanding rookie. After his death, the league presented the Calder Memorial Trophy to be awarded in perpetuity. Elected 1945.

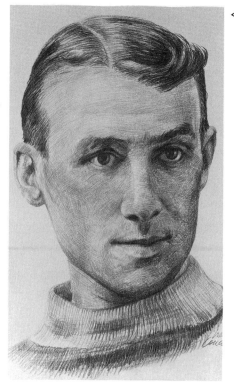

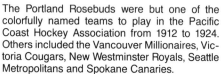

The Portland Rosebuds were but one of the colorfully named teams to play in the Pacific Coast Hockey Association from 1912 to 1924. Others included the Vancouver Millionaires, Victoria Cougars, New Westminster Royals, Seattle Metropolitans and Spokane Canaries.

Hockey's roots as a town game in northern climes is clearly illustrated in this photograph taken on a sunny day in Dawson City in the Yukon Territory in 1910. Note the absence of high boards or markings on the natural ice. Bare goal posts without any sort of netting are just visible at the far end of the ice.

◁While playing goal for the Montreal Nationals against Chicoutimi, **Joseph Cattarinich** could not help but notice the sensational play of the opposing netminder. He prevailed upon his manager to sign the Chicoutimi goalie — replacing himself. Cattarinich unselfishly gave up his position to someone he felt was better. That other goalie was Georges Vezina, who became a legend for the Canadiens.

Cattarinich went on to play an important role in the development of the National Hockey League. On November 3, 1921, Cattarinich, Leo Dandurand and Louis Letourneau purchased the Montreal Canadiens for $11,000. They built the club into the "Flying Frenchmen" with many of the era's great stars, including Newsy Lalonde, Howie Morenz, Joe Malone, Aurel Joliat and Vezina.

Under the partners' management the club enjoyed glorious years, winning the NHL title and the Stanley Cup on three occasions. Letourneau retired in 1931 but Cattarinich and Dandurand managed the Canadiens until 1935 when they sold the team for $165,000. Cattarinich would like to have retained the club but the economics of the time made it impossible. Joseph Cattarinich was born November 13, 1881, in Levis, Quebec. On December 7, 1938, while recovering from an eye operation, he suffered a heart attack and died. Elected 1977.

Sprague Cleghorn was one of the greatest but roughest defense players the game of hockey has ever known. Born in Montreal, in 1890, he played in either the National Hockey Association or the National Hockey League from 1911 to 1928.

He played with the New York Crescents in 1909-10 and moved to Renfrew of the NHA the following season. He went on to play six seasons with the Montreal Wanderers, a season split between Ottawa and Toronto, two full seasons with Ottawa, four with the Canadiens and three with Boston. He started out as a forward but was moved back to defense to play alongside Cyclone Taylor at Renfrew. He tried to emulate Taylor's great rushing style and for five years was the darling of the Wanderers' fans, once scoring five goals in one game. In 17 seasons — he missed 1918 because of a broken leg — Cleghorn scored 163 goals. He played on two Stanley Cup championship teams, the Ottawa club of 1920 and the Canadiens of 1924.

Cleghorn had not been a popular player in Ottawa and, in 1922, when he joined the Canadiens, he appeared to have a vendetta against his former teammates. Many brawls broke out between these two teams, climaxing in the 1923 playoffs when Cleghorn assaulted Lionel Hitchman with a vicious cross-check. He drew a match penalty and suspension from the final game along with a $200 fine levied by his own manager. He died in Montreal on July 11, 1956. Elected 1958.

Samuel Russell (Rusty) Crawford was born in Cardinal, Ontario, on November 7, 1884, and played hockey until he was 45 years of age. A fast-skating forward with a lefthanded shot, Crawford was capable of playing at center or either wing with equal dexterity.

His talent attracted the Quebec Bulldogs and he joined them for the 1912-13 season, helping them win the Stanley Cup.

Crawford remained with Quebec until 1918, when he went to Ottawa for four games before joining the Toronto Arenas. Toronto won the Stanley Cup that year, defeating Vancouver in a five-game series. Rusty stayed another season with Toronto, then went to Saskatoon in 1920. He played with Calgary 1922-25, joined Vancouver in 1926, and ended his career with Minneapolis in 1929. He died December 19, 1971. Elected 1962.

John Proctor (Jack) Darragh was another product of Ottawa, a city that produced many great hockey players in the early 1900s. He was born in Canada's capital city on December 4, 1890, and became a master mechanic of the game.

In 1911, he joined the Ottawa Senators, who immediately won a Stanley Cup. He went on to play for three more teams that won hockey's top prize, in 1920, 1921 and 1923. He also played on the Ottawa team that was defeated by Vancouver in the 1914-15 playoffs. One of Darragh's cleverest moves was an adroit backhand. He was also noted for clean play, slick stickhandling and an ability to turn on the speed when required.

Jack Darragh was also a fine scorer; he had 24 goals in the 22-game schedule of 1919-20 and 195 in his pro career. He died suddenly on June 25, 1924, in Ottawa. Elected 1962.

◁ The name of Leo Joseph Viateur Dandurand was synonymous with the promotion and development of major sports, not only in Quebec but across North America. Born July 9, 1889, in Bourbonnais, Illinois, he came to Canada in 1905.

He became associated with Joseph Cattarinich, and later with Louis Letourneau, in a partnership known as the "Three Musketeers of Sport." This trio bought the Montreal Canadiens on November 3, 1921, for $11,000 and built the club into the "Flying Frenchmen," featuring many of the top players of the day. Fourteen years later, the club was sold for $165,000. He died June 26, 1964. Elected 1963.

and to encourage development of the fledgling sport. They called themselves the Canadian Amateur Hockey League, and historians have traced a winding but unbroken line in the development of the game and its governing bodies from this organization to those of today.

The Montreal Rules called for seven-man hockey. One very brave soul would guard the pair of posts set in the ice that marked the goal; two half-backs or defensemen would play close to the goal; a rover would switch from defense to attack as the play shifted; and three forwards would play positions very similar to those of today.

Stickhandling was the order of the day, as no forward passing was allowed. Forward passes were ruled off-side. The principal occupation of the half-back was clearing the puck up into the rafters of the building and down the ice into the neutral zone, where the offensive men would regroup and begin the process of working the puck back into scoring position.

A match under the Montreal Rules consisted of two half-hour periods, with a ten-minute break in between. Once the first half had commenced, a player could not be replaced by a substitute unless he was injured during the play. In the second half, an injured player could either be replaced, or both teams would play short-handed, at the discretion of the opposing captain.

By the 1890s, there were numerous teams and leagues competing with varying degrees of serious intent. The most prestigious award was the Canadian Senior Amateur Trophy, a tall and attractive icon that can be found today at the Hockey Hall of Fame.

Serious competition for the Senior Amateur Trophy started in 1893. The two teams vying for the championship of the

Alan M. (Scotty) Davidson shot like a meteor from junior ranks and starred as a professional until his life was snuffed out while serving in Belgium during World War I. Davidson was born in Kingston, Ontario, in 1892. He was a strong, powerful skater, played very cleanly, possessed an overpowering shot and was a tremendous back-checker. Although he played only two years as a pro before the War, he was and still is considered one of the great rightwingers of all time.

He signed to play the 1912-13 season with Jack Marshall's Toronto team in the National Hockey Association, immediately starring at right wing. That team won the Stanley Cup in 1914. Davidson scored 19 goals in 20 games in his first season as a pro, and increased his output in the Cup-winning season. Elected 1950.

Thomas Dunderdale is the first Australian to achieve the honor of being elected to the Hockey Hall of Fame. He was born May 6, 1887, in Benella, Australia.

When the National Hockey Association formed in 1910, he joined the Shamrocks in Montreal, moving to Quebec to play for the Bulldogs in 1911. Lured to Victoria, British Columbia, in 1912, Dunderdale remained in the Pacific Coast Hockey Association through 1923 and wrapped up his playing career in 1924 with Saskatoon and Edmonton of the Western Canada Hockey League.

During his 12 seasons with the PCHL he scored more goals than any other player in the league. He scored in every one of Victoria's 15 games in 1914 and was named the league's all-star center. His career totals are 225 goals in 290 regular-season games, plus six goals in 12 playoff games. When he finished playing, Dunderdale coached and managed teams in Los Angeles, Edmonton and Winnipeg and resided in the latter city at the time of his death in 1960. Elected 1974.

◁ Although he was not a fast skater, **Cyril Joseph (Cy) Denneny's** accurate shot enabled him to rank among the greats of professional hockey. He was born December 23, 1891, in Farran's Point, Ontario, a village since covered by the St. Lawrence seaway system. In 1897, his family moved to Cornwall where Denneny played his early hockey.

In 1912, he played for Russell, Ontario, in the Lower Ottawa Valley League and a year later joined the O'Brien Mine team in the Cobalt Mining League. Denneny's pro career began in 1914, with the Toronto Shamrocks of the National Hockey Association, and he played there for two seasons before joining the Ottawa Senators in 1916. He stayed with the Senators through their transition into the NHL, leaving them in 1928 to become a player, coach and assistant manager of the Boston Bruins for one season. The Bruins won the Stanley Cup that year, making a total of five Cups for Denneny in his 14-year playing career. His best individual season was 1917-18, when he scored 36 goals in 22 games. During 11 NHL seasons, Cy scored a total of 246 goals.

Cy retired as a player after one year at Boston and became an NHL referee for a year. He coached junior and senior amateur teams in Ottawa during 1931-32, coached the Ottawa Senators in 1932-33 and retired for good when the team left the league after that season. He died in September, 1970. Elected 1959.

Long before hockey became a professional sport, one of the greatest stars of the game was **Charles Graham Drinkwater.** Although he never played professionally, Drinkwater played for four teams that won the Stanley Cup.

When the Cup was first presented in 1893, he was still at McGill University, gaining fame as a hockey and football standout. His first championship came in 1893, while he was a member of the Montreal AAA (Amateur Athletic Association) junior team. The following autumn, Drinkwater played on the McGill junior football championship team and in 1894 was a member of the McGill intermediate hockey team that also won a title. He left McGill to join the Montreal Victorias in 1895 and his winning ways followed him. The Victorias won the Stanley Cup, lost it to the Winnipeg Victorias in 1896, and then came back to claim three Cup triumphs. Drinkwater was team captain in the 1899 victory.

Drinkwater was born in Montreal on February 22, 1875. He died September 26, 1946, in Montreal. Elected 1950.

◁ In the beginning. Montreal's Victoria rink in 1893 featured hockey games played between seven-man teams on ice with dasher boards about one foot high. The goal posts are exactly that.

Amateur Hockey Association of Canada were the Montreal Amateur Athletic Association and the Ottawa Hockey Club. The AHA of Canada was at that time considered to be the country's premier league.

In the same year, Canada's Governor General, Lord Stanley of Preston, decided to present a trophy that would symbolize dominion hockey supremacy. P.D. Ross, a principal civil servant on Lord Stanley's staff, was convinced that the Ottawa club would win, and encouraged his boss to lend his patronage to the sport and be the sponsor of the new trophy. Lord Stanley agreed, and Ross set about having a suitable bowl manufactured. Much to the chagrin of Ross and his fellow Ottawans, the season finished with Montreal on top, and the Cup was awarded for the first time to the Montreal AAA after the close of the season.

From its inception in 1893 the Dominion Challenge Trophy, which eventually became known as the Stanley Cup, stood for absolute supremacy in the game. Unlike today's annual playoff system, each league produced its own champions, who would apply to the Trustees of the Dominion Challenge Trophy for an opportunity to challenge the incumbent Cup holder at any point during the season. Lord Stanley's intention was to foster competition between clubs from all parts of the country, and to raise the game above its regional encampments.

Phillip Ross and Sheriff John Sweetland of Ottawa were made trustees of the trophy, responsible for governing the challenges to the Cup. Stanley had made it clear that the trustees should have unquestioned authority. They would arbitrate all challenges, and they would appoint their successors. To date there have been only seven trustees of the Stanley Cup: Ross and Sweetland, William Foran, Mervyn Dutton, Cooper Smeaton,

Although small in stature — 5′,8″ 150 pounds — **Cecil Henry Dye** had a distinguished athletic career. Born May 13, 1898, in Hamilton, Ontario, he moved to Toronto before he was one year old. He became a star halfback with the Toronto Argonauts and was good enough at baseball to be offered $25,000 (a fabulous sum in those days) by Connie Mack of the Philadelphia Athletics.

He joined the Toronto St. Pats for the 1919-20 season, where he found it difficult to break the starting lineup but still scored 11 goals in 21 games. In the next six seasons, he led the league in scoring four times, twice scored in 11 consecutive games and twice scored five goals in a game. He went on to play for Chicago in the expanded NHL of 1926-27, but to all intents his career ended when he broke a leg in the 1927 training camp and missed the season.

Babe played for one Stanley Cup winner, the St. Pats of 1922, and scored nine goals in the five-game final against Vancouver. He died on January 2, 1962. Elected 1970.

Edwin S. (Chaucer) Elliott succumbed to cancer on March 13, 1913, at the age of 34. Although his life was brief, he was tremendously respected as an outstanding athlete and sportsman.

Born in Kingston, Ontario, he was a natural athlete with great achievements in many sports, including hockey, baseball and football.

Chaucer Elliott became a hockey referee in 1903 and for 10 years was regarded as one of the best in Canada. Wherever he went, Elliott made friends and held them with a magnetic personality. As a referee, he enjoyed the complete confidence of the players, and as a result was always in great demand. Elected 1961.

A forward throughout his short but productive career with the Montreal Shamrocks, **Arthur F. Farrell** played on two first-place teams in the Canadian Amateur Hockey League as well as on two Stanley Cup champions. Farrell was a stylish player and is considered to be one of the men responsible for changing hockey. Farrell's play shifted hockey from an individual's game to one that favored complete team effort.

He joined the Montreal Shamrocks in 1897 and played with the club through the 1901 playoffs. The Shamrocks captured the first of their two straight Stanley Cups in 1899, when they also finished in first place in the league.

On March 2, 1901, Farrell had the best game of his career as he scored five goals against the Quebec Bulldogs. The Shamrocks finished third that season and lost to the Winnipeg Victorias in the playoffs. Elected 1965.

Frank C. Foyston was born February 2, 1891, in the small village of Minesing, Ontario, about 60 miles north of Toronto.

In 1912, Frank became a professional with the Toronto Blueshirts of the National Hockey Association and played center for that team when it won the Stanley Cup in 1914. By 1915-16 he was on his way to the Seattle Metropolitans and a year later was part of the first American team to win the Stanley Cup. He stayed with Seattle for nine years, shifting to Victoria for two seasons, and was once again on a Stanley Cup winner with the Cougars in 1925. When Detroit purchased the team, Foyston went east and stayed in the Motor City for two seasons, retiring as a player in 1928.

During his 11 seasons in the PCHA and WCHL, Frank Foyston scored 186 goals. He added 17 in his first year in Detroit and seven in his final season. As well as playing for three Stanley Cup champions, he reached the finals three other times. He lived in Seattle, Washington, until his death on January 24, 1966. Elected 1958.

The exact site and date of the first hockey game is subject to debate, but it is clear that some of the earliest organized games were played near Kingston, Ontario, by members of Her Majesty's Royal Canadian Rifles regiment in the 1860s. This is one of the sticks used in these early matches.

Brian F. O'Neill and Judge Willard Estey.

Champions from a number of leagues competed for the Cup over the next few years. Teams from Sydney and Halifax, Nova Scotia, tried for the Cup, as did squads from central Canada, but only the Manitoba Senior Hockey League was able to send a winning challenger to the "world hockey court" in Montreal. In 1896, the Winnipeg Victorias, led by Dan Bain and George Merrit, took the prize silverware west after the first of two successful Winnipeg bids.

George Merrit of the Winnipeg club was the first goaltender to wear protective pads in a Stanley Cup game. He came to his post sporting white cricket pads, which rapidly became standard goalkeepers' attire.

The eastern rivals of the Winnipeg Vics were their namesakes from Montreal. The Montreal Victorias gave up the Cup to Winnipeg in 1896, and took it back the following season. When Montreal came to the West to reclaim the Cup, Winnipeggers paid upwards of 12 dollars a seat to watch their local heroes. In Montreal, telegraph operators were kept busy with what might have been the first play-by-play transmissions, and the streets were stormed by fans awaiting news of their successful challenge. Many players on the Montreal Victorias of those days are not well known names today, but along with Hall of Famers Mike Grant and Graham Drinkwater, the Vics dressed goalscorers Shirley Davidson, Robert McDougall and Ernie McLea.

The Manitoba League squad from Kenora, Ontario, took the Cup from eastern Canada. In 1907, an aggregation of regulars and "ringers" won the Cup from the Montreal Wanderers, and kept it at the Lake of the Woods for the season. Both these teams were packed with future

CONTINUED ON PAGE 28

Frank Fredrickson was born in Winnipeg in 1895 and established himself as an amateur standout before becoming a professional in 1920.

Fredrickson played his first senior hockey with the Winnipeg Falcons during the 1913-14 season. He took time out from hockey to serve in the Canadian forces in World War I, and in 1919, joined the Falcons and captained them to both an Allan Cup triumph and the 1920 Olympic crown at Antwerp.

Frank signed with Lester Patrick's Victoria Aristocrats (later renamed the Cougars) at Christmas of the same year. The Cougars defeated the Montreal Canadiens to win the 1925 Stanley Cup playoff but lost the next year's final to the Montreal Maroons. His career took him to Detroit for half a season, to Boston, and, in 1928-29, to Pittsburgh. He was coach, manager and center for Pittsburgh when a leg injury virtually ended his playing days. Fredrickson retired in 1931, after a short stint with Detroit. In the PCHA and WCHL, Frank scored 142 goals and led the league in 1920 and 1923. He died May 28, 1979, in Toronto. Elected 1958.

The true hockey potential of **Herbert Martin (Herb) Gardiner** will never be known. He didn't arrive in the NHL until he was 35 when he quickly established his credentials by winning the Hart Trophy as most valuable player.

Herb was born May 8, 1891, in Winnipeg, and began his hockey career in 1908 with the Winnipeg Victorias. In 1909 and 1910 he played for the Northern Crown Bank in the Bankers' League but was out of hockey until he joined the Calgary Tigers of the Western Canada Hockey League in 1918.

In 1924, his team unsuccessfully challenged the Montreal Canadiens for the Stanley Cup. Herb so impressed his opponents that he was asked to join the Canadiens for the 1926-27 season. He stayed with the Canadiens until, during the 1929 season, he was loaned to Chicago, where he acted as manager. Montreal recalled him for the playoffs but later sold him to Boston, which in turn, sold him to the Philadelphia Arrows of the Canadian-American League. He died January 11, 1972. Elected 1958.

James Henry (Jimmy) Gardner was born in Montreal on May 21, 1881. Gardner was to enjoy more than a decade as an outstanding player and was associated with two great teams, the Montreal Hockey Club's "Little Men of Iron" and the Montreal Wanderers. Those "Little Men of Iron" won the Stanley Cup in 1902 after a stubborn stand against Winnipeg. The Wanderers won in 1910.

A talented leftwinger, Gardner played for several different clubs. After one season with the Montreal HC and another with the Wanderers, he went to Calumet, Michigan, where he played two seasons. In 1907, he moved on to Pittsburgh and after one season there, returned to Montreal and played with the Shamrocks. He rejoined the Wanderers just in time to be on his second Stanley Cup winner. In 1911 he went to New Westminster of the Pacific Coast League, but after two seasons he again returned to Montreal. Jimmy played for the Canadiens for two seasons, then retired to a coaching role with that club for another two years.

Gardner shifted to officiating in 1917, refereeing in the minors and then the Western Canada Hockey League in 1923-24. He took another fling at coaching with the Hamilton Tigers of 1924-25 but that team withdrew from the league in a celebrated salary dispute. He died in Montreal, on November 7, 1940. Elected 1962.

A star participant in football, paddling, cricket, tennis, lacrosse and hockey, **Edward George (Eddie) Gerard** was born in Ottawa on February 22, 1890.

Eddie turned professional with the Ottawa Senators in the 1913-14 season and became their captain in 1920. During his 10 years with the team he was on four Stanley Cup winners, although one championship was won while he was on loan to the Toronto St. Pats.

Known as a gentleman on and off the ice, he played his defense position well and cleanly. Gerard retired in 1923 because of asthma and coached the Montreal Maroons to a Stanley Cup victory in 1926. He remained with the Maroons until 1930, then joined the New York Americans as manager. He went back to the Maroons in 1932 and joined the St. Louis Eagles in 1934 but was forced to quit halfway through the season. Gerard died in Ottawa at the age of 47 on August 7, 1937. Elected 1945.

The romance of the early days of hockey is ▷ evident in this school notebook cover circa 1910. The handsome players are dashing down the open-air rink with smiles on their faces and not one hair out of place on their brilliantined heads.

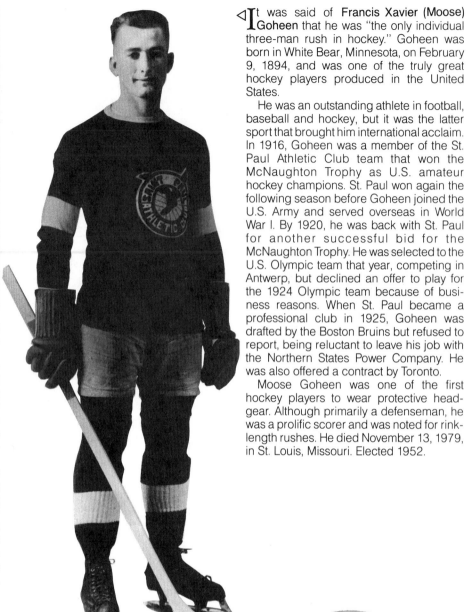

John L. (Jack) Gibson organized the first pro hockey league in the world — the International League of 1903-07.

Born September 10, 1880, in Berlin (now known as Kitchener), Ontario, he graduated from Detroit Medical School and set up a dental practice at Houghton. A fine player and a member of Ontario's 1897 Intermediate champions, he organized the Portage Lake team in 1902 and soon became captain as well as leading scorer.

That Portage Lake team is considered by many oldtimers to be one of the greatest ever assembled. Portage Lake, in the spring of 1905, challenged Ottawa's famous Silver Seven to a championship series and in 1906 a similar challenge was issued to Montreal. Both were refused. Gibson eventually set up practice in Calgary where he resided until his death on October 7, 1955. Elected 1976.

It was said of Francis Xavier (Moose) Goheen that he was "the only individual three-man rush in hockey." Goheen was born in White Bear, Minnesota, on February 9, 1894, and was one of the truly great hockey players produced in the United States.

He was an outstanding athlete in football, baseball and hockey, but it was the latter sport that brought him international acclaim. In 1916, Goheen was a member of the St. Paul Athletic Club team that won the McNaughton Trophy as U.S. amateur hockey champions. St. Paul won again the following season before Goheen joined the U.S. Army and served overseas in World War I. By 1920, he was back with St. Paul for another successful bid for the McNaughton Trophy. He was selected to the U.S. Olympic team that year, competing in Antwerp, but declined an offer to play for the 1924 Olympic team because of business reasons. When St. Paul became a professional club in 1925, Goheen was drafted by the Boston Bruins but refused to report, being reluctant to leave his job with the Northern States Power Company. He was also offered a contract by Toronto.

Moose Goheen was one of the first hockey players to wear protective headgear. Although primarily a defenseman, he was a prolific scorer and was noted for rink-length rushes. He died November 13, 1979, in St. Louis, Missouri. Elected 1952.

Goaltender Percy LeSueur won two Stanley Cups with Ottawa. His cricket pads adapted for hockey are shown here.

A talented rightwinger for the Ottawa Hockey Club, Hamilton Livingstone (Billy) Gilmour was born in Ottawa on March 21, 1885. Gilmour joined the Ottawa Silver Seven in 1902 from McGill University and stayed with the club for three consecutive Stanley Cup victories.

In 1907-08 he played with the Montreal Victorias of the Eastern Canada Amateur Hockey Association, and the following season joined the Ottawa Senators in the ECHA. The Senators won the Stanley Cup in 1909 and Gilmour finished the season with 11 goals in 11 games. He died in Mount Royal, Quebec, on March 13, 1959. Elected 1962.

Hockey, lacrosse, horse racing (flat and harness), baseball and figure skating — Thomas Patrick Gorman worked in all of these during his long career. For many years he was sports editor of the Ottawa *Citizen*, so it can be said that this Ottawa Irishman — born there on June 9, 1886 — was surrounded by sports activity all his life.

Tommy helped to hold the old NHA together when he picked up the Ottawa franchise during World War I. In 1917, he was a founder of the NHL. Tommy managed or coached seven Stanley Cup teams: three in Ottawa, two for the Canadiens and one each with Chicago and the Montreal Maroons. He died May 15, 1961. Elected 1963.

Although best known for his ability and leadership in hockey, Michael (Mike) Grant was also an outstanding speedskater.

In 1894, Grant joined the Montreal Victorias and soon was elected captain. He led them to a Stanley Cup victory in 1894 but the club lost the Cup the following season to Winnipeg. Montreal recaptured the Cup in 1896 and retained it in 1897-98. During his career, Mike Grant played with three Montreal teams — the Crystals, Shamrocks and Victorias — and was the captain of each. When his career came to a close he had been captain on three Stanley Cup victors.

When he was not playing, Grant often refereed games in the same league. He became one of the first Canadian hockey ambassadors after he retired, demonstrating and organizing hockey exhibitions in the U.S. He died in 1961. Elected 1950.

Often remembered as the Hamilton Tigers' captain who led the first player strike in the history of the NHL, Wilfred Thomas (Shorty) Green had many other claims to fame. Green was born in Sudbury, Ontario, on July 17, 1896, and showed such good early form that he never played junior hockey.

In 1923, Green turned professional with the Hamilton Tigers. The Tigers won league honors in 1925 and Shorty, as captain, was spokesman for the players who refused to participate in a playoff game unless the club paid $200 per player. The owners refused to give in and Toronto and the Canadiens played a series to decide the title.

The Hamilton franchise was shifted to New York and Green scored the first goal in Madison Square Garden as the newly formed New York Americans bowed 3-1 to the Canadiens on December 19, 1925. He continued with the Americans until a serious injury sidelined him in 1927. He coached until retiring in 1933. Shorty Green died April 19, 1960. Elected 1962.

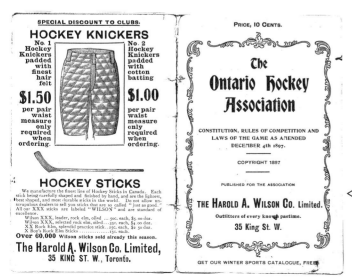

◁ The Ontario Hockey Association was organized in 1890, though it was not formally incorporated until 1896. This constitution and rule book is the amended 1897 edition. Like all organized hockey of this era, the OHA played an "on-side" game in which forward passing wasn't permitted. Substitutions were allowed only if injury occurred. The OHA was amateur hockey's governing body throughout Ontario. Teams at this time included Queen's University, Osgoode Hall, Ottawa, Stratford, Barrie, Guelph, Kingston, Peterborough, Cornwall and Windsor.

Hall of Famers: the Wanderers featured Ernie Russell, Lester Patrick, Riley Hern, Ernie Johnstone and Hod Stuart, while Kenora called on the likes of Si Griffis, Harry Westwick, Alf Smith, Frank Whitcroft and Art Ross. This game may have seen more Hall of Famers than any before or since in a battle for the legendary Stanley Cup.

Most of us cannot remember when Ottawa was home to an enduring big-league hockey team, but the Ottawa Hockey Club (popularly known as the "Silver Seven") defended the Cup successfully on ten separate occasions between 1903 and 1906, until they finally gave it up to the Montreal Wanderers in a two-game total-goal series won by the Wanderers 12-10. This Ottawa club boasted a powerful lineup — including Frank McGee, the three Gilmour brothers (David, Billy and Suddy), Alf and Harry Smith, and Harry Westwick — and blazed a trail for a long tradition of big-league hockey in Canada's national capital. Dr. J.L. (Doc) Gibson, a dentist in Portage Lake, Michigan, had long been barred from amateur play in Ontario, because he, along with the other boys on his team, had once accepted an award of ten dollars in silver from the mayor of Berlin, Ontario. After studying dentistry in Michigan and making a home for himself among the mining men there, he brought together several local teams to form the world's first professional hockey league.

By 1903, the International Professional Hockey League (IHL) had amassed a large following and money enough to attract many Canadian stars. Hod and Bruce Stuart, Jimmy Gardner, Cyclone Taylor and Hugh Lehman — all eventual Hall of Famers — drew their first acknowledged paychecks from the gold mines of northern Michigan.

CONTINUED ON PAGE 32

Silas Seth (Si) Griffis brought a combination of dazzling speed and intelligence to hockey, first coming to prominence with the great Kenora, Ontario, team that successfully challenged for the Stanley Cup in 1906-07.

Griffis was born in Kansas on September 22, 1883. He was a big man, 195 pounds, but became known as the fastest man in the game. Griffis started as a rover in the seven-man game of that era but later moved back to play cover point (defense). Griffis was given a purse of gold by the citizens of Kenora and offered a fine home but moved to Vancouver after the Cup-winning season. He retired from hockey until 1911, when the Patricks started the Pacific Coast Hockey Association. On his opening night with the Millionaires he played the full 60 minutes, scoring three goals and assisting on two others. Griffis was captain of the Vancouver Millionaires that won in 1915, although he did not play in the Cup series due to a broken leg sustained in the final game of the schedule. He remained with the team until 1918 when he retired permanently.

Si was outstanding in several other sports. He won many events as an oarsman and, in 1905, successfully stroked the Junior Four at the Canadian Henley Regatta in St. Catharines, Ontario. Si was a champion lefthanded golfer and in later life became a great ten-pin bowler. He died in July, 1950, at the age of 67. Elected 1950.

◁Didier Pitre had one of the hardest shots of his day, scoring 240 goals in 282 games from 1904 to 1923. Note the dark blue and white jersey of the 1910 Canadiens.

One of the true slam-bang defensemen in the game, past or present, **Joseph Henry (Joe) Hall** was a professional hockey player for 14 years until tragedy claimed him on April 5, 1919.

Joe was born May 3, 1882, in Staffordshire, England, but his family moved to western Canada. Joe, who had started playing hockey in 1897, joined the Winnipeg Rowing Club and Rat Portage teams until turning pro in the 1905-06 season with Kenora. He played for Brandon in 1907. Kenora took him east for the Cup series against the Montreal Wanderers, although he did not play.

Hall moved east to play for the Montreal Shamrocks from 1907 to 1910. He played for the Quebec Bulldogs from 1910-11 through 1915-16, winning Stanley Cups in 1911 and 1913. He finished his career with the Montreal Canadiens. The Canadiens won the NHL title in 1919 and went west to play for the Stanley Cup in Seattle.

The series with Seattle, winners of the Pacific Coast Hockey Association title, was deadlocked after five games with each team having two wins and a tie when the local Department of Health cancelled further play because of an influenza epidemic. Joe Hall was the most seriously stricken of several players, dying from influenza on April 5, 1919. Elected 1961.

The Montreal Wanderers were known as the "Redbands" because of the crimson chestband on their sweaters. Uniform numbers were a recent innovation in 1913, the year of this photo. It's apparent that the numbers shown here were added to existing numberless sweaters. The Wanderers never solved their goaltending problems in this season, allowing 125 goals against in 20 games. Top row, from left: Lefebvre, Harry Hyland, Gordon Roberts, unknown; bottom row, from left: Art Ross, Sprague Cleghorn, Carl Kendall, Billy Nicholson, Ernie Russell, and Odie Cleghorn.

William Milton (Riley) Hern played on seven championship teams in his first nine years in hockey.

He was born in St. Mary's, Ontario, on December 5, 1880, and started playing hockey with the local Ontario Hockey Association junior team as a goaltender. He moved up through intermediate and senior ranks and for a time played forward with a team in London, Ontario. Riley went to Houghton, Michigan, in 1904 as goaltender for the Portage Lake team. The Montreal Wanderers signed him as a goalie in 1906 and he made that city his permanent home. Hern received much credit for the Wanderers winning the Stanley Cup that year. During the next five years he was one of the outstanding players on the team as the Wanderers won the Stanley Cup again in 1908 and 1910.

Hern died in Montreal on June 24, 1929. Elected 1962.

Robert W. (Bobby) Hewitson was born January 23, 1892, in Toronto. He became a referee prior to 1920, handling games not only in hockey but in lacrosse and football as well. He went on to officiate for 10 years in the NHL. He was also active in many other areas of sport. He was secretary of the Canadian Rugby Union for almost 25 years, was closely associated with horse racing and was an original member of the Hot Stove League on hockey broadcasts. He became the first curator of both the Hockey Hall of Fame and Canada's Sports Hall of Fame, retiring in 1967. He died January 9, 1969. Elected 1963.

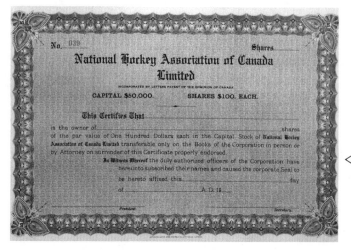

◁These share certificates were part of the $50,000 capitalization of the National Hockey Association, which was the NHL's immediate predecessor. The NHA operated from 1910 to 1917 and absorbed clubs from the rival Canadian Hockey Association during its first year of operation. By the mid-1910s, the NHA and the Pacific Coast Hockey Association in the west were the game's top leagues. The NHA never did sell all of its shares. More than half of the certificates in the original share book were never filled out.

If there had been a trophy for the leading netminder during the period that **Harry (Hap) Holmes** played, he would have won it eight times. This outstanding goalie starred in five professional hockey leagues: National Hockey Association, Pacific Coast Hockey Association, Western Canada Hockey League, Western Hockey League and NHL.

Born in Aurora, Ontario, in 1889, Holmes turned pro with the new Toronto franchise in the NHA in 1912-13. His career spanned 15 years with teams in Toronto, Seattle, Victoria and Detroit. He played on seven championship teams and four Stanley Cup winners.

Holmes had a goals-against average of 2.90 in 405 league games. His Cup teams included Toronto in 1914 and 1918, Seattle in 1917 and Victoria in 1925.

After three seasons and one Stanley Cup in Toronto, Holmes moved to Seattle, where he was a standout for the first team to take the Stanley Cup to a U.S. city. The Cup seemed to follow Holmes around as he returned to Toronto and helped the Arenas win it in 1918. He then returned to the west and for eight seasons was a standout in the PCHA.

He was Seattle's goalie in the 1919 Cup series that finished without a winner due to an influenza epidemic. With the windup of the WHL in 1926, players went en masse to the expanded NHL and Holmes shifted to Detroit, where he played two years before retiring.

The memory of this great goalie, who died while vacationing in Florida in 1940, is perpetuated through the Harry Holmes Memorial Trophy, awarded annually since 1941 to the leading goalie in the American Hockey League. Elected 1972.

Christened **William Abraham Hewitt** at birth on May 15, 1875, in Cobourg, Ontario, he was seldom referred to as anything but W.A. Hewitt in more than 60 years of association with hockey. His family moved to Toronto in 1879, where he later joined the Toronto *News* as a sportswriter and spent 41 years in the newspaper business, 32 of those as sports editor of the Toronto *Star*.

As well as being head of one of Canadian sports' most famous families — son Foster is also a Hockey Hall of Fame member — he was secretary of the Ontario Hockey Association from 1903 to 1961, registrar and treasurer of the CAHA for 39 years and manager of three champion Canadian teams in Olympic hockey.

He was responsible for an important hockey innovation: tired of disputes over whether a puck had gone between the goal posts, he came up with the idea of draping a fish net over them, so shots would be caught. He died September 8, 1966. Elected 1945.

This 1910 cigarette card shows ▷ Fred "Cyclone" Taylor, who earned his nickname from his powerful rushes up the ice from his defenseman's position. He's shown here in the uniform of the Renfrew Club in the NHA.

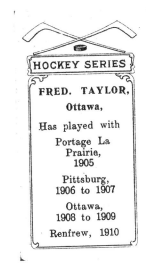

HOCKEY SERIES

FRED. TAYLOR,
Ottawa,
Has played with
Portage La Prairie, 1905
Pittsburg, 1906 to 1907
Ottawa, 1908 to 1909
Renfrew, 1910

FRED. TAYLOR of RENFREW CLUB.

These were powerful hockey teams, as good as the best in Canada. They did well in exhibition matches against the touring Montreal Wanderers in 1905, but although they are said to have applied for a Stanley Cup challenge, Trustees Ross and Sweetland were not yet prepared to risk the Cup title to an upstart pro team from the United States.

In 1903, the Canadian Sault (The Soo) became the first Canadian pro team. Other early circuits included the Manitoba Pro League, the Maritime Professional League, the Ontario Pro League (the so-called "Trolley League"), and the Intercollegiate Hockey League in the northeastern U.S. in which the St. Nicholas Street Club of New York played, and where the great Hobey Baker played his hockey.

By the time the century was a decade old, hockey was being played across northern North America and throughout Europe. In 1904, there were teams in the great cities of Europe, and by 1908, they had organized themselves into an association, the International Ice Hockey Federation (IIHF), which continues to govern international play today. France, England, Switzerland, Belgium, Germany and Bohemia signed the IIHF charter in 1908. Today the IIHF is the longest-running hockey association in the world.

The year 1910 saw the first ice hockey world championship. For years, Stanley Cup winners had been calling themselves "World Champions," but the IIHF did not sanction an official competition until the end of the first decade of the century. In dispute at the time was whether or not Canadians would be allowed to play in the tournament. Specifically, the Oxford University team was fortified by players who had learned the game in Canada, and the organizers felt that the superior strength of Oxford would put the competition on

CONTINUED ON PAGE 36

The team from Kenora, Ontario, challenged three times for the Stanley Cup before finally winning in January, 1907. One of the key members of that Cup-winning team was **Charles Thomas (Tom) Hooper**, a hometown boy who was to play on one other world championship team, the Montreal Wanderers of 1908.

Hooper was born in Kenora on November 24, 1883. In 1901, Hooper and Tommy Phillips moved up to the senior club and helped it win the Manitoba and Northwestern League championship. That team was known as the Thistles and by 1903 it challenged Ottawa for the Stanley Cup, losing a two-game series.

Kenora again challenged for the Cup in 1905. This time the Thistles won the first game but lost the next two in Ottawa. In 1907, the Thistles' persistence paid off in a Cup victory. Two months later, however, the Thistles and Wanderers met again in Winnipeg and the Cup returned to Montreal. Hooper switched to the Wanderers in 1907-08 after his team folded, retiring at the end of the season. Elected 1962.

Although he is chiefly remembered and honored as a hockey goaltender, **John Bower (Bouse) Hutton** was a great performer in many sports. Hutton was born on October 24, 1877. He was a goalie in both hockey and lacrosse, and a fine fullback in football. In 1907 he had the unique distinction of being the only man to play on a Stanley Cup winner, a Canadian lacrosse championship team and a Canadian football championship team in the same year.

Hutton played goal for the Ottawa team that won the Canadian Amateur Hockey Association intermediate title in 1899 and moved up to play two games with the Silver Seven that same year. He stayed with that club for six seasons, averaging 2.90 goals against in 36 games. Hutton also played in 12 Stanley Cup games, allowing 28 goals. Bouse Hutton was in goal when Ottawa won the Stanley Cup in 1903 and 1904. He died on October 27, 1962. Elected 1962.

Very few athletes can boast that they have played on two national championship teams in the same year. **Harry Hyland,** a very versatile performer, played on the 1910 Montreal Wanderers team that won the Stanley Cup. The same year, he was also a member of the Salmonbellies team that won the Minto Cup, symbolic of Canadian professional lacrosse supremacy.

Harry was born in Montreal on January 2, 1889. He turned professional with the Shamrocks for the 1908-09 season, although still within junior age limits. He shifted to the Wanderers in time to play on their Stanley Cup-winning team but was lured to the Pacific Coast Hockey League for the 1911-12 season. He joined New Westminster and this team went on to win the league championship, with Hyland scoring 16 goals in 12 games. Hyland rejoined his former Montreal team in 1913 and on January 27 of that year scored eight goals in the Wanderers' 10-6 victory over Quebec. In 1918, he left the Wanderers to join Ottawa, where he finished his active career. He died August 8, 1969, in Montreal. Elected 1962.

James Dickenson Irvin was an outstanding player and coach. Known as Dick throughout his athletic career, he was born on July 19, 1892, in Limestone Ridge, near Hamilton, Ontario. In 1899 his family moved to Winnipeg, where he embarked on a hockey career.

Dick was a standout through church league and junior hockey with the Strathconas. He moved up to the senior Monarchs in 1912, as an emergency replacement, and scored six goals in two games of the Allan Cup final, although his team lost to the Winnipeg Victorias. The Monarchs played an exhibition series in 1914 against the Toronto Rugby and Athletic Association. In one of those games Irvin scored all nine goals in a 9-1 victory. He remained with the Monarchs for the 1914-15 season, when they won the Allan Cup.

He turned pro with the Portland Rosebuds the next season and finished third in the league scoring race. Irvin joined the Canadian army and went overseas in World War I. He returned to pro hockey in 1921 and played four seasons with the Regina Caps before returning to Portland, where he scored 30 goals in 30 games. Irvin moved to Chicago for three seasons as a player beginning in 1926. He was the first captain of the Hawks and collected 18 goals and 18 assists, finishing second to Bill Cook in the league scoring race. He fractured his skull in the 12th game of the next season, ending his playing career.

After coaching Chicago, he moved to Toronto in 1931 for a Stanley Cup-winning season. He coached the Montreal Canadiens from 1940-55, his teams winning the Stanley Cup three times, before returning to the Blackhawks for one final season. He died in Montreal on May 16, 1957. Elected 1958.

The Stanley Cup, resplendent in bowler, overcoat, furled umbrella and spats, is seen purchasing a one-way ticket from Ottawa to Montreal in this 1906 cartoon. The Montreal Shamrocks defeated Ottawa 12-10 in a two-game total goals series to win the Stanley Cup in March of that year. Montreal won game one 9-1, but Ottawa made it close with a 9-3 win in game two.

◁ Ernest (Moose) Johnson was born in Montreal in 1886 and, as his name implies, grew to be a big man. He started playing as a junior around 1900, and by 1904 was playing for the Montreal Amateur Athletic Association (AAA).

"As a beginner, I once played junior Friday night, intermediate Saturday afternoon and senior Saturday night," Johnson recalled in later days. He turned professional with the Montreal Wanderers and played with them on four Stanley Cup championship winners — 1906, 1907, 1908 and 1910. He joined the New Westminster Royals of the Pacific Coast League in 1912. This team moved to Portland at the beginning of World War I. The club, led by Johnson, won its league title in 1916. He later played with Victoria, Los Angeles and other teams of the Western Hockey League. He finished his pro career in 1931.

He earned the nickname Moose while with the Victoria hockey club, and also became known as the player with the longest reach in hockey history. Moose had the longest stick in the game and his reach, fully extended, was 99 inches. "The year I quit they buried my stick," he said. "It was the longest stick ever used. In those days, there were no size regulations and they couldn't take it away from me because it was my means of livelihood." He died in White Rock, British Columbia, on March 25, 1963. Elected 1952.

It is doubtful that any great hockey player ever bounced through ▷ more teams in more leagues than **Gordon Blanchard (Duke) Keats**.

Duke was born in Montreal on March 1, 1895, but his family moved to North Bay, Ontario, where he started his itinerant hockey career. At the age of 14 he was paid $75 a month to play in the Cobalt area. He went on to North Bay and, at 17, jumped to the National Hockey Association with Toronto. Keats credits the coaching of Eddie Livingstone at Toronto with making him a great center. Subsequently, he returned to amateur play with Peterborough, Ontario, went back to Toronto and then into the Canadian army to serve overseas in World War I.

Following the war, he went to Edmonton and played for a first-class amateur team. Keats stayed with Edmonton when the team turned pro in 1919, leading the Western Canada League in scoring in 1923. The WCHL was sold by the Patricks in 1926, so Keats joined Boston of the NHL and transferred to Detroit part way through the season. The next season, he was with Chicago but after an argument with the owner, Major Frederic McLaughlin, moved to the American Association. Tulsa paid $5,000 for his transfer, which proved to be money well spent as Keats won the scoring title. Keats remained in hockey in various capacities across western Canada for many years. He scored 119 goals in 128 games prior to playing in the NHL where, in two years, he added another 30 goals. He died January 16, 1972. Elected 1958.

E douard Charles Lalonde was born in Cornwall, Ontario, on  October 31, 1887, and as a youth worked in a newsprint plant. That's where he acquired the nickname Newsy — and it stuck with him through an outstanding athletic career.

In 1950, Lalonde was named Canada's outstanding lacrosse player of the half-century. Lalonde began a somewhat riotous professional hockey career in Cornwall in 1905, and he was to be a dominant figure for almost 30 seasons. His hockey travels took him to play in Toronto, Woodstock, Sault Ste. Marie and Renfrew in Ontario, as well as in Vancouver and Saskatoon in western Canada, for the New York Americans and, of course, for the Montreal Canadiens in the NHL. He completed his active connection with the game as coach of the Canadiens.

He was a brilliant goal-scorer but also was known as one of the roughest players of his day. Feuds between Lalonde and Joe Hall, when the latter played with the Quebec Bulldogs, helped fill Montreal's old Westmount Arena. Newsy scored 441 goals in 365 games and was a scoring champion five times while playing in the National Hockey Association, Pacific Coast Hockey Association and NHL. He once scored 38 goals in an 11-game schedule and, while with Vancouver, scored 27 goals in 15 games. He died November 21, 1970, in Montreal. Elected 1950.

The 1906 Portage Lakers, champions of the International (Pro) League, challenged to play for the Stanley Cup, but weren't permitted to play for the Trophy. The Lakers iced a team that included top stars of the day: Joe Hall, Bruce Stuart, Riley Hern and Cyclone Taylor.

such an uneven footing that other teams would be reluctant to enter the fray. In the end, the Oxford Canadians were admitted to the tournament, but were not allowed to compete. Instead they were only allowed to play in exhibition games to show their skills. Results of their games did not register in the standings.

The tournament took the form of a round robin between the entries from Belgium, Germany, Switzerland and England, and was held at Les Avants, Switzerland. The Princes' Club of London won the series, yet refused to play the Oxford Canadians, to maintain their reputation as champions.

In 1920, North Americans finally came to be represented in the European form of world competition. Although Canadians had been claiming world championship status for Stanley Cup winners for years, it was not until that year that ice hockey became part of the Olympics (at Antwerp), and Canada and the United States entered teams. Neither country belonged to the IIHF at the time, but they were permitted to join at the next congress, in April of that same year.

The stars of these early competitions in Europe included Frank Frederickson of Winnipeg, who led the Canadian side to the first Olympic championship in 1920, and Moose Goheen, who was part of the American team that won silver in that same year. Both were made members of the Hockey Hall of Fame. Undoubtedly there were outstanding European players in these competitions, but their stories have remained unknown on this side of the ocean.

No one on the roster of the Oxford team in 1922 seemed particularly remarkable at the time (they did not win any notable competition), but the team did include two Canadians who went on to do

CONTINUED ON PAGE 40

Frederic Hugh (Hughie) Lehman was born in Pembroke, Ontario, on October 27, 1885, and became one of the outstanding netminders of his era. Lehman played goal for 23 years, 21 as a professional, and earned the nickname "Old Eagle Eyes."

When the Pacific Coast Hockey Association League was formed in 1911, Lehman joined the New Westminster Royals and stayed with them for three seasons. He joined the Vancouver Millionaires in 1914 and played with that team until the league was sold by the Patricks after the 1925-26 season.

Hughie returned east with most of the PCHA players and spent the 1926-27 season with Chicago of the NHL. He retired after the 1927-28 season, when he was co-coach of Chicago with Barney Stanley. Lehman played on eight Stanley Cup challengers but was successful only once, with Vancouver in 1915. He died April 8, 1961, in Toronto. Elected 1958.

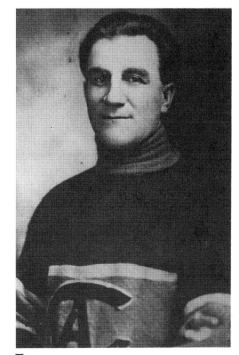

J ean Baptiste (Jack) Laviolette is one of only three athletes named to both the Hockey Hall of Fame and Canada's Sports Hall of Fame prior to 1970. He was named to the latter as a lacrosse player. Born in Belleville, Ontario, on July 27, 1879, he moved to Valleyfield, Quebec, at an early age.

Laviolette formed the Montreal Canadiens in 1909 and played point (defense), but later moved up to play on a line with Didier Pitre and Newsy Lalonde. Jack had great speed and earned the nickname "Speed Merchant." He played on a Stanley Cup winner in 1916 and retired at the end of the 1917-18 season. Laviolette lost a foot in an accident in the summer of 1918 but, amazingly, came back to do some refereeing. He died January 10, 1960, in Montreal. Elected 1962.

◁ T he hockey career of **Percy LeSueur** spanned 50 years, but he gained his fame as the goaltender of the Ottawa Senators from 1906 to 1913.

LeSueur was born in Quebec City on November 18, 1881, and died in Hamilton, Ontario, on January 27, 1962. He acted in many capacities connected with hockey: player, coach, manager, referee, inventor, arena manager, broadcaster and columnist. Peerless Percy, as he was nicknamed, played on Stanley Cup winners in 1909 and 1911.

He was captain of the Senators for three years and manager and coach for part of the 1913-14 season. He was traded to the Toronto Ontarios in 1914, playing two seasons before joining the 48th Highlanders in 1916. After a tour of duty overseas, he did not return to play. He became a referee, then coached in Ontario. He was the first manager of the Detroit Olympia. LeSueur is credited with inventing the gauntlet-type glove for goalies and the net used by the National Association and the NHL from 1912 to 1925. LeSueur was also an original member of radio's Hot Stove League. Elected 1961.

The Portland Rosebuds lost a five-game total goals Stanley Cup final series to the Montreal Canadiens in 1916, but shocked the Canadiens with a 2-0 win in game one. Portland's Ernie "Moose" Johnson is on his knees in the center of this photoengraving, which ran in the Montreal *Daily Star.* The headline read, "Johnson Must have found the Spring of the Elixir of Youth in Oregon For He Was Better Than Ever."

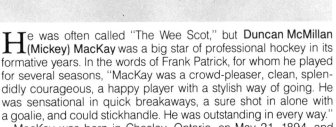

He was often called "The Wee Scot," but **Duncan McMillan (Mickey) MacKay** was a big star of professional hockey in its formative years. In the words of Frank Patrick, for whom he played for several seasons, "MacKay was a crowd-pleaser, clean, splendidly courageous, a happy player with a stylish way of going. He was sensational in quick breakaways, a sure shot in alone with a goalie, and could stickhandle. He was outstanding in every way."

MacKay was born in Chesley, Ontario, on May 21, 1894, and played with the Chesley Colts until Barney Stanley lured him to western Canada. Still a junior, he played senior hockey at Edmonton and at Grand Forks, British Columbia, until Patrick hired him to play for the Vancouver Millionaires of the Pacific Coast Hockey Association. In his rookie season there, MacKay scored 33 goals, 10 more than Cyclone Taylor, and missed the scoring title by one point. He played with Vancouver through the 1925-26 season, won the goal-scoring title three times and scored 202 goals in 242 games. The Millionaires won the Stanley Cup 1915.

Mickey moved to Chicago for the 1926-27 season and was the team's leading scorer in 1927-28. After half a season with Pittsburgh, Mickey joined Boston in time to help them win the Stanley Cup. He retired after the start of the next season, but finished the year with Boston as business manager. On May 21, 1940, Mickey suffered a heart attack while driving a car near Nelson, British Columbia. The car was involved in an accident and he died. Elected 1952.

Maurice Joseph (Joe) Malone was a remarkable marksman who performed scoring miracles in both the National Hockey Association and the NHL. The late Charles L. Coleman, author of *The Trail of the Stanley Cup*, credits Malone with 379 goals between his first professional game in Waterloo in 1909 and his retirement in 1924.

In his eight biggest seasons — five with Quebec, two with Hamilton and one with the Montreal Canadiens — he scored 280 goals in 172 games. Malone led the NHA in scoring in 1912-13, and tied Frank Nighbor in 1916-17 with 41 goals in 20 games. Malone topped the NHL in its first season, 1917-18, with the phenomenal total of 44 goals in 20 games. Some of his outstanding single-game performances include: nine goals againt the Sydney Millionaires in a 1913 Stanley Cup playoff game; eight against the Montreal Wanderers in 1917; and seven against Toronto in 1920, a mark that still stands as an NHL single-game record.

Joe Malone was born in Quebec City on February 28, 1890. He played his first organized hockey with the junior Crescents in 1907. In 1909-10, he played with the Quebec seniors and for Waterloo, Ontario. He went on to play seven seasons with the Quebec Bulldogs, two with the Montreal Canadiens, and two with Hamilton, where he added the duties of coach and manager. He retired in 1924 after playing a few home games for the Canadiens. He died May 15, 1969. Elected 1950.

The name of **Francis (Frank) McGee** was written into the hockey record book with one spectacular scoring splurge. On January 16, 1905, McGee scored 14 goals in a Stanley Cup game as Ottawa trounced a weary Dawson City, Yukon, team, 23-2. Of McGee's 14 goals, eight were scored consecutively in a span of eight minutes and 20 seconds. Three of these were scored in 90 seconds and the fourth came just 50 seconds later, Cup records for three-goal and four-goal individual performances.

Frank McGee played center and rover for the famous Ottawa Silver Seven between 1903 and 1906 and, although he had lost the sight of one eye prior to joining the club, became one of the best forwards in the game.

Ottawa won the Stanley Cup in McGee's first season with the club, but he didn't play a prominent role until 1903-04, when he scored 21 goals in eight Cup games. The Silver Seven made it three Stanley Cups in a row when they whipped Dawson City at the end of the 1904-05 season. McGee was a lieutenant in the Canadian army when he was killed in action on September 16, 1916. Elected 1945.

John C. (Jack) Marshall was associated with five Stanley Cup winners and two other teams that challenged for the Cup during his 17-year hockey career. Born in St. Vallier, Quebec, on March 14, 1877, Marshall is first noted in hockey record books as having played with the Winnipeg Victorias when they won the Cup in 1901.

An outstanding center at that time, he played the next two seasons with the Montreal AAA. He moved to the Montreal Wanderers for two seasons but, by 1906-07, was playing for the Montreal Montagnards. Jack was back with the Wanderers in 1907, switched to the Montreal Shamrocks for the following two seasons, and then returned once again to the Wanderers, where he stayed through 1912. By that time, he had shifted to defense.

Shortly after the Toronto Blueshirts entered the National Hockey Association in 1913, Marshall was hired as playing manager, winning the Stanley Cup in 1914. It was Marshall's fifth and last Cup, although he played another year in Toronto and two with the Wanderers before retiring. He died in Montreal on August 7, 1965. Elected 1965.

Although he had several offers to become a professional hockey player, **Fred G. Maxwell** remained an amateur throughout his career. He picked up the nickname "Steamer" because of his tremendous ability to skate.

He was born in Winnipeg on May 19, 1890, and developed as a rover in the seven-man game then in vogue. Maxwell joined the Winnipeg Monarchs in 1914. This team went on to win the Allan Cup, defeating Melville, Saskatchewan, in the final series. He shifted over to coach the Winnipeg Falcons in 1918-19 and took that team to an Allan Cup triumph. The following year, the Falcons won both the Olympic and World hockey championships. In 1925-26, he coached the Winnipeg Rangers to the Manitoba championship. He next coached the Winnipeg Maroons of the American Professional Hockey League, staying with the club until the league terminated in 1928.

Maxwell returned to coaching amateur teams, both junior and senior, and in 1929-30 he coached the Elmwood Millionaires to both the junior and senior Manitoba championships. He coached another World championship club in 1934-35 when the Winnipeg Monarchs won the title at Davos, Switzerland. He died September 11, 1975. Elected 1962.

rather well. One was Roland Michener, a future Governor General of Canada, and the other was Mike Pearson, Canada's Prime Minister from 1963 to 1968.

With North American teams participating in IIHF play, European hockey organizers feared their clubs would always be second best. Seeing this situation as an impediment to the progress of the sport, Carl Spengler, a Swiss physician, set up a cup competition in 1923 to represent the European championship of ice hockey. Oxford won the premier series, and the tradition of Spengler Cup competition continues to this day.

A Hall of Famer to have real impact on the European hockey scene was John Francis (Bunny) Ahearn. Ahearn was the driving force behind the British semi-professional league, was secretary to the British Ice Hockey Association from 1933 to 1973, and served as both president and vice-president of the IIHF.

In the first decade of the century, hockey was an amateur game throughout most of the world. But in central Canada, more and more entrepreneurs were following the lead of the International Pro League in Michigan by paying their players and charging admission. It was clear that this was the way of the future. The Eastern Canadian Amateur Hockey Association was riddled with questionable payment of players, and the use of "ringers" was so frequent that the Stanley Cup trustees issued a warning that clubs must challenge using the players who skated during the regular season.

By 1909 the situation had become so murky, and so many entrepreneurs wanted into the game, that the ECAHA disbanded and in its place sprung two leagues, the Canadian Hockey Association and the National Hockey Association. The CHA was based in Montreal, while the

CONTINUED ON PAGE 44

Born in Penetang, Ontario, on August 26, 1886, **George McNamara** moved to Sault Ste. Marie, Ontario, at an early age. In 1908-09 he joined the Montreal Shamrocks of the Eastern Canada League as a defenseman.

McNamara's next three seasons were spent with the Halifax Crescents of the Maritime Pro League before he joined the Toronto Tecumsehs for the 1912-13 campaign. In 1913-14, he played one game for Ottawa and the balance with the Toronto Ontarios, who went on to win the Stanley Cup. George remained in Toronto and joined the Canadian army for World War I. After the war, he returned to the Canadian Soo and coached the Sault Ste. Marie Greyhounds to the Allan Cup in 1924.

George McNamara died March 10, 1952. Elected 1958.

Francis Nelson became an important member of the Ontario Hockey Association in its struggling years. When John Robertson became president of the OHA in its tenth year of existence, Robertson realized that he needed capable men around him to make the organization a success. He called upon Nelson, sports editor of the Toronto *Globe*, for assistance. Nelson served as a OHA vice-president from 1903 to 1905, retiring with Robertson after the 1905 season.

The following season he was named OHA Governor to the Amateur Athletic Union of Canada and the Union later awarded him a life membership. Francis Nelson died in April, 1932. Elected 1945.

Many of hockey's great players achieved their fame as members of several teams, but William George (Billy) McGimsie was an exception. He played all of his major league hockey with one team, the Kenora Thistles.

The Thistles challenged Ottawa for the Stanley Cup in 1903 but lost a two-game series. Two years later, they challenged Ottawa again with the same result. Undaunted, they came back a third time in January, 1907. A two-game series was played in Montreal against the Wanderers and Kenora won both, the first by a score of 4-2 and the second, 8-6. This achievement put Kenora into the record book as the smallest town ever to win the Cup. Two months later, in March, 1907, the Thistles and Wanderers played a challenge series in Winnipeg and the Wanderers triumphed to take the Stanley Cup back to Montreal.

McGimsie's career ended when he dislocated his shoulder in an exhibition game in Ottawa. He died in Calgary on October 28, 1968. Elected 1962.

Patrick Joseph (Paddy) Moran played top-level hockey for 16 seasons. He was a member of the Quebec Bulldogs for 15 years and, although he retired a year before the NHL was formed, is regarded as one of the greatest standup goaltenders in the game.

Paddy was born in Quebec City, on March 11, 1877. Moran began his career with the Quebec Bulldogs in 1901-02 and, except for a one-season fling with Haileybury, Ontario, in 1909-10, he remained with that team. His standup style earned him a reputation as a stick-stopping goalie good enough to help the Bulldogs win two consecutive Stanley Cups, in 1912 and 1913.

Moran died in Quebec, on January 14, 1966. Elected 1958.

He was often called the Flying Dutchman or the Pembroke Peach, but by whatever name he was known, Frank Nighbor was a slick 160-pound package of stickhandling ability.

He was a 60-minute center with the Ottawa Senators from 1915 to 1929, and was one of the game's great exponents of the poke check. He was shifty and always ready with a lightning thrust of his oversize stick.

Nighbor was born in Pembroke, Ontario, in 1893, and played his early hockey there. He played the 1910-11 season in Port Arthur, Ontario, and turned professional with the Toronto Blueshirts in 1913. His first Stanley Cup triumph came with the Vancouver Millionaires when they defeated Ottawa in the 1915 final. The next season, he returned to Ottawa and remained with the Senators until the last half of 1928-29, his final season as a player, when he played for Toronto.

While with the Senators, Nighbor played on four more Stanley Cup champions: 1920, 1921, 1923, and 1927. He was also the initial winner of two of the league's great trophies, the Hart and the Lady Byng. Nighbor won the Hart, awarded to the MVP to his team, in 1924, and the Lady Byng in 1925 and 1926.

Frank Nighbor died at his home in Pembroke on April 13, 1966. Elected 1945.

◁ Edward Reginald Noble was born in Collingwood, Ontario, on June 23, 1895, and went on to become one of the finest leftwingers in hockey. Championships seemed to follow him wherever he went. His career began with Collingwood Business College and he moved up to the town's junior team and helped it win the OHA Group title in 1915 before losing to Berlin in the provincial semi-finals. The following season, he played for the Toronto Riversides, winning OHA senior honors.

Noble moved into professional hockey with Toronto in 1916-17 but the Blueshirts disbanded part way through the season. He was sent to the Montreal Canadiens but the league ruled that he had arrived too late in the season to play in the Stanley Cup finals, which the Canadiens lost to Seattle. The NHL was organized the following year and Reg played for the Toronto Arenas, who won the Stanley Cup. He scored 28 goals in 22 games that season.

The Arenas became the St. Patrick's in 1919-20 and Noble played for this team when it defeated Vancouver in the Cup final of 1922. He was traded to the Montreal Maroons in 1924 and came out a winner again when the Maroons won the Cup in 1926.

A trade took him to the Detroit Cougars, where he played five years as a defenseman, returning to the Maroons early in 1933 to finish out his NHL playing career with a total of 170 goals. Noble played one more season with Cleveland of the International League. He refereed in the NHL for two seasons.

He died in Alliston, Ontario, on January 19, 1962. Elected 1962.

William M. Northey presided over the Montreal Amateur Athletic Association during some of the Association's greatest years and was named a life member of the Canadian Amateur Hockey Association. He also supervised construction of the original Montreal Forum and managed the building for many years.

Northey's main interest was amateur hockey and, in 1908 when the Stanley Cup was taken over by professional interests, he prevailed upon Sir Montagu Allan to donate the Allan Cup. He was born in Leeds, Quebec, on April 29, 1872, and died April 9, 1963. Elected 1945.

Conn Smythe, manager of the Toronto Maple Leafs and builder of Maple Leaf Gardens, started in college hockey with the University of Toronto Varsity team. After a stint as captain in 1915, Smythe, shown at the extreme left in this photo, coached the team to the Allan Cup and Canadian Senior Hockey Championship in 1927. The same club, renamed the Varsity Grads, won the Olympic gold medal for Canada in 1928.

The National Hockey League rule book contains 22 pieces of legislation that were introduced by **Frank Patrick**. The most important one established the blue line. Frank was born in Ottawa on December 21, 1885, and learned his hockey in Montreal where he starred with McGill University's team.

Frank visualized artificial ice arenas and the operation of a pro league on the Pacific Coast. The Patricks built the first artificial rinks in Canada — Vancouver's cost $350,000, seated 10,000 and was the largest building in the country. He became president of the Pacific Coast League when it was formed in 1911, owned, managed and coached the Vancouver club and also played defense. This team won a Stanley Cup in 1915. In 1926, he engineered the biggest deal in hockey to that time, selling the entire league to eastern interests. He later served as managing-director of the NHL, as a coach with Boston and manager with the Canadiens. Frank Patrick died June 29, 1960. Elected 1958.

John Ambrose O'Brien took part in hockey from his earliest years, playing on junior, intermediate and senior teams in his home town, Renfrew, Ontario. He later played with the University of Toronto Varsity Blues.

In 1909, the Eastern Canada Association was the only professional hockey league in that part of the country and the ECA rejected Renfrew's application for admission. O'Brien responded by organizing the rival National Hockey Association. His father Senator Michael J. O'Brien, financed four clubs in the new league, but John O'Brien's main interest was in bringing the Stanley Cup to Renfrew. He then helped launch one of the most famous teams in NHL history — the Montreal Canadiens.

The O'Brien Cup, a silver trophy given by Senator M. J. O'Brien, was awarded to the champion of the NHA. This trophy was adopted by the NHL but is no longer awarded and rests in the Hockey Hall of Fame. J.Ambrose O'Brien was born May 27, 1885, and died April 25, 1968, in Ottawa. Elected 1962.

HAMILTON TIGER HOCKEY CLUB
SENIOR CHAMPIONS O.H.A. 1918-1919.
HOLDERS of the ALLAN CUP ~ CHAMPIONS of CANADA

The Hamilton Tigers won Canada's senior championship in 1919 led by Shorty Green, depicted here in the top left oval portrait. Green was a top amateur player until 1923, when he turned pro with Hamilton in the NHL. As team captain, he led his fellow players in their demands for additional pay for playoff games in 1925.

NHA was concentrated in the mining centers of Northern Ontario. The CHA began its short life with five teams: Ottawa Senators, Shamrocks, Quebec Bulldogs, Nationals and All Montreal. However, after less than 20 days of regular-season play it became apparent that because of poor fan support they would not survive. The NHA won the day, with the big winners being J. Ambrose O'Brien and his father, M.J. O'Brien, who had made a fortune in mining. M.J. financed the NHA, owning franchises in Renfrew, Haileybury and Cobalt. The O'Brien Trophy, considered by many to be the most beautiful trophy ever awarded in hockey, was donated by Senator Michael O'Brien in 1909 and was initially awarded to the champion of the NHA. This trophy is now displayed at the Hockey Hall of Fame.

The NHA's first season saw five teams — Renfrew, Cobalt, Haileybury, the Montreal Wanderers, and Les Canadiens — begin the schedule. That same season they were joined by Ottawa and the Montreal Shamrocks from the CHA. The Wanderers won the league championship, and, later that year, the Stanley Cup.

These may not have been the golden days of ice hockey, but they were surely the silver ones. The boom-and-bust spirit of the mining towns now at the center of the hockey world had a real effect on the game. Hockey was big-time entertainment, with large sums wagered on every game. Pioneer players like Frank and Lester Patrick, Cyclone Taylor, Percy LeSueur, Newsy Lalonde, Ernie Russell, Riley Hern, Didier Pitre and "Bad" Joe Hall played for big money.

The NHA had some pretty good seasons. Although by 1911 they were reduced to four teams (Wanderers, Ottawa, Canadiens and Quebec), they were the unri-

CONTINUED ON PAGE 48

◁ It would take a separate book to describe the many contributions **Lester Patrick** made to the game of hockey as a player, coach, manager, owner and NHL governor. He was one of hockey's immortals and is identified with many of the major developments in style of play, organization and expansion of the game.

He was one of the first rushing defensemen in hockey. As a coach and executive, he inaugurated hockey's first major farm system. With his brother Frank, he devised the profitable playoff system still in use today and was responsible for many rule improvements. He introduced pro hockey to British Columbia and was a guiding force behind its rise in the northeastern United States.

Lester Patrick was born on December 30, 1883, in Drummondville, Quebec, where he developed into a tremendous skater and stickhandler. He broke into pro hockey as a defenseman with Brandon, Manitoba, in 1903, and in 1905-06 joined the Montreal Wanderers, where he played on two successive Stanley Cup winners before moving to Canada's west coast.

Lester and Frank both played for Renfrew, Ontario, and then built arenas in Vancouver and Victoria, British Columbia, where they formed the Pacific Coast Hockey Association. Lester captained and managed the Victoria Aristocrats in 1912-13 when they defeated Quebec for the world title, although the Stanley Cup was not at stake.

When he and Frank sold the Western Hockey League in 1926, Lester became manager of the New York Rangers. The Rangers won three Stanley Cups under his guidance, in 1928, 1933, and 1940. He died in Victoria, British Columbia, on June 1, 1960. Elected 1945.

During the early decades of the century of number of major hockey leagues ▷ existed, including the Pacific Coast Hockey Association, the Western Canada Hockey League and the National Hockey Association, which in 1917 evolved into the NHL. Any of the various leagues' teams could, and did, challenge for the coveted Stanley Cup. The NHA's top award, the O'Brien Trophy, was also highly valued, and was awarded by the NHL for excellence in the regular season until 1950. The silver, bronze and wood trophy is on display in the Hockey Hall of Fame.

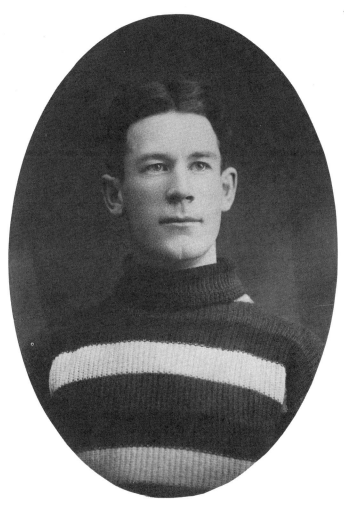

◁ Hockey oldtimers who could recall the game as it was played in the early 1900s agreed that **Thomas Neil Phillips** was perhaps the greatest hockey player they had ever seen.

Tommy was born in Kenora, Ontario, on May 22, 1880. He played hockey as a schoolboy in Kenora before going east to attend McGill University. He played for both McGill and the Montreal AAA, signing with the latter in 1902. Tommy, or "Nibs" as he was often called, attended college in Toronto in 1904 and helped the Marlboros win the Ontario Hockey Association senior championship.

By 1905, Phillips was back in Kenora and was captain of the Thistles when that team made two strong challenges for the Stanley Cup. They lost their first bid, despite Phillips' best efforts. Invading Ottawa, they scored a sensational 9-3 upset in the first game. Ottawa came back to take the second 4-2 and the third 5-4 to retain the Cup. In 1907, Kenora travelled to Montreal to play the Wanderers and Phillips scored all the goals in a first-game 4-2 triumph. Kenora also won the second game, 8-6, and the Stanley Cup was theirs. Two months later, the Wanderers challenged the Thistles again and regained the trophy.

Phillips played right wing for Ottawa in 1907-08, having been converted to the position because captain Alf Smith refused to relinquish Phillips' customary spot on the left side. As a rightwinger, he scored 26 goals in 10 games. Phillips had everything a good player should have — whirlwind speed, a bullet-like shot and stickhandling wizardry — and he was regarded as being without peer as a back-checker. He died in Toronto on November 30, 1923. Elected 1945.

Didier **Pitre** was the idol of ▷ French-Canadian hockey followers in the early, rough-and-ready days of the game. He weighed about 200 pounds, had a shot "like a cannonball," and could skate with tremendous speed for a big man.

He was born September 1, 1883, in Valleyfield, Quebec, and entered big-league hockey as a defenseman with the Montreal Nationals of the Federal Amateur Hockey League.

When Jack Laviolette formed the Canadiens in 1909, Pitre was the first player he signed. He remained with the team until his retirement in 1923, except for the 1913-14 season when he played for Vancouver. Laviolette moved to left wing on a line with Pitre and Newsy Lalonde and the trio led the Canadiens to the Stanley Cup in 1916.

A veteran of 19 seasons, Pitre played in 282 games and scored 240 goals. His playoff record included 14 goals in 27 games. He died July 29, 1934. Elected 1962.

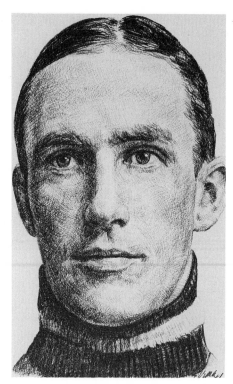

◁ Few men in Canadian sport can equal the great all-round record of athletic achievement set by **Harvey Pulford**. He was outstanding in many sports: hockey, football, lacrosse, boxing, paddling, rowing and squash.

Although born in Toronto in 1875, he spent most of his life in Ottawa, where he won championships in virtually every sport he tried. He was a defense star of Ottawa's Silver Seven from 1893 to 1908 and played on Stanley Cup winners in 1902-03, 1903-04, and 1904-05.

He played for the Ottawa Rough Riders, who won Canadian football titles in 1898, 1899, 1900 and 1902. He played for the Capitals, who ruled Canadian lacrosse from 1897 to 1900. He was light-heavy and heavyweight boxing champion of eastern Canada from 1896 to 1898. He was eastern Canadian double- and single-blade champion in paddling in 1898.

Pulford is best remembered in hockey as a clean but hard-hitting defenseman who contributed to Ottawa's Stanley Cup victories over Kenora and Dawson City.

He died in Ottawa, Ontario, on October 31, 1940. Elected 1945.

The Oxford Canadians were a successful team of Canadian-born players studying in England. They were easily able to defeat the best European teams of the 1920s and played in France, Sweden, Switzerland, Germany and other countries. Hall of Fame archives contain pictures of this club playing on outdoor rinks in Davos, Switzerland. From left: E.A. Nanton, Dick Bonnycastle, Mike Pearson, E.B. Pitblado, Ken Taylor, Jack Farthing, Roly Michener, Ron McCall, F.M. Bacon III. The names of these players read like a Who's Who of Canadian political and business life in subsequent decades.

Frank Rankin was born April 1, 1889, and right from the start was destined to play for championship teams. He was a rover in the era of seven-man hockey and played a very prominent role in Stratford's winning the OHA junior championship in three consecutive seasons — 1907, 1908 and 1909. When department-store owner John C. (later Sir John) Eaton formed the Eaton Athletic Association in Toronto in 1910, Frank Rankin played rover and captained the Eaton's hockey team to the Ontario title in both 1911 and 1912.

Rankin joined Toronto St. Michael's and played in three consecutive OHA finals from 1913 to 1915. He later went on to become a successful coach and, in 1924, directed the Toronto Granites to an Olympic championship, winning the world amateur title in a series played at Chamonix, France. Elected 1961.

Gordon Roberts was a great leftwinger who played professional hockey while acquiring a medical degree at McGill University in Montreal. He joined Ottawa in 1910, and helped them defend the Stanley Cup against Edmonton.

He entered McGill in 1911 and played six seasons with the Wanderers, reaching the playoffs only once. A strong and tireless player, he had a tremendous shot that Clint Benedict, the Ottawa goalie, claimed would curve as a result of Roberts' powerful wrist action.

On graduation from McGill in 1916, he left for the west coast, where he practiced medicine and continued to play hockey. Roberts signed with Vancouver and was sensational with the Millionaires. In 1917, he scored 43 goals in 23 games, an all-time scoring record for the Pacific Coast Hockey Association. The next year his hospital duties took him to Seattle, where he starred with the Metropolitans. He didn't play in 1919 but returned to Vancouver in 1920 and wound up his playing career that year on a team with Jack Adams and Cyclone Taylor. Born September 5, 1891, Roberts died September 2, 1966. Elected 1971.

George Taylor Richardson was born in Kingston in the 1880s, and gained early fame as a member of the Queen's University team that won the Canadian Amateur Hockey Association senior championship in 1909. Most of his senior hockey was played with the 14th Regiment of Kingston. This team lost the Ontario Hockey Association final series to Stratford in 1907 but came right back the following season to win the OHA senior title. In the 1909 Allan Cup final, Queen's University, representing the OHA, added Richardson to its roster and won the Cup.

Richardson entered the army during World War I. He went overseas as a company commanding officer of the Canadian Expeditionary Force and was killed in action on the night of February 9, 1916. Elected 1950.

In 1917 the Seattle Metropolitans of the Pacific Coast Hockey Association became the first American-based team to win the Stanley Cup. Their championship series with the Montreal Canadiens was a rough four-game encounter in which the Canadiens drew numerous costly penalties. One of Montreal's stars, Newsy Lalonde, was ejected from the third game for butt-ending the referee with his stick. The Metropolitans took three of the four games and, in returning to the U.S. with the Cup, defied Lord Stanley's original stipulation that the trophy be awarded to the top team in the Dominion of Canada.

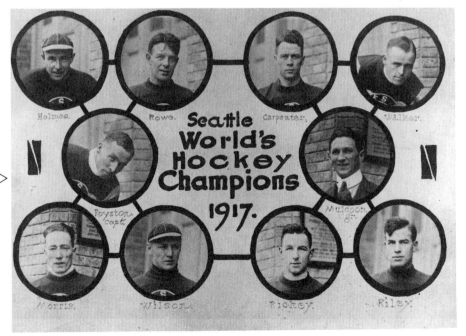

valed first division of hockey, and set salary standards for professional leagues everywhere. Hockey was good business and the O'Brien family knew it, but they were by no means the only entrepreneurs in the game.

In 1911, two Ontario-born players sold the family lumber mill to finance a professional hockey league on Canada's west coast, where first-rate hockey had never been seen before. Frank and Lester Patrick built the first artificial ice rink in Canada, raised player salaries by raiding the NHA, and built one of the most important organizations in the history of the game: the Pacific Coast Hockey Association. PCHA teams from Vancouver, Victoria, Seattle, Spokane, Portland and New Westminister competed for 15 years, and although these clubs won the Stanley Cup on only three occasions, the hockey played was equal to that of the NHA. January, 1912, saw the first ice hockey played on artificial ice in Canada. Three teams - Vancouver, Victoria and New Westminister - were included in the original schedule. The winners intended to challenge for the Stanley Cup following the season, but due to warm spring weather in the east, the PCHA did not play for the Cup until 1913.

Considerable wrangling went on behind closed doors to allow the PCHA challenge to take place. The west coast league still played seven-man hockey, while the NHA had switched to a six-man game. As well, NHA owners still resented the roster raiding carried out by the PCHA two years earlier. In 1915, the Vancouver Millionaires were the first PCHA team to win the Stanley Cup, defeating Ottawa 26-8 in a three-game total-goal series. The Millionaires were the best team money could buy, and featured seven future Hall of Famers.

CONTINUED ON PAGE 52

There are three great monuments to the memory of **John Ross Robertson**: the Ontario Hockey Association, the now-defunct Toronto *Telegram* newspaper and Toronto's Hospital for Sick Children.

Though never a player, Robertson looked upon hockey as a worthy sport and in 1898 began a six-year term as president of the OHA. A Member of Parliament, Robertson was offered a knighthood but declined. He died May 31, 1918. Elected 1945.

Claude C. Robinson was born December 17, 1881, in Harrison, Ontario, but at an early age moved to Winnipeg, where he made his great contribution to hockey. It was Robinson who first suggested the formation of a national association to compete for amateur hockey championships and he became the first secretary of the Canadian Amateur Hockey Association when it was formed in 1914.

Robinson managed the Canadian team at the 1932 Winter Olympics, held in Lake Placid, New York. He died June 27, 1976, in Vancouver. Elected 1945.

◁ By his own count, **Michael J. (Mike) Rodden** refereed 2,864 hockey games, 1,187 of which were in the NHL. Rodden was born April 24, 1891, in Mattawa, Ontario, and had a long and illustrious record in Canadian sport.

Although he was elected to the Hockey Hall of Fame in 1962 as a hockey referee, he was associated with many other aspects of sport — as a player, coach and sportswriter.

It was in football that Mike Rodden gained his greatest coaching glories. He was the guiding hand behind 27 championship teams in that game, including five in the Inter-Provincial Union, two in the Ontario Rugby Football Union and two winners of the Grey Cup.

He died January 11, 1978, in Kingston, Ontario. Elected 1962.

ARTHUR ROSS

A rthur Howie Ross was many things to the game of hockey. He was a pioneer, innovator, strategist, promoter, coach, manager and outstanding player.

Art was born in Naughton, Ontario, on January 13, 1886, and was a defenseman during a 14-year playing career that started with Westmount of the Canadian Amateur Hockey League in 1905. He played for Brandon, Manitoba, and for Kenora, Ontario, in 1907, and led the latter club to a Stanley Cup victory. His only other Stanley Cup as a player came the next year with the Montreal Wanderers. Ross subsequently played for Edmonton, Haileybury (Ontario), the Wanderers again, Ottawa, and then once more with the Wanderers, where he finished his playing career in 1918. He scored 85 goals in 167 games and added six in 16 playoff encounters.

Ross refined many aspects of the sport. He improved the design of both the puck and goal net used in the NHL and left his mark on the game in many other ways. The Art Ross Trophy is awarded annually to the scoring champion of the NHL. Ross died in Boston on August 5, 1964. Elected 1945.

W hen Lord Stanley of Preston donated a challenge cup for Canadian hockey supremacy in 1893 he named **Philip Dansken Ross** of Ottawa as one of its trustees. Ross remained a trustee for 56 years and made many important decisions concerning the Cup and the early development of hockey.

Born in Montreal in 1858, his love of the game stemmed from his playing career. Ross played with the Honorable Edward Stanley on the Rebels, a team that introduced and popularized hockey in Ontario and also prompted Edward's father, the Governor-General, to present the world's most famous hockey trophy.

Ross died in July, 1949, but not before delegating to the NHL "full authority to determine and amend . . . conditions of competition for the Stanley Cup . . . providing always that the winners . . . shall be acknowledged 'World's Professional Hockey Champions.'" Elected 1976.

An excellent two-way player throughout his career as an amateur with the Montreal Victorias, **Blair Russel** was often overshadowed by Russell Bowie. Russel played center when Bowie was at his usual position of rover, but he shifted to right wing when Bowie moved up. This pair made up the most potent scoring threat in hockey at that time.

When the Eastern Canada Amateur Hockey Association became a fully professional league in 1909, Russel refused offers to play for the Montreal Wanderers and retired. He coached the Montreal Victorias in 1910.

Blair Russel was born in Montreal on September 17, 1880, and played all his major hockey with the Victorias. He scored 110 goals in 67 games and once registered seven in a game against the Montreal Shamrocks in 1904. He died in Montreal on December 7, 1961. Elected 1965.

Ernie Russell was a fast skater and an accomplished stickhandler, equally at home playing center or rover. Although he weighed only 140 pounds, he proved to be a very proficient scoring machine, collecting 180 goals in 98 league games. He is remembered in Montreal, where he was born October 21, 1883, for his feat of scoring three goals in each of five successive games.

Ernie first appeared in senior hockey with the Montreal Winged Wheelers in 1905, but the remainder of his playing career was spent with the Montreal Wanderers. This team won the Stanley Cup four times with Russell in the lineup — 1906, 1907, 1908 and 1910. Although he played for the Wanderers, Ernie maintained membership in the AAA for other sports. This didn't suit the Wanderers, who expelled him from their membership. Because of this he didn't play hockey in 1908-09. When he returned in 1909-10, Russell and Newsy Lalonde engaged in a furious struggle for the scoring championship, which Lalonde won by scoring nine goals in the last game of the season. Russell had won a scoring title of his own in 1906-07 with 42 goals. He scored at least one goal in 10 consecutive games in 1911-12. He died in Montreal on February 23, 1963. Elected 1965.

Jack D. Ruttan was born in Winnipeg on April 5, 1889. He enjoyed a long and illustrious career in hockey, as both a player and a coach in the amateur ranks.

Ruttan's playing career began with the Armstrong's Point team which won the juvenile championship of Winnipeg in 1905-06. He switched to the Rustler club the following season and played on another city juvenile winner. By 1907-08, Jack was playing for the St. John's College team, winners of the Manitoba University Hockey League. Rattan joined the Manitoba Varsity team which won the 1909-10 championship of the Winnipeg Senior Hockey League. He stayed with the Varsity through two more seasons and then played for the Winnipeg Hockey Club. This team was exceedingly successful, winning everything from the Winnipeg League championship to the Allan Cup national senior title.

Ruttan remained in hockey as a coach for many years. He died January 7, 1973. Elected 1962.

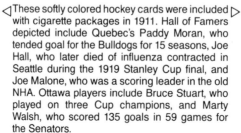

These softly colored hockey cards were included with cigarette packages in 1911. Hall of Famers depicted include Quebec's Paddy Moran, who tended goal for the Bulldogs for 15 seasons, Joe Hall, who later died of influenza contracted in Seattle during the 1919 Stanley Cup final, and Joe Malone, who was a scoring leader in the old NHA. Ottawa players include Bruce Stuart, who played on three Cup champions, and Marty Walsh, who scored 135 goals in 59 games for the Senators.

One of the great forward lines in the early days of hockey played for the Montreal Shamrocks. Each member of this line — Harry Trihey, Arthur Farrell and **Frederick Scanlan** — went on to the Hockey Hall of Fame.

Scanlan joined the club in 1897 and quickly became part of the forward foursome, which also included rover Jack Brannen. The Shamrocks, a team that began play in 1893 at St. Mary's College, won consecutive Stanley Cup victories in 1899 and 1900 after finishing in first place in their league in both seasons. Scanlan remained with the Shamrocks through 1901, and then shifted to the Winnipeg Victorias, with whom he remained until he decided to retire in 1903. At the close of his career, he was credited with having scored 16 goals in 31 games. He also scored six goals in 17 playoff contests. Elected 1965.

Joe Simpson was a man who proved himself on the ice and on the battlefield, where he won the Military Medal. He was born Harold Edward Simpson in Selkirk, Manitoba, on August 13, 1893, and became an outstanding defenseman in both amateur and professional hockey.

In his prime, "Bullet Joe" Simpson was described by Newsy Lalonde as "the greatest living hockey player." Simpson was not exceptionally big for a defenseman, but had speed to burn, earning him the nickname Bullet Joe. He played amateur hockey in 1914-15 with the Winnipeg Victorias before joining the Winnipeg 61st Battalion hockey club, which went on to win the Allan Cup.

The Battalion went overseas in 1916. Joe served with the 43rd Cameron Highlanders and rose to the rank of lieutenant. He was wounded twice in battles at the Somme and Amiens, where he won the Military Medal. Returning to hockey following World War I, Simpson played a season with the Selkirk Fishermen in 1919-20. He joined the Edmonton Eskimos in 1921-22 and played four seasons with that club. Twice during his tenure with the Eskimos, the team won the Western Canada Hockey Association championship with Simpson a major contributor to the team's success.

Joe joined the New York Americans of the NHL in 1925-26. Edmonton had received many offers for his services from both the Vancouver Maroons and the Ottawa Senators before finally selling him to New York. He remained with that team as a player until 1931, managed the Americans from 1932 until 1935, and then managed New Haven and Minneapolis before retiring from the game. He died in December, 1973. Elected 1962.

MARTY WALSH

JOE MALONE

J. HALL

The first American team to win the Cup was Seattle of the PCHA, who defeated Montreal in 1917. This created a dicey situation. No one of the Canadian hockey establishment really wanted the Cup to go south, but the Seattle organizers had extracted a promise from the Cup trustees before agreeing to play. Seattle was victorious; the promise was kept; and the Stanley Cup became an emblem of international hockey supremacy.

Fall 1916 brought some changes to the operation of the NHA. The 228th Battalion (Northern Fusiliers) had recruited a large number of sportsmen to their ranks, including a number of formidable hockey stars. The Fusiliers included George McNamara, Goldie Prodgers, Art Duncan and Eddie Oatman. With this sort of strength, the 228th was seen as a viable competitor in the NHA, and was awarded a franchise. Major Frank Robinson of the 228th succeeded the outgoing president Emmet Quinn, and Frank Calder was appointed secretary-treasurer of the NHA. After the first half of the schedule, the 228th was sent overseas, the Toronto club suspended operations, and the league was forced to draw up a four-team format.

The NHA faced a crisis the following autumn. League officials were confronted with an uncooperative owner, Toronto hockey boss Eddie Livingstone, who was so disliked that the NHA voluntarily decided to disband their league and form a new league without him. On November 26, 1917, the National Hockey League was voted into existence. As the Toronto franchise changed hands just prior to the demise of the NHA, and as it appeared that Livingstone would no longer be involved, Toronto was granted an NHL franchise along with Ottawa, Montreal Wanderers, and Les Canadiens.

CONTINUED ON PAGE 56

Skating and hockey were traditions of the Seibert family of Berlin, Ontario. Berlin was later renamed Kitchener, but the Seibert name has remained over the years as one of the greatest in the area. Oliver was a very speedy and versatile player. He started as a goaltender for Berlin, but switched to forward and starred for many years.

Born **Oliver Levi Seibert** on March 18, 1881, he at one time played on a team composed entirely of members of his family. Oliver was a leader in many respects. He was one of the first Canadians to play on artifical ice when he took part in an exhibition game in St. Louis. He also fashioned his own pair of skates made by cutting blades out of a piece of solid steel and fastening them to his shoes with screws.

After playing for the Berlin Rangers, champions of the Western Ontario Hockey Association for seven successive seasons (1900-1906), Oliver became a pro with Houghton, Michigan. He also played professionally with London and Guelph in the Ontario Pro League and with teams in the Northwestern Michigan League. Oldtimers like to recall the time Oliver skated against a trotter. The horse had a one-mile record of 2:13, but Oliver, wearing his old rocker skates, won a match race of one mile over a course laid on the ice of the Grand River. It was claimed he could skate as fast backward as forward.

Oliver was the father of Earl Seibert, another Hall of Fame member. Oliver Seibert died May 15, 1944. Elected 1961.

Although he had more than one offer to become a professional hockey player, **J. Cooper Smeaton** instead became an outstanding official, refereeing for more than a quarter of a century. In 1913 Emmett Quinn appointed Smeaton to the staff of the National Hockey Association. In that capacity, he handled many Allan and Stanley Cup games.

He managed the Philadelphia Quakers of the NHL in the 1930-31 season, but returned to refereeing the following year when Philadelphia withdrew from the league. Smeaton was appointed head referee of the NHL and continued until 1937, when he retired to devote his time to business.

Born July 22, 1890, in Carleton Place, Ontario, Smeaton moved to Montreal as a child. He played baseball, football, basketball and hockey for the Westmount AAA, and went overseas in World War I. Smeaton died on October 3, 1978, in Montreal. Elected 1961.

Thomas James Smith was born September 27, 1885, in Ottawa, one of 13 children. Five of the seven boys in his family became proficient hockey players. His brother Alf was inducted into the Hockey Hall of Fame in 1962. Tommy was known as a little bulldog of a player at 5' 4" and 150 pounds.

Smith played school and junior hockey in Ottawa and moved up to senior with the Ottawa Vics of the Federal Amateur Hockey League in 1906. He led the league in scoring and added six goals playing with the Senators in three games at the end of the season. In 1907, he joined Pittsburgh in the International League, led the team with 23 goals in 22 games and, in 1909, led all scorers in the Ontario Professional Hockey League, playing rover for Brantford. He played for Cobalt in the NHA in 1910, and led the scoring race in 1911, playing center for Galt, which won the league title but lost to Ottawa in a challenge for the Stanley Cup.

In 1912, he moved to Moncton, New Brunswick, of the Maritime Pro League. Again, Smith's team won the league title but lost in another Cup challenge to the NHA champion Quebec Bulldogs. Smith played for Quebec the next season, finally being part of a Stanley Cup triumph. He was a linemate of Joe Malone and Jack Marks, finishing just four goals behind Malone, who had 43 to win the scoring crown.

Smith was dealt to the Canadiens in 1917, retiring from hockey when the NHA dissolved the next year. He came back to play ten games with Quebec in 1919-20, but was scoreless and retired as a player at age 35. He scored 239 goals in 171 recorded league games, though records from his year in the Maritime Pro League are not available. He added 15 more goals in 15 playoff games.

He was leading scorer in his league five times and scored in 14 consecutive games in 1913. He scored nine goals in a game twice, in 1909 and 1914, and scored eight in a game in 1906. In addition, he had four five-goal performances. Tommy Smith died August 1, 1966. Elected 1973.

The Metropolitan Toronto Hockey League, a sprawling organization of minor amateur teams and probably the biggest minor hockey league in the world, had a very humble beginning. Four days after Christmas, 1911, a group of men met in the living room of a Toronto home to form a hockey league. The home belonged to Frank D. Smith and he became secretary of the Beaches Hockey League, which eventually grew into the MTHL.

Smith was a good organizer, and good secretary; so good that he held the position for more than 50 years, resigning in 1962. Frank D. Smith was born June 1, 1894, and died June 11, 1964. Elected 1962.

Alfred E. Smith was born in Ottawa, Ontario, on June 3, 1873, and played his first hockey with the Ottawa Electrics. He then played for the Ottawa Capitals and moved on to Pittsburgh, which played in a well-organized professional league. He returned to Ottawa in 1895 and showed an early penchant for rough play. After three seasons, Smith dropped out of hockey but returned, at the age of 30, after Ottawa won the Stanley Cup in 1903. He helped the team win the league championship and the Stanley Cup in the next two seasons, playing right wing on a line with Frank McGee at center.

While still a player, he coached the Ottawa Cliffsides, Allan Cup winners in 1909. He died in Ottawa, on August 21, 1953. Elected 1962.

Lord Stanley of Preston was Governor-General of Canada from 1888 to 1893. During his final year of office, he donated a trophy to be awarded to the championship hockey club of Canada. This Stanley Cup, a bowl originally costing ten guineas (equivalent to $50 at the time), has been augmented and altered over the years at a cost of many thousands of dollars. It now stands almost three feet high and has become the oldest trophy competed for by North American professional athletes. Elected 1945.

A new team, the Pittsburgh Pirates, entered the NHL in 1925 and took third place in the standings, behind the Montreal Maroons and Ottawa Hockey Club. Coach Odie Cleghorn altered the course of hockey that year by instituting fast line changes, which apparently confused the opposition. At one point in the season, Cleghorn took over for Hall of Fame goaltender Roy Worters, who was threatened with pneumonia. The Pirates' top scorer in that first season was a spry forward with the unlikely name of Hib Milks. The franchise lasted just five years.

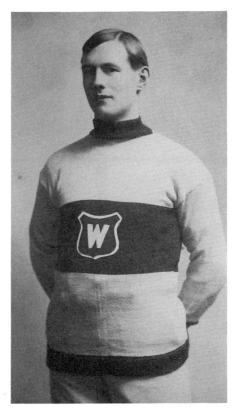

In more than a decade of professional hockey career, **Russell (Barney) Stanley** played every position on the ice except goaltender. Despite his long and successful tenure in the game, his only Stanley Cup win came in his first year as a pro.

He joined the Vancouver Millionaires on February 15, 1915, and this club went on to win the Cup.

Stanley remained with the Millionaires through the 1918-19 season and then played a season with the Edmonton Eskimos, an amateur club that he also coached. In 1920-21, he returned to pro ranks as coach of the Calgary Tigers. Barney coached and managed the Chicago Blackhawks in 1927-28.

He scored 144 goals in 216 games, twice scoring five goals in a game. Stanley was born in Paisley, Ontario, on June 1, 1893, and died May 16, 1971, in Edmonton. Elected 1962.

Born in Ottawa in 1882, **Bruce Stuart** joined the Ottawa Senators in 1898-99 and played with them for two seasons before joining the Quebec Bulldogs. During his two years with Ottawa, he scored 12 goals in six games. After a season in Quebec, he rejoined the Senators for the 1901-02 schedule before moving on to play in the International Hockey League with Pittsburgh, Houghton, and Portage Lakes.

Bruce moved to the Montreal Wanderers in 1907-08 and helped them win a Stanley Cup. In 1908-09, he became captain of the Ottawa Senators and led that team to another Stanley Cup triumph. After losing out the following year, Stuart and the Senators came back to win the Cup again in 1911. In his three Cup victories, Stuart scored 17 goals in seven games. In 45 scheduled games during his career, Stuart scored 63 goals and once scored six in a game against Quebec. He also had two five-goal games. Stuart died in Ottawa, on October 28, 1961. Elected 1961.

A tragic diving accident on June 23, 1907, in Belleville, Ontario, ended the life and hockey career of **William Hodgson (Hod) Stuart,** one of hockey's first great defensemen.

Rated one of the best of his or any other time, Hod Stuart was born in Ottawa and rose up through the minor ranks in that city. With his brother, Bruce, he broke into big-time hockey with the Ottawa Senators in 1898-99. They moved together to the Quebec Bulldogs in 1900 and while Bruce returned to Ottawa after a season, Hod remained in Quebec.

In 1902 he accepted an offer to play for Calumet, Michigan, in the International Pro League, where he also acted as captain and manager. The Montreal Wanderers negotiated for his services in December 1906 but he turned them down, stating that he had signed a contract to captain and play for Pittsburgh that winter. On December 27, 1906, he was scheduled to play a game against the Michigan Soo but refused to go on the ice because of a disagreement with the referee. He packed his bags and joined the Wanderers for what was to be his final season.

The Wanderers won the Stanley Cup in March, 1907, defeating the Kenora Thistles. Kenora had won the Cup only two months previously. During his playing career, Hod scored a total of 16 goals in 33 games for which records are available. Elected 1945.

After six games, the Wanderers gave up their franchise, as their arena had burned to the ground. This left the fledgling league with three clubs to finish its first season. Much to the chagrin of the NHL governors, Toronto, which still appeared to be controlled by Eddie Livingstone, went on to win the Stanley Cup.

In 1920 the new league added a team from Quebec, which sported Joe Malone, Harry Mummery (who played defense, tended goal for two games, and still scored 9 goals in 24 games!), Jack McDonald and Jack Marks. The following year the Quebec team was transferred to Hamilton, where they became the Tigers.

By 1923 the financial picture had changed considerably: the NHL was thriving, while support for teams on the west coast had waned. The Patrick brothers had forged a link with the Western Canada Hockey League, with teams in Calgary, Edmonton, Saskatoon and Regina, yet by the close of the 1925 season, big-league hockey in western Canada was in trouble.

In 1926, the Patricks turned their dying hockey league into hard cash and put top PCHAers into the NHL. The actual dollar amounts involved in the Patricks' dealings may never be known, but we do know that they sold the contracts of some of the PCHA's biggest stars, and that they were compensated for the sale of the Portland Rosebuds team to Chicago and the Victoria Cougars to Detroit. George Hainsworth, Art Gagne, Mickey McKay, Cully Wilson, Dick Irvin and George Hay were among the players sent east to join the swelling ranks of the NHL. Frank Patrick went north to find gold, while Lester Patrick went east to continue his quest for the elusive Stanley Cup silver as general manager of the New York Rangers.

CONTINUED ON PAGE 60

The Father of Hockey, Captain **James T. Sutherland**, was an ardent supporter of the game who worked diligently on its behalf. He made his home town of Kingston, Ontario, a famous hockey center during the years before World War I.

As a coach of the Kingston Frontenac Juniors, Sutherland guided several championship teams and fanned the hockey flame throughout Eastern Ontario. He first joined the Ontario Hockey Association as a district representative and rose through the organization's ranks to become president in 1915. He served two years in that office, and moved on to become president of the Canadian Amateur Hockey Association in 1919. He died in Kingston on September 30, 1955. Elected 1945.

The 1924-25 Boston Bruins were the first U.S.-based team to compete in the NHL. Owned by Charles Adams (top row, far left) and managed by hockey pioneer Art Ross (top row, far right), the Bruins managed only 12 points in 30 games in their first season. But Ross was a master team-builder who steadily improved the Bruins by acquiring talented amateurs and players from the Western Canada and Pacific Coast leagues.

Fred Eric (Cyclone) Taylor, O.B.E., was a ▷
brilliant hockey player in every phase of
the game and starred at defense, center
and rover. When he played defense for
Ottawa and Renfrew, his furious rushes
earned him his famous nickname.

Taylor was born in Tara, Ontario, on June
23, 1883, but first attracted attention while
playing in Listowel, Ontario. He also played
in Thessalon, Ontario, and Portage La Prairie, Manitoba, before turning pro with
Houghton, Michigan, in 1906. He spent two-
year hitches with Ottawa and Renfrew and
then joined Vancouver in 1912. He played
in Vancouver until the end of his playing
career in 1921.

Cyclone's scoring feats are legend. He
collected 194 goals in 186 league games
and another 15 in 19 playoff games. Taylor
seemed to be like old wine — he improved
with age. He was 29 when he joined Vancouver and at the age of 35 was in the
process of winning two consecutive scoring
titles, playing as a rover and center. In the
18-game schedule of 1917-18, Taylor
rapped home 32 goals. The previous season, he scored six goals in one game
against Victoria. Taylor played on two Stanley Cup-winning teams, Ottawa in 1909 and
Vancouver in 1915.

Cyclone Taylor was honored by King
George VI, who awarded him the Order of
the British Empire for his services during
World War II. In 1960, Cyclone turned the
sod for the Hockey Hall of Fame building
in Toronto. He died June 9, 1979, in Vancouver. Elected 1945.

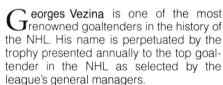

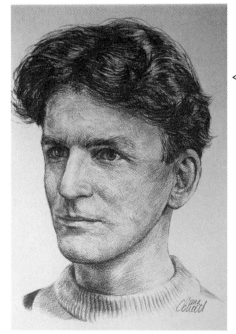

Georges Vezina is one of the most
renowned goaltenders in the history of
the NHL. His name is perpetuated by the
trophy presented annually to the top goaltender in the NHL as selected by the
league's general managers.

He was born in Chicoutimi, Quebec, in
January of 1887, and was so cool under
pressure that he came to be known as the
"Chicoutimi Cucumber." Vezina was the
nearest thing to the perfect athlete, never
missing a game from the time he broke into
the NHL until he retired 15 years later. He
was a strong competitor on the ice, and
always as gentleman, seldom becoming
excited in the heat of sustained goal-mouth
action.

Vezina first played goal in his hometown
and turned pro with the Montreal Canadiens
in 1910. He played a total of 328 consecutive league games and 39 more in the
playoffs, allowing 1,267 goals against. He
was very adroit and was able to muffle a
drive and clear it while seldom allowing a
rebound. Until 1922, goalies were not
allowed to drop to their knees to stop the
puck, making his 3.45 goals-against average even more remarkable. Georges
played on five championship teams and on
Stanley Cup winners in 1916 and 1924. His
final game was played November 28, 1925,
when he started against Pittsburgh despite
severe chest pains. He had to retire after
one period. This was the first indication of
tuberculosis, which claimed him on March
24, 1926. Elected 1945.

◁Born December 25, 1877, **Henry J.
(Harry) Trihey** starred in hockey,
lacrosse and football. A powerful man, he
was a smart stickhandler and strategist, and
was the first to utilize a three-man line,
leaving the rover free to roam. He also
encouraged defensemen to carry the puck.
On February 4, 1899, he scored 10 goals
when the Shamrocks downed Quebec 13-
4, one of the highest single game totals in
Stanley Cup play. He was rover and captain
of the Montreal Shamrocks when they won
the Cup in 1899 and 1900, and had earlier
starred at McGill University.

After retiring as a player, Trihey became
secretary-treasurer of the Canadian Amateur Hockey League and, later, the league
president. He refereed many league and
Stanley Cup games. Trihey died in Montreal
on December 9, 1942. Elected 1950.

◁J ohn Phillip Walker played only two seasons in the NHL, but he enjoyed 30 years of close association with the game and won many honors as a left wing and rover.

He was born in Silver Mountain, Ontario, on November 28, 1888. He played for the Toronto Blueshirts, who won the Stanley Cup in 1914. After two seasons in Toronto, he went west to Seattle and, in 1917, again contributed to a Stanley Cup victory. Walker's third Stanley Cup came with the 1925 Victoria Cougars. Detroit purchased his contract in 1926. He played two seasons with them before returning west to join the Edmonton Eskimos. He died in Seattle, on February 16, 1950. Elected 1960.

◁H arry E. (Moose) Watson is considered one of the greatest all-round forwards in the history of hockey. He was born in St. John's, Newfoundland, on July 14, 1898.

Watson played for the Toronto Dentals in 1919, moving over to the Toronto Granites the following year. The Granites won the Allan Cup in 1922 and 1923, adding the Olympic championship in 1924. Watson was an outstanding player for Canada in the Olympics, scoring 13 of 30 goals in one game against Czechoslovakia. A fast man for his huge size, Watson was offered a $30,000 contract to play the 1925-26 season with the Montreal Maroons. He was regarded as the best amateur center in Canada at the time. Harry had previously declined the offer of a pro contract from the Toronto St. Pats.

Watson retired as a player in 1925 but came back in 1931 with the Toronto National Sea Fleas, as both player and coach, as that team went on to win the Allan Cup. He died in Toronto, on September 11, 1957. Elected 1962.

I n his 50 years of officiating Fred C. Waghorne took part in more than 2,000 hockey games and 1,500 lacrosse games, and contributed several innovations and rule changes.

He initiated the practice of dropping the puck during faceoffs; previously the puck had been placed on the ice between the players' stick blades. He also implemented the use of a whistle rather than a handbell to stop play.

Fred C. Waghorne was one of the pioneers of the Toronto Hockey League, which was organized in 1911. Born in Tunbridge Wells, England, in 1866, he died in 1956 at the age of 90. Elected 1961.

Frederick Whitcroft was a rover in the days of seven-man hockey.

Although he was born in Port Perry, Ontario, Fred first drew attention to his playing ability in the Peterborough, Ontario, area. He played for the Peterborough Colts in 1901 when they won the Ontario Hockey Association junior championship, defeating a good Stratford team in the final series. He shifted his services to the Manitoba Senior Hockey League, playing for the Kenora Thistles when they won the Stanley Cup in January, 1907.

At the end of the 1907 season, Whitcroft moved to Edmonton, scoring 49 goals as captain of a senior club that unsuccessfully challenged Ottawa for the Stanley Cup.

After retiring as a player, Whitcroft moved to Vancouver, where he died in 1931. Elected 1962.

Although he entertained numerous offers to become a professional hockey player, Gordon Allan (Phat) Wilson remained an amateur throughout a lengthy career as a player and coach. Wilson was born in Port Arthur, Ontario, on December 29, 1895, and developed into one of the finest defensemen of his era.

His first senior team was the Port Arthur War Veterans. He joined the club in 1918 and remained with it until 1920. The following season he played with Iroquois Falls of the Northern Ontario Hockey Association, defeating the Soo Greyhounds for the league title. He returned to the Port Arthur Bearcats and was a member of the team that won the Allan Cup in 1925, 1926 and 1929. In 1930, Wilson played with the same team, winning the western Canada title.

He lived in Thunder Bay until his death in August, 1970. Elected 1962.

Born in Egmondville, Ontario, on November 5, 1904, Ralph Weiland acquired the nickname "Cooney" as a child. He played 11 seasons in the NHL with Boston, Detroit and the Ottawa Senators and was a member of two Stanley Cup champions with the Bruins of 1929 and 1939, his first and last seasons in the NHL.

In 11 seasons, he totalled 173 goals and 160 assists in 509 regular-season games and 12 goals and 10 assists in the playoffs. His best season saw him score 43 goals in 44 games in 1930. He was voted to the NHL's second all-star team in 1935.

A very slick stickhandler, Weiland came to the Bruins from Minneapolis. In Boston, he became part of the "Dynamite Line" with Dit Clapper and Dutch Gainor. Cooney was sold to Ottawa for the 1932-33 season and then went to Detroit, but returned to Boston in 1935-36 in a trade for Marty Barry. He remained with Boston until his retirement as a player. He coached the Bruins beginning in 1939. They won their third Stanley Cup — and last until 1970 — under his guidance in 1941. Elected 1971.

◁Lester Patrick opened up the west coast to pro hockey, building arenas in Vancouver and Victoria and founding the Pacific Coast Hockey Association with his brother Frank. When the league foundered in 1925, Patrick took his team, the Victoria Cougars, into the new Western Canada Hockey League. In March 1925 in Vancouver the Cougars faced off against the Montreal Canadiens — Morenz, Joliat, Vezina, and company — for the Stanley Cup, which they won handily in a four-game series. Crowds are said to have stood at the corner of Peel and Ste. Catharine streets in Montreal until 2 a.m. to get telegraphic reports of the games as they came over the wire. Four Victoria players — "Happy" Holmes, Frank Fredrickson, Frank Foyston and Jack Walker, as well as manager Lester Patrick — are members of the Hockey Hall of Fame.

With the demise of the PCHA, the NHL became hockey's undisputed major league and sole proprietor of the Stanley Cup. Fortified by highly skilled players from the western teams, the NHL expansion clubs — Chicago, Detroit, Boston and the New York Rangers — were a powerful force. From 1927 to 1946, American expansion teams won 11 of 20 Stanley Cups.

Marty Walsh was born in Kingston, Ontario, in 1883, and gained his first hockey notoriety with Queen's University of the Ontario Hockey Association. Queen's challenged Ottawa's Silver Seven in 1906. Ottawa's great center, Frank McGee, found himself playing against Walsh. Queen's lost, but Walsh made such a fine impression that Ottawa tried to sign him after McGee retired.

Walsh didn't immediately accept the Ottawa offer. Instead, he joined the International Pro League, where he broke a leg. When his leg mended, he joined Ottawa in 1908.

Walsh was a very nimble and tricky skater with a knack for always being in the right position for a shot. In five seasons with Ottawa, he played in 59 league games and scored 135 goals. He also had 26 goals in eight playoff games and played on Stanley Cup winners in 1909 and 1911. Walsh had many games in which he scored a large number of goals, including ten against Port Arthur on March 16, 1911. Marty Walsh died in Gravenhurst, Ontario, in 1915. Elected 1962.

An elusive style for a man of comparatively small physique earned **Harry Westwick** the nickname "Rat" during his early days as a member of the Ottawa Senators.

Westwick was born in Ottawa, Ontario, on April 23, 1876, and started his hockey career as a goaltender. He was also a fine lacrosse player, starring with the famous Ottawa Capitals for several seasons. In hockey, he played goal for the Ottawa Seconds but was soon converted to play rover and went on to become one of the game's outstanding competitors at this position. He played for the Aberdeens of the Ottawa City League and graduated to the Senators in 1895. He played for that team when it won three consecutive Stanley Cups, starting in 1903.

Westwick had his most productive season in 1905, scoring a total of 24 goals in 13 games, as the Senators, who were also known as the Silver Seven, won their third consecutive Stanley Cup.

Westwick retired before another Cup came to Ottawa in 1909. Following his retirement as a player, he retained a close connection with the sport, refereeing briefly in the National Hockey Association. He died in Ottawa on April 3, 1957. Elected 1962.

The NHL Emerges
1927-1945

The NHL Emerges *(clockwise from top left)*
The Prince of Wales Trophy was first awarded to the regular-season champion of the NHL in 1924. Today it is awarded to the club winning the Prince of Wales Conference Championship. The New York Americans always wore patriotic *sweaters*. The Amerks were a part of the NHL from 1925 to 1942. Goaltender Lorne Chabot used these *padded gloves* with rigid protective cuffs. Two of the NHL's top scorers of the 1930s — Charlie Conacher and Nels Stewart — used these *sticks* in their last NHL games. Both were leading stars, depicted here on the cover of *programs* sold at the Montreal Forum. The *tube skate* had taken over by the 1930's. This example belonged to U.S.-born defenseman Alex Levinsky who played with Toronto, the Rangers and Chicago.

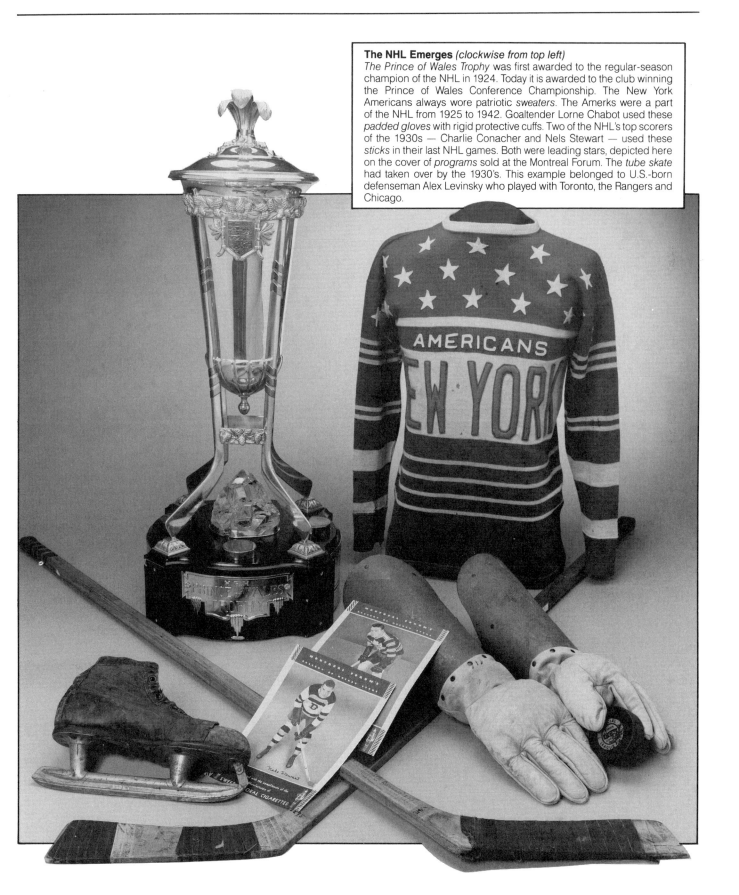

In 1927, hockey was half a century old. With the NHL established as the sport's elite league, hockey had grown from being a game that entertained a few high-spirited McGill students to an amateur sport popular among the upper classes, and through a period of unacknowledged professionalism to become an international entertainment circuit.

The 1920s were a period of unprecedented growth in professional sports. NHL expansion began in 1924 when two new teams, the Montreal Maroons and the Boston Bruins, purchased franchises. The Maroons became established as the English Montrealers' counterpart to Les Canadiens, and captured the Stanley Cup in their second NHL season. The Maroons were not a team of big names, but they were hard workers who, under coach Eddie Gerard, regularly turned in respectable results. Their top players included Hall of Fame members Nels Stewart, Red Dutton, George Boucher and Clint Benedict.

As expected, the introduction of the Maroons put a new spark into the game in Montreal. Both Montreal teams played at the Forum, where the biggest games were always those involving the crosstown rivals. A generation of Montreal hockey fans remember this period as a time of intense, but friendly, rivalry.

The Maroons would take one more Cup, in 1935, under the tutelage of Tommy Gorman, before disbanding at the close of the 1937-38 season. King Clancy, retired as a player, coached the Maroons in their last season.

The Boston Bruins also entered the NHL in 1924. Managed by former star player Art Ross, they quickly climbed the rankings until in 1929 they took the first of the three Stanley Cups they would win in this early period. Ross, who had been a rushing defenseman in his playing days,

There is little in hockey that Sidney Gerald (Sid) Abel has not done — and done well. He began his NHL career in 1938 with the Detroit Red Wings and spent nine full seasons in a Detroit uniform. He was an all-star at two different positions, won the Hart Trophy, and captained the Wings at 24.

Abel scored 189 NHL goals, including a personal high of 34 in the 1949-50 season and a league-leading 28 in 1948-49. He left Detroit in 1952 to become playing coach of the Chicago Blackhawks, leading that team to its first playoff berth in nine seasons.

In eleven seasons behind the Wings' bench, his teams won a league championship and made the Stanley Cup playoffs seven times. Elected 1969.

From November 1, 1924, (when his father Charles was awarded an NHL franchise) until his death on March 19, 1973, **Weston W. Adams** was intimately associated with the Boston Bruins. After graduating from Harvard, where he played goal, he became a director of the Bruins. In 1932 he took over as president of the Boston Tigers, a Bruins' farm team. He succeeded his father as Bruins' president in 1936 but gave up an active role when the U.S. entered World War II. He served in the Pacific with the navy, retiring at war's end with the rank of Commander. At this time the club merged with the Boston Garden Arena Corporation and its corporate structure changed. Weston Adams, Sr., relinquished his club presidency although he remained a majority stockholder at the Garden.

He became chairman of the board of the Boston Garden in 1956 and two years later was elected chairman of the hockey club as well. By 1964 he was club president again, remaining in office until 1969, when he retired in favor of his son, Weston, Jr. Elected 1972.

Franklin (Frank) Ahearn was the pride, the power and the passion behind Ottawa's great NHL days of the 1920s. Ahearn bought out his partner Tommy Gorman in 1924, became sole owner of the NHL Ottawa Senators and assembled a lineup of such stars as Hooley Smith, Alex Connell, Allan Shields, Alex Smith, Jack Adams, Frank Finnigan, Hec Kilrea, George Boucher, Frank Nighbor and Syd Howe. His team won the Stanley Cup in 1927.

The Depression years halted his benevolence and he was forced to sell off his star attractions. He eventually disposed of his rink holdings as well but, despite his shrewd player sales, his hockey losses were estimated at $200,000. Ahearn was born May 10, 1886, in Ottawa and died November 17, 1962. Elected 1962.

◁ **Charles Francis Adams** made hockey and the Adams name synonymous in Boston. Always an ardent fan, he saw the Stanley Cup finals of 1924 in Montreal and immediately set out to get an NHL franchise for Boston. With partner Art Ross, he formed the Bruins and the team played the first NHL game in the United States in December of the same year.

Born October 18, 1876, in Newport, Vermont, he purchased the entire Western Canada League from the Patrick brothers in 1926, for about one quarter of a million dollars. This secured such stars as Eddie Shore, Harry Oliver, Mickey MacKay and Duke Keats for the Bruins and provided Detroit, Chicago and New York with numerous other fine players.

In 1927, Adams guaranteed $500,000 over five years for the 24 home games the Bruins would play in each NHL season. This guarantee financed the construction of the Boston Garden, where the Bruins still play, and where Adams saw them win three Stanley Cups before his death in 1947. Elected 1960.

▷ The Philadelphia Quakers were a one-season entry in the NHL, playing in the League's American Division in 1930-31. The Quakers weren't successful on the ice, winning only four of 44 games played.

THE NHL EMERGES

knew the value of solid checkers and stocked the roster with the likes of Lionel Conacher, Lionel Hitchman, Sprague Cleghorn and the stalwart Eddie Shore. Bringing defenseman Dit Clapper up across the blue line to join Cooney Weiland proved a very productive move, and created an emphasis on offense that would culminate in the "Kraut Line" of Woody Dumart, Milt Schmidt and Bobby Bauer. The Krauts finished 1-2-3 in the 1939-40 NHL scoring race, their first year as linemates, and led Boston to a Stanley Cup victory in 1939 and again in 1941. The Bruins of this period were a tough team — the single-mindedness of Eddie Shore would cause the team a good deal of grief, as he spent lots of time in the penalty box. Since he often played sixty-minute shifts, he perhaps saw the penalty box as his only chance to catch his breath without losing face.

Hockey was as tough in the boardroom as it was on the ice. In 1925, the Hamilton Tigers led the overall standings by one point over Toronto, who were two points up on the Canadiens. Fourth place finisher Ottawa was only one point back of Montreal. The Hamilton players were scheduled to play more than the number of games stipulated in their contracts because of the playoffs, so they asked management for more cash. When the request was denied, it was replaced by a demand, and backed by the threat of a strike. In a stunning power play, League president Frank Calder and the NHL Board of Governors ordered the next-best teams, Toronto and the Canadiens, to play off for the League title. The Hamilton franchise was disbanded, and emerged as the New York Americans the following season.

The New York Americans looked a lot like the Hamilton team but failed to deliver the results of earlier years. Under

Charles Joseph Sylvanus Apps was born January 18, 1915, in Paris, Ontario, and was an exceptionally fine athlete, even as a youngster. He played hockey and football for McMaster University in Hamilton, excelling at both. In his final junior year, he played amateur hockey with the Hamilton Tigers. He was also a great pole-vaulter, winning the Canadian and British Empire championships in 1934 and the Canadian again in 1935. He finished sixth in the 1936 Olympic Games to earn a point for Canada.

Although a modest, quiet type, Apps was a great inspirational leader of the Toronto Maple Leafs. His entire professional career was spent with Toronto, most of it as team captain. He joined the Leafs in 1936 and became the first winner of the Calder Trophy, awarded at that time by NHL president Frank Calder to the outstanding rookie in the league.

Apps played seven more seasons before becoming a member of the Canadian Armed Forces during World War II. In his pre-war career, he played on one Stanley Cup winner, was voted to the first all-star team at center twice and to the second team three times, and won the Lady Byng Trophy in 1941-42.

Returning to the Leafs for the 1945-46 season, Apps continued his fine play and in the next three seasons scored 24, 25 and 26 goals to bring his career total to 201 — an average of 20 per season. He also led the Leafs to two more Stanley Cup triumphs, retiring after the 1947-48 season. Elected 1961.

Irvine W. (Ace) Bailey's NHL career was relatively brief, due to a disastrous incident on December 12, 1933, when a collision with Eddie Shore resulted in a fractured skull that terminated his playing days. In eight seasons as an outstanding winger with the Toronto Maple Leafs, Bailey had established himself as both a scorer and a defensive star.

He signed with the Toronto St. Pats. When they became the Maple Leafs, he, along with Hap Day and Babe Dye, were the cornerstones of the new club. Bailey was the club's top scorer, leading the NHL in both scoring and points in 1928-29. He also played on the Cup-winning team of 1932-33.

Ace later coached, then joined the staff of minor officials at Maple Leaf Gardens, where he was still active at the time of his induction. In 313 NHL games, Ace scored 111 goals and had 82 assists. Elected 1975.

The record books show that **Martin J. (Marty) Barry** was almost 26 years old before he made it to the NHL to stay. Once there, however, he achieved great success.

He earned a regular spot with the Boston Bruins in 1929 and remained with them until 1935-36, when he was traded to Detroit.

With the Red Wings he played on a line with Herbie Lewis and Larry Aurie that was one of the most effective combinations in the league. The Wings won the Stanley Cup in 1935-36 and 1936-37. Barry won the Lady Byng Trophy and was named to the first all-star team. He died August 20, 1969, at his home in Halifax, Nova Scotia. Elected 1965.

Hector (Toe) Blake was tabbed very early in life as a coming superstar of hockey. Ensuing events bore this out, for he succeeded not only in becoming a great player, but an outstanding coach, too.

Blake joined the Montreal Maroons in February, 1934. The Maroons won the Stanley Cup in 1935, but Blake sat on the bench. He started the next season with Providence but joined the Canadiens in February when the Maroons traded him and Bill Miller for goalie Lorne Chabot. The rest is NHL history as Blake starred with the Canadiens until retiring on January 11, 1948, when he broke his leg.

Blake won the NHL scoring title and the Hart Trophy in 1939 and the Lady Byng Trophy in 1946. For several seasons he was part of one of the NHL's greatest forward combinations, the Punch Line, with Elmer Lach and Maurice Richard. He scored 235 goals in 572 league games, and played on two Stanley Cup winners.

He returned to the Canadiens as coach in 1955. His teams won eight more Stanley Cups before he retired in 1968. Elected 1966.

Tommy Gorman in their first season in New York, they finished with a 12-20-4 record, good enough for fifth place in the seven-team NHL.

The Americans did everything to win and attract fans. They had respectable rosters, with the likes of Red Dutton, Roy Worters, Jakie Forbes, Normie Himes, Sweeney Schriner, Lorne Carr, Nels Stewart, Baldy Cotton, Carl Voss, Ching Johnson and even Eddie Shore making appearances over the years. They changed the uniform style more times in their 16 years than most clubs change in a lifetime. They were coached by many former stars: Tommy Gorman, Newsy Lalonde, Wilf Green, Lionel Conacher, Eddie Gerard, Bullet Joe Simpson and Red Dutton all had a go at making something of the Americans. They even tried moving the franchise to Brooklyn in 1941, but the effort was futile, and the Americans finally left the NHL at the close of the 1941-42 season. Despite plans to revive the franchise after the war, the Americans were finished in 1942.

Pittsburgh arrived in the NHL in 1925 with some fresh faces. The team had been known as the "Yellow Jackets," and was led by Lionel Conacher, the Canadian football star who was studying on an athletic scholarship in Pittsburgh. The Yellow Jackets had been a good local team and had won the U.S. Amateur Championship. When they joined the NHL, they were further bolstered by some seasoned skaters and by Oddie Cleghorn, a playing coach who is credited with introducing the first successful system of rapid line changes.

However, the Pittsburgh team, called the Pirates, never achieved the kind of results necessary to keep the fans coming, and in 1930 the franchise was shifted to Philadelphia where they played as the

CONTINUED ON PAGE 72

John Paris Bickell's hockey involvement came in a roundabout manner. Bickell was a silent partner in the Toronto St. Pats hockey club. When the St. Pats were purchased by the newly formed Maple Leaf hockey club in 1927, Conn Smythe convinced Bickell to transfer his interests, both financial and personal, to the Leafs. Bickell supported Smythe's view that a new arena was needed and provided financial knowledge and support to float an issue of Maple Leaf Gardens stock. The building was erected in five months during the worst economic depression of the 20th century.

Bickell became the first president and chairman of the board of Maple Leaf Gardens, serving until his death on August 22, 1951. Elected 1978.

Frank Boucher devoted more than a half-century to hockey and, above all else, was a gentleman. Considered one of the great playmakers of all time, Boucher won the Lady Byng Trophy seven times in eight seasons and was finally given permanent possession of the original trophy.

Born October 7, 1901, in Ottawa, he was a member of a hockey-playing family. At one time, four Bouchers were playing major league hockey — George with Ottawa, Billy and Bob with the Canadiens and Frank with Vancouver.

Tommy Gorman offered him $1,200 a year to play for Ottawa and he leapt at the chance. At first Frank rode the bench with another fellow named King Clancy. He played the next four years with the Vancouver Maroons, but when the team folded, he went to New York and wound up centering Bill and Bun Cook on one of the great lines of the era.

Frank stayed with the Rangers' organization from 1926 until 1944 and played on two Stanley Cup winners. Although retired as a player, he coached the Rangers to a Stanley Cup win in 1939-40. He died December 12, 1977, in Kemptville, Ontario. Elected 1958.

Francis Charles (Frank) Brimsek was a star virtually from the day he stepped into the NHL. He was also one of the first players born in the United States who rose to stardom in the sport.

Born September 26, 1915, in Eveleth, Minnesota, he replaced the great Cecil (Tiny) Thompson in the Boston nets in 1938 and went on to win both the Vezina Trophy as the league's top goalie and the Calder Trophy as the outstanding rookie. He was almost immediately tabbed "Mr. Zero" because he twice registered shutout strings of three games in a row. Brimsek played in the NHL until 1950, finishing his career with a one-year stint in Chicago.

It would be difficult to exceed that success of his first season, but Brimsek remained a star, playing on another Stanley Cup winner in 1940-41 and winning another Vezina Trophy in 1941-42. Elected 1966.

◁ An outstanding defenseman from a celebrated hockey family, George (Buck) Boucher played pro for 20 years, 17 in the NHL. Before turning to pro hockey, George had played three years of football with the Ottawa Rough Riders and was considered a great halfback.

He was born in Ottawa in 1896, and joined the Senators in 1915. This Ottawa Senators team won the Stanley Cup four times between 1920 and 1927. Midway through the 1928-29 season, George was sold to the Montreal Maroons. Two years later he went to Chicago.

During his career, George scored 122 goals, an outstanding total for a defenseman of that era. He died October 17, 1960, in Ottawa. Elected 1960.

◁ Anyone for tea? The NHL's first twenty-year man, Dit Clapper of the Bruins, was presented with a silver tea set prior to a game at Maple Leaf Gardens in 1946. Clapper scored 41 goals in a 44-game season for Boston in 1939-40. He was instrumental in three Stanley Cup victories with the Bruins between 1929 and 1941.

68

Walter A. Brown made a large contribution to the sports world. At the time of his death on September 7, 1964, he was president of Boston Garden, chairman of the Basketball Hall of Fame Corporation, member of the Hockey Hall of Fame Governing Committee and past president of the International Ice Hockey Federation. He was also co-owner and president of the Boston Bruins hockey club and the Boston Celtics basketball team.

Born February 10, 1905, he followed in the footsteps of his father, George V. Brown, as a strong promoter of hockey in schools and colleges. He succeeded his father as general manager of Boston Garden in 1937. Elected 1962.

Angus Daniel Campbell was born March 19, 1884, in Stayner, Ontario. He played hockey and lacrosse while at the University of Toronto and was on championship teams in both sports. During the 1909-10 season he was in Cobalt, Ontario, playing on a team with such greats as Walter Smaill, Art Ross, Herb Clarke and Bruce Ridpath. He returned to Cobalt after graduation and played hockey there until 1914.

After his hockey career, Campbell concentrated on the development of amateur hockey in northern Ontario. He was first president of the Northern Ontario Hockey Association when it was formed in 1919. He later became an executive on the Ontario Hockey Association. He died in 1976, in Toronto. Elected 1964.

The Oxford Canadians were a successful team of Canadian-born players studying in England. They were easily able to defeat the best European teams of the 1920s and played in France, Sweden, Switzerland, Germany and other countries. Hall of Fame archives contain pictures of this club playing on outdoor rinks in Davos, Switzerland. From left: E.A. Nanton, Dick Bonnycastle, Mike Pearson, E.B. Pitblado, Ken Taylor, Jack Farthing, Roly Michener, Ron McCall, F.M. Bacon III. The names of these players read like a Who's Who of Canadian political and business life in subsequent decades.

William (Billy) Burch was born in Yonkers, New York, on November 20, 1900, but came to Canada as a boy and learned his hockey around Toronto. He turned pro with the Hamilton Tigers in 1923 and centered a line of the Green brothers, Redvers (Red) and Wilfred (Shorty), which carried the team to first place in the NHL in 1925. Burch was awarded the Hart Trophy that season as the most valuable player to his team.

The Hamilton team was shifted to the U.S. where it became the New York Americans in 1926 and Burch, an excellent playmaker and stickhandler, was made captain. In 1927, he was winner of the Lady Byng Trophy, but missed much of the 1928 season because of a knee injury. Billy remained with the Americans until 1932, when he was sold to Boston, who in turn let him go to Chicago. This was his last active year as, near the end of the season, he broke a leg and decided to retire.

Billy Burch led his teams in scoring in the seasons of 1924, 1925, 1926, 1927 and 1929. In 390 regular season games, he scored 135 goals and earned 42 assists. A strike and lockout of Hamilton players over playoff bonus money in 1925 cost Burch his best chance to be on a Stanley Cup winner. The Tigers had finished first but were dropped from the playoffs when they could not come to terms with management regarding payment for the series. He died in December, 1950. Elected 1974.

The Irish of Ottawa produced many fine athletes, but none more outstanding than Francis Michael (King) Clancy. He was one of the most refreshing athletes ever to compete in the NHL. Clancy was born February 25, 1903, and inherited the name King from an equally outstanding father.

He played amateur hockey with St. Brigid's, but signed to play professionally at the age of 18 with the Ottawa Senators. King became a regular with that club after the retirement of Eddie Gerard and quickly established himself as an outstanding player. In 1930, Clancy was the key figure in what has since been called "the best deal in hockey." Conn Smythe, manager of the Toronto Maple Leafs, paid the then-unheard-of sum of $35,000 and two players to acquire Clancy from Ottawa. Smythe obviously saw the leadership qualities he desired in Clancy and the King repaid him by leading the Leafs to their first Stanley Cup victory in 1931-32.

He was twice named to each of the first and second NHL all-star teams and remained an outstanding rushing defenseman until he retired early in the 1936-37 season. Clancy coached the Montreal Maroons for the first half of the 1937-38 season and then became a referee. He returned to the Leaf's organization in 1950, coaching the team from 1953 to 1956. "The time to quit is when it's no longer fun," King once said, and hockey remained fun for him throughout his life. He died November 8, 1986, in Toronto. Elected 1958.

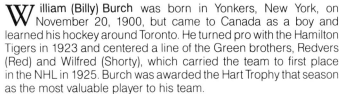

◁ In 1930, Conn Smythe paid $35,000 and traded two players to Ottawa to obtain the services of defenseman King Clancy. These cancelled cheques add up to $25,000. Smythe raised the last $10,000 by hitting a long-shot winner at the racetrack.

During his 12-year stay in the NHL, William Osser (Bill) Cook scored 228 goals and 140 assists. Cook was a member of one of the all-time great lines, with brother Bun Cook and playmaking center Frank Boucher. He was a strong sharpshooter who played his entire NHL career with the New York Rangers. In that span he was on Stanley Cup champions in 1928 and 1933.

Born October 8, 1896, in Brantford, Ontario, Bill broke into organized hockey in Kingston with the Frontenac Juniors in 1916. He served overseas during World War I, but returned to play intermediate hockey with the Frontenacs in 1919. He spent a year with the Sault Ste. Marie Greyhounds before turning professional in 1922 with the Saskatoon Sheiks. Cook became a star during four years in the Western Canada Hockey League, winning the scoring championship on three occasions. In the 1924-25 season, he scored 31 goals in 30 games.

The New York Rangers entered the NHL in 1926, coinciding with the demise of the WCHL, and the Rangers purchased the contracts of both Cook brothers, later adding Boucher to form their great scoring unit. Bill Cook added the NHL scoring crown to his laurels in that first season, scoring 33 goals in 44 games. He tied Charlie Conacher with 34 goals to lead the league in 1932 and won the honors outright the following season with 28 goals. He retired from the NHL in 1937 after being named to the first all-star team three times and to the second team on one occasion. His WCHL record was 87 goals and 58 assists. Cook also scored 16 goals and earned 10 assists in Stanley Cup playoffs. He died March 5, 1986, in Kingston, Ontario. Elected 1952.

Neil MacNeil Colville played his entire pro career with the New York Rangers. He is best remembered as a member of New York's famous "Bread Line" with his brother Mac and Alex Shibicky. Born August 4, 1914, in Edmonton, he played three seasons of junior hockey in and around Edmonton before moving into the Rangers' organization.

Colville moved up to the Rangers in 1936 and played on the Bread Line for six years. During these years, the Rangers won the Stanley Cup in 1940 and the NHL championship in 1942. From 1942 to 1945, he was stationed with the Canadian armed forces in Ottawa, where he captained the 1942-43 Allan Cup-winning Ottawa Commandos. When he was discharged, he returned to play four more seasons on defense with the Rangers. Elected 1967.

Alex Connell set a goaltending record during the 1927-28 season that has stood the test of time. He registered six consecutive shutouts and was not scored upon for 446 minutes and nine seconds. He was known as the "Ottawa Fireman," partly because of his position as secretary of the Ottawa Fire Department and partly because he often put out the fire of opposition marksmen.

Born in Ottawa in 1900, Connell was also a standout baseball and lacrosse player. He was a catcher in the Interprovincial League and played on Ottawa's Eastern Canada lacrosse champions of the 1920s. Connell entered hockey almost by accident, being talked into playing goal while serving in the army at Kingston in World War I. Returning to civilian life, he played in the St. Brigid's League and for the Cliffsides, where his trademark became the small black cap he wore while tending goal.

He turned pro with the Ottawa Senators in 1924 when the team's regular goalie, Clint Benedict, went to the Montreal Maroons. With Connell in goal, Ottawa won the Stanley Cup in 1927. The following year he set his fabulous shutout streak, allowing only 57 goals in 44 games. Alex retired in 1933 but came back in 1934 to help the Montreal Maroons win the Stanley Cup. He continued to coach junior teams until 1949, spending several seasons with the St. Patrick's College juniors. He died in Ottawa on May 10, 1958. Elected 1958.

F̲ew players have accomplished as much in their hockey careers as **Aubrey Vere (Dit) Clapper,** who was the first NHLer to play in the league for 20 years. His steady genius graced NHL arenas from 1927 to 1947.

Born in Newmarket, Ontario, on February 9, 1907, he moved to Hastings, Ontario, while quite young and soon embarked on a hockey career that few will equal. He was only 13 when he played junior at Oshawa and 19 when he became a regular with the Boston Bruins. In between, he played for the Toronto Parkdale Canoe Club. Through his 20 seasons with Boston, Clapper played nine seasons at right wing and 11 on defense and was regarded as "an athlete's athlete." He was a big player, over six feet and 200 pounds, but most often used his heft to stop fights.

Dit scored his 200th goal in Toronto in 1941, giving his Bruins a 1-0 victory over the Maple Leafs. He finished with 228 goals and 246 assists in the regular season along with 12 goals and 23 assists in the playoffs. His highest single-season scoring mark was 41 goals in the 44-game schedule of 1929-30. Clapper played on three Stanley Cup championship teams with Boston: 1929, 1939, and 1941. He was also named three times to each of the first and second NHL all-star teams.

On February 12, 1947, Dit Clapper officially retired from playing hockey. The Boston Bruins retired his number 5 sweater and he was elected to the Hockey Hall of Fame. He coached the Bruins for two years and returned to hockey from business life to coach the Buffalo Bisons of the American Hockey League for one season in 1960. He died January 21, 1978, in Peterborough, Ontario. Elected 1947.

The forerunner of modern NHL all-star contests, ▷ the Ace Bailey benefit game saw the Toronto Maple Leafs, wearing dark "ACE" jerseys, take on the best of the rest of the NHL. This photo is a "who's who" of hockey in the 1930s.

H̲e was big and strong, and with a heavy shot that was the nemesis of every goaltender in the NHL. That was **Charlie Conacher,** member of a famous athletic family, who played 13 seasons in the league before retiring.

Considered one of the greatest rightwingers of any era, Conacher was born December 10, 1909, in Toronto. He was as neat and shifty around the net as he was adept at blasting through with a bullet-like shot. He made the jump into the NHL directly from junior hockey. He last played amateur for the Toronto Marlboros in the 1928-29 season, joining the Maple Leafs after the Marlboros had won the Memorial Cup. Conacher played nine seasons with Toronto before being traded to Detroit,

where he played for a year.

From 1939 until 1941, he was with the New York Americans, retiring at the end of that season. During his NHL career, Conacher scored 225 goals and won the scoring title in 1934 and 1935. In all, he was the league's top goal scorer for four consecutive seasons, sharing the lead with Bill Cook in 1932 and Bill Thoms in 1936. He was a first all-star three times and second all-star twice.

Charlie turned to coaching junior hockey after leaving the NHL but returned in 1947 to coach the Chicago Blackhawks. He left Chicago after the 1949-50 season and retired into the business world. He died December 30, 1967, in Toronto. Elected 1961.

Quakers. Philadelphia's first NHL franchise would play exactly one desperate season, finishing with only four wins in 44 games. With the addition of the Rangers, Detroit Cougars and Blackhawks in the fall of 1926, the NHL had become a ten-team league, split into two divisions. The Canadian Division included all the Canadian teams — Toronto, Montreal Canadiens, Montreal Maroons and Ottawa Senators — plus the New York Americans. The American Division consisted of the remaining American franchises: Detroit, Boston, New York Rangers, Pittsburgh and Chicago. The increase in the number of teams meant that each team would now play 44 games, an increase from the 36 played previously. The two-division system remained in place until 1938.

While the NHL was booming in the USA in the 1920s and 1930s, the league's Canadian teams were developing their own star attractions. In Montreal, legends were being written around the likes of Aurel Joliat and Howie Morenz. When Leo Dandurand brought Joliat up from the amateur club in Iroquois Falls in a deal for Newsy Lalonde, people thought he was crazy. What could this little pipsqueak do better than Newsy, who was one of hockey's greatest stars? But Joliat, who would play for another 16 years, could fly like the wind, and from the start the Canadiens fans loved him. Joliat would doff his peaked cap and rush up the wing at full tilt. When in the next season Dandurand matched Joliat with rookie Howie Morenz, he created a recipe for magic. Skating first with Billy Boucher and later with Art Gagne, Nick Wasne and finally with Johnny Gagnon, Joliat and Morenz produced a forward line that was the crowd-pleaser of the era. They won three Cups, playing very watchable hockey.

CONTINUED ON PAGE 76

◁ **A**rthur Edmund Coulter was born in Winnipeg on May 31, 1909, and started his hockey career with the Pilgrim Athletic Club in that city in 1924. He became a pro in 1929 in Philadelphia and entered the NHL with the Chicago Blackhawks in 1931-32.

A defenseman, he partnered Taffy Abel as a strong unit when Chicago won the Stanley Cup in 1934. He made the second NHL all-star team in 1935, but in mid-season of the following year was traded to the Rangers for Earl Seibert in a deal that was to prove beneficial to both clubs. A prototype of the solid defensive defenseman, Coulter was chosen to the second all-star team three more times. He played on another Stanley Cup winner with the Rangers in 1940 and, after two more seasons, entered the Canadian Armed Forces during World War II, ending his pro career. Elected 1974.

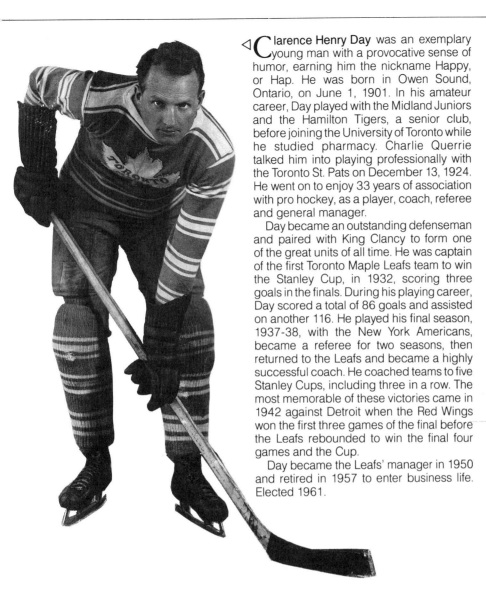

Clarence Henry Day was an exemplary young man with a provocative sense of humor, earning him the nickname Happy, or Hap. He was born in Owen Sound, Ontario, on June 1, 1901. In his amateur career, Day played with the Midland Juniors and the Hamilton Tigers, a senior club, before joining the University of Toronto while he studied pharmacy. Charlie Querrie talked him into playing professionally with the Toronto St. Pats on December 13, 1924. He went on to enjoy 33 years of association with pro hockey, as a player, coach, referee and general manager.

Day became an outstanding defenseman and paired with King Clancy to form one of the great units of all time. He was captain of the first Toronto Maple Leafs team to win the Stanley Cup, in 1932, scoring three goals in the finals. During his playing career, Day scored a total of 86 goals and assisted on another 116. He played his final season, 1937-38, with the New York Americans, became a referee for two seasons, then returned to the Leafs and became a highly successful coach. He coached teams to five Stanley Cups, including three in a row. The most memorable of these victories came in 1942 against Detroit when the Red Wings won the first three games of the final before the Leafs rebounded to win the final four games and the Cup.

Day became the Leafs' manager in 1950 and retired in 1957 to enter business life. Elected 1961.

Gordon Arthur Drillon played only seven seasons in the NHL — six with Toronto and one with the Canadiens — but in that time scored 155 goals for an average of more than 22 a season. This was in an era when a 20-goal season was outstanding. Drillon led the league in both goals and points in 1937-38 and was a member of the 1941-42 Cup-winning Leafs.

Born October 23, 1914, in Moncton, New Brunswick, he broke into the Leafs' lineup in 1936-37 as a temporary replacement for the ailing Charlie Conacher.

The Leafs won the league championship in 1938, sparked by the lines of Drillon, Syl Apps and Bob Davidson. In 1940-41 he led the team in scoring for the third straight season and in his final season with the Leafs earned a berth on the second all-star team. He was sold to Montreal and played one more season, finishing his NHL career with a 50-point effort from 28 goals and 22 assists. He died September 22, 1986. Elected 1975.

In a 13-year NHL career, William Mailes (Bill) Cowley established a reputation as a remarkable playmaker able to pass the puck "on a dime" to his wingmen. Cowley turned professional with the St. Louis Eagles for the 1934-35 season. One year later, he was purchased by the Boston Bruins and remained with them until retiring in 1947.

He played on championship teams in 1938-39, 1939-40 and 1940-41, and on Stanley Cup winners the first and third year of that skein. His lifetime regular-season record in the NHL is 195 goals and 353 assists, plus 12 goals and 34 assists in playoff competition. Indicative of his great playmaking, he won the NHL scoring title in 1940-41. In the 1943-44 season he amassed 72 points in 36 games, only to lose the scoring title when injury sidelined him for the next six weeks of the schedule.

Born in Bristol, Quebec, on June 12, 1912, Cowley moved to Ottawa, where he still resides, in 1920. Elected 1968.

Often referred to as "the best man amateur hockey ever had", George S. Dudley was active in the sport for more than 50 years. He was born in Midland, Ontario, April 19, 1894, and played hockey in his home town. He moved up to the executive level after obtaining his law degree in 1917.

At the time of his death on May 8, 1960, he was treasurer of the Ontario Hockey Association, president of the International Ice Hockey Federation and head of the hockey section of the 1960 Olympic Games. Elected 1958.

THE NHL EMERGES

At the time of his induction into the Hockey Hall of Fame, **James A. (Jimmie) Dunn** had completed 50 years of service to hockey.

Jimmie was acting as league secretary, convener and timekeeper when his league became part of the Manitoba Amateur Hockey Association in 1927. In 1942 he became MAHA vice-president and three years later began a six-year tenure as president. Later, he served as CAHA vice-president and president.

Nevertheless, he retained his interest in Manitoba hockey affairs, acting as convener of international tournaments in 1967 and 1968 and as secretary-treasurer of the Manitoba Hockey Players' Federation, Inc.

Born March 24, 1898, he resided in Winnipeg until his death in 1979. Elected 1968.

Mervyn (Red) Dutton was one of the most penalized players in hockey. Opposing forwards had plenty of respect for this crashing defenseman. He later served as NHL president from 1943 to 1946, continuing to earn great respect both for himself and for the NHL.

Red was born July 23, 1898, in Russell, Manitoba, but for most of his life made Calgary his home. His hockey career almost ended before it began. He stopped a shrapnel blast at Vimy in World War I and barely avoided amputation of his leg. Miraculously, he recovered and diligently practiced seven hours a day to strengthen the leg so he could play hockey. This hard work paid off as Dutton played professionally with Calgary from 1921 through 1925.

When the Patricks sold the Western Canada Hockey League to eastern interests, Dutton signed with Eddie Gerard and the Montreal Maroons. Dutton stayed with the Maroons until 1930, when he shifted to the New York Americans. In 1936, he took over coaching and managing the club and remained with the Amerks until 1942, when the team ceased operations.

When Frank Calder, the NHL president, died in 1943, Dutton was asked to fill the post and remained as head of the league until Clarence Campbell assumed the position in 1946. Although a rugged, fiery player, Dutton was a model of decorum as president. His executive abilities carried on into his business life, where he was equally successful. He died March 15, 1987. Elected 1958.

Charles Robert (Chuck) Gardiner was at the height of his career when tragedy struck. Rated by many as the outstanding goaltender of his generation, he died of a brain tumor at the age of 30, at his home in Winnipeg. Gardiner was born in Edinburgh, Scotland, on December 31, 1904, and became one of the few U.K.-born players to win a steady job in the NHL. The curly-headed Scot came to Canada with his family in 1911 and because he was a poor skater, took up goaltending. He was so good at this, however, that he played competitive intermediate hockey at the age of 14. By 1925 he was playing senior hockey in Selkirk, Manitoba, and moved up to the pro ranks with the Winnipeg Maroons the following year.

He joined the Chicago Blackhawks in 1927, as an understudy to the great Hughie Lehman. In a seven-year career with the Hawks, Gardiner played in 315 games, allowed only 673 goals for an average of 2.13 goals against, and registered 42 shutouts. He also played in 21 Stanley Cup contests, posting five shutouts and giving up only 35 goals for a phenomenal 1.66 goals-against average. Gardiner won the Vezina Trophy twice, in 1931-32 and 1933-34. He was selected to the first all-star team three times and to the second all-star team once.

He died on June 13, 1934. Elected 1945.

These beer coasters, printed in blue and black on white blotting paper, utilized the cartooning skills of Toronto's Lou Skuce. Depicted here is Busher Jackson of Toronto's Kid Line.

One of the many players who came out of Ottawa to star in the NHL, **Ebenezer Ralston (Ebbie) Goodfellow** was born in Canada's capital city on April 9, 1907. He started playing for Detroit in 1929 and scored 17 goals. The next season, Goodfellow led the American Division of the league with 25 goals.

Ebbie moved to defense in 1934 and continued to star. He was named to the NHL's second all-star team in 1936 and the first team in 1937 and 1940. Goodfellow also won the Hart Trophy as NHL MVP in 1940. He played on three Stanley Cup winners: 1936, 1937 and 1943.

He was captain of the Red Wings for five seasons, turning that post over to Sid Abel in 1943 when he retired. Goodfellow retired to Florida and was a member of the Hockey Hall of Fame Selection Committee. He died September 10, 1985. Elected 1963.

Goaltender **George Hainsworth** established two brilliant records during 11 seasons in the NHL. Both came during the 1928-29 season.

Hainsworth allowed only 43 goals in 44 games and recorded a remarkable total of 22 shutouts. Ironically, his team won 22 games that season.

Born in Toronto on June 26, 1895, Hainsworth moved as a youth to Kitchener, Ontario, and made his debut in both hockey and baseball in that city. His composure under fire and his unquestionable skill brought him to the attention of the Kitchener Juniors in 1912. He quickly moved up through intermediate and senior teams, winning championships at every level, including an Allan Cup in 1918.

Hainsworth turned professional with Saskatoon in 1923 and remained with that team until shifting to the Canadiens in 1926. He was an immediate sensation in Montreal, winning the Vezina Trophy in his first three seasons with the team.

The Canadiens ran into difficulties in the early 1930s and traded Hainsworth to Toronto for Lorne Chabot. He remained with the Maple Leafs until his retirement midway through the 1936-37 season. He came back to appear in a few games for the Canadiens before retiring permanently.

He died October 9, 1950. Elected 1961.

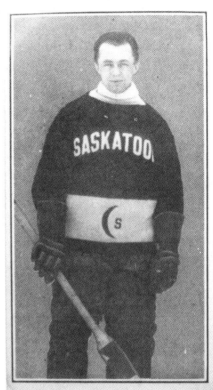

Many experts called **George William Hay** the greatest stickhandler in hockey when he played in the NHL during the 1920s. He was one of the so-called little men — he weighed around 156 pounds — who thrived on professional competition. Although born in Listowel, Ontario, on January 10, 1898, George's early hockey was played in Winnipeg.

George turned professional in 1921 with the Regina Caps. He moved on to the Portland Rosebuds, where he scored 18 goals and, when the team was sold to Chicago, he moved into the NHL. Hay had a poor season with Chicago, playing much of it with torn ligaments in his left shoulder, and was dealt to Detroit prior to the 1927-28 season. With the Cougars (later the Red Wings), Hay led the club with 22 goals and 13 assists. The NHL's ten coaches selected an all-star team that year and Hay was named to the forward unit with center Howie Morenz and rightwinger Bill Cook. In his five NHL seasons, Hay scored 73 goals and collected 54 assists. He died July 13, 1975, in Stratford, Ontario. Elected 1958.

When Conn Smythe took over coaching duties in Toronto, the team there was mediocre. It had talent, however: Hap Day, Jack Adams and Babe Dye (all future Hall of Famers) had been former coach Eddie Powers' forwards. Smythe began to build his team slowly. He put Hap Day behind the blue line and made him captain. He brought up Ace Bailey and Cy Denneny, and kept John Ross Roach in net until he found Lorne Chabot in 1928. The 1920s were a time of building, and Smythe's Maple Leafs burst into the 1930s with the "Kid Line" of Busher Jackson, Charlie Conacher and Joe Primeau.

Ottawa's lineup looks, in retrospect, like a program from a future Hall of Fame induction ceremony, with such notables as King Clancy, George Boucher, Jack Adams, Punch Broadbent and Frank Nighbor making appearances during the 1920s. Before surrendering their NHL franchise in 1934, Ottawa would take home four Stanley Cups, which when combined with their previous NHA wins total six successful Stanley Cup challenges for the Ottawa Senators.

Six U.S.-based expansion teams dominated in the 1930s. The New York Rangers sported the "Bread Line" — Bun Cook, Frank Boucher and Bill Cook — which was bested only by Toronto's "Kid Line." Their defensive skaters included Earl Seibert, Ching Johnston, Hib Milks, Ott Heller, Babe Siebert and Art Coulter, while their goaltender was Dave Kerr, Vezina Trophy winner for 1939-40.

Ranger coach Lester Patrick took his men to the playoffs in nine out of ten seasons in the 1930s, and New York City saw Ranger Stanley Cup parades in 1933 and 1940. In March 1938, the Rangers faced their cross-town rivals, the New York Americans, in a first-round playoff that ended in a match lasting 120 min-

CONTINUED ON PAGE 80

On March 22, 1923, **Foster William Hewitt** aired one of hockey's first radio broadcasts, from Toronto's Mutual Street Arena. On that night he became the eyes of his radio listeners and later continued to supply commentary for television viewers across Canada. Foster described thousands of hockey games, including national, world and Olympic championships in Canada, the United States and in Europe. He also described important contests in almost all major sports for North American fans.

Son of William A Hewitt, Foster was born November 21, 1902, in Toronto. He was intercollegiate boxing champion while attending the University of Toronto. Foster also had a successful business career, owning and operating his own radio station until he retired in 1981. He died April 21, 1985. Elected 1965.

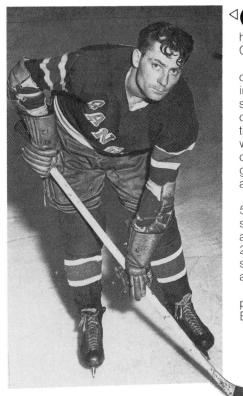

On and off the ice, **Bryan Aldwyn Hextall** has been a credit to the game of hockey. Hextall was born July 31, 1913, in Grenfell, Saskatchewan.

He turned professional with the Vancouver Lions of the Western Hockey League in 1934. The Lions won the WHL championship in 1936. Hextall transferred to Philadelphia the next season and moved up to the New York Rangers in 1937. He played with the Rangers through 1947-48 and during that span played in 449 league games, recording 187 goals and 175 assists.

He led the NHL in points in 1941-42 with 56 on 24 goals and 32 assists and was selected to the first all-star team three times and to the second team twice. He scored 20 or more goals in seven of his 12 NHL seasons and scored the overtime winner in a 1940 Stanley Cup game against Toronto.

Two of his sons and one of his grandsons played in the NHL. He died July 25, 1984. Elected 1969.

James Cecil Valdamar (Jim) Hendy originated the hockey statistics that are now a vital part of both the game's publicity and the player evaluation process. Born in Barbados on May 6, 1905, his family emigrated to Vancouver when he was six.

Hendy first published hockey statistics in *The Hockey Guide* in 1933 and continued to produce the book annually until 1951, when the pressure of other work forced him to give it up. He turned his records and the rights to the *Hockey Guide* over to the National Hockey League, asking only that they continue his work.

He worked in hockey in various capacities, serving as publicist for the New York Rangers, president of the U.S. Hockey League, and general manager of a highly successful AHL franchise in Cleveland, where he resided at the time of his death on January 14, 1961. Elected 1968.

Until the 1940s, no face-off circles were painted on the ice, which gave rinks a rather sparse look compared to today's more colourful surfaces. Here the Bruins and Rangers battle in front of Boston goalie Tiny Thompson in 1938. Eddie Shore, wearing number 2 for the Bruins, emerges from behind the net to assist his goaltender.

George Reginald (Red) Horner is one of the few members of the Hockey Hall of Fame who was known as one of the NHL "badmen" during his playing days.

An aggressive 6'1" and 200 pounds, Horner led the NHL in penalties for eight successive seasons — 1932-33 through 1939-40. He set a league record for penalties in a single season, spending 167 minutes in the box in 43 games in 1935-36, a mark that stood for 20 years.

Born May 28, 1909, in Lynden, Ontario, Horner moved up to the Leafs directly from the Marlboro juniors in the 1928-29 season. He became the Leafs' captain in 1937, an honor he considers the highest of his playing career. Red scored 42 goals and added 110 assists but, more important, his play provided an inspirational force behind the colorful Toronto teams of the 1930s. Elected 1965.

Sydney Harris Howe was born September 28, 1911, in Ottawa and died May 20, 1976, in the same city. Howe turned pro with the Ottawa Senators of the NHL in 1930. He followed a nomadic career for some time, being loaned to the Philadelphia Quakers and then the Toronto Maple Leafs before returning to Ottawa at the start of the 1932-33 season.

Syd was with the Senators when they transferred to St. Louis in 1935. Jack Adams then purchased him for the Detroit Red Wings. Howe set a modern record on February 3, 1944, when he scored six goals in one game against the Rangers in Detroit. He was also on the ice when Mud Bruneteau scored the goal that ended the longest game in Stanley Cup history. During his 16-year NHL career, Howe played center, wing and defense, and scored 237 goals and 291 assists. Elected 1965.

Fred J. (Mickey) Ion became a hockey referee in 1913, handling his first professional game in New Westminster, British Columbia.

Mickey Ion was born February 25, 1886, in Paris, Ontario, and grew into a fine baseball and lacrosse player.

He began to referee amateur hockey games on Canada's west coast where he caught the eye of Frank Patrick, who gave him the opportunity to work professional matches. Mickey became a top official of the Pacific Coast League, and moved east and joined the NHL staff when the PCL folded. He refereed the memorable Howie Morenz memorial game, played in the Montreal Forum on November 2, 1937, and continued as an NHL official until 1941. He died October 26, 1964, in Seattle, Washington. Elected 1961.

An excellent leftwinger, Harvey (Busher) Jackson collected 241 goals and 234 assists in 633 NHL games. In playoff competition he had 18 goals and 12 assists in 72 games.

Born in Toronto on January 19, 1911, Jackson signed with the Toronto Maple Leafs in 1930. He combined with Charlie Conacher and Joe Primeau to form the brilliant "Kid Line." He was on three league champions and one Cup winner (1932) in Toronto. He led the league in scoring with 28 goals and 25 assists in 1933 and was named to NHL all-star teams on five occasions.

When Conacher suffered injuries and Primeau retired in 1936, Busher played on a unit with his brother Art and Pep Kelly. The following year he was teamed on a potent line with Syl Apps and Gordie Drillon. Although great on the ice, Jackson's off-ice antics often got him into difficulties with management. He injured his shoulder in the 1939 season finals against Boston in what proved to be his last appearance with Toronto. He was dealt with three other players to the New York Americans for Sweeney Schriner. In 1942 he went to the Bruins, closing out his playing career in 1944. Jackson died June 25, 1966, in Toronto. Elected 1971.

General John Reed Kilpatrick always proudly boasted that he was New York's number one hockey fan.

Born June 15, 1889, Kilpatrick had his name inscribed in the record books of both track and football while attending Yale University.

As president of Madison Square Garden and the New York Rangers for 22 years, he was not only a keen hockey fan but an astute executive. He was an original director of the NHL Players' Pension Society, which was established in 1946, and remained on the Board until his death on May 7, 1960. He was elected an NHL Governor in 1936 and during his years with the Rangers saw them win two Stanley Cups. Elected 1960.

◁From fall 1926 until spring 1938, Ivan Wilfred (Ching) Johnson stood out as one of the most colorful defensemen in the NHL. He spent 11 years with the New York Rangers and was named to the first all-star team twice and the second team twice.

Johnson's NHL career ended with the New York Americans in 1937-38. He played in 463 games and acquired 969 minutes in penalties. Ching, who picked up his nickname as a boy, was born in Winnipeg, Manitoba, on December 7, 1897. Although he was already a 28-year-old, the Rangers signed him when the New York franchise was formed in 1926, starting Johnson on his colorful pro career.

He played defense with a zest for hard-hitting that led to several injuries, such as a broken leg, broken collarbone and broken jaw. He retired from the NHL at 41 but continued to play until he was 46 for teams in Minneapolis, in Marquette, Michigan, in Washington, D.C., and in Hollywood, California. He died June 16, 1979, in Takoma Park, Maryland. Elected 1958.

George Alfred (Al) Leader devoted his life to hockey. After 25 years of service, Al Leader stepped down from the job of president of the Western Hockey League in 1969. During those years the league experienced financial and internal strain, but he maintained its position as one of hockey's top minor pro leagues.

Born December 4, 1903, in Barnsley, Manitoba, Al's hockey career began as a 16-year-old player near Watson, Saskatchewan. He died May 8, 1982. Elected 1969.

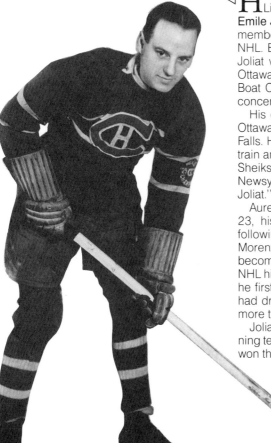

◁He was called the Mighty Atom or the Little Giant, this man named Aurel Emile Joliat who spent 16 seasons as a member of the Montreal Canadiens in the NHL. Born in Ottawa on August 29, 1901, Joliat was a star kicking fullback with the Ottawa Rough Riders and Regina Wascana Boat Club before a broken leg led him to concentrate on hockey.

His early ice experience came with the Ottawa New Edinburghs and with Iroquois Falls. He went west on a harvest excursion train and stayed to play with the Saskatoon Sheiks, but the Canadiens dealt off the great Newsy Lalonde for this "unknown kid, Joliat."

Aurel warmed the bench most of 1922-23, his first season in Montreal, but the following year was teamed with Howie Morenz and Billy Boucher. He went on to become one of the greatest leftwingers in NHL history. He weighed 160 pounds when he first joined the Canadiens but by 1925, had dropped to 125 and seldom weighed more than 135 in subsequent years.

Joliat played on three Stanley Cup-winning teams — 1924, 1930 and 1931 — and won the Hart Trophy in 1934. He died June 2, 1986, in Ottawa. Elected 1945.

The New York Rangers used this painting of a dashing skater thundering out of the darkness on their program cover. Note the exposed elbow pads, which were the fashion in the NHL in the late 1930s and early 1940s.

utes, 40 seconds. The Americans, after six periods of very close and careful hockey, defeated the Rangers on a seventh-period goal by Lorne Carr.

Fred McLaughlin, owner of the Chicago Blackhawks, was a man some might call a visionary. He wanted a championship team, but unlike most of his fellow club owners, he tried to do it with an all-American roster. It was his hobby to follow the talent in the northern U.S. backwaters. In the end, he produced a Cup winner on which half the players and coach Bill Stewart were American-born.

The Chicago club, which had won the Cup four years earlier with Charlie Gardiner in net and the line of Doc Romnes, "Mush" March and Paul Thompson, was the dark horse of 1938. Yet rookie coach Bill Stewart had reason to be hopeful going into the playoffs. He had finished the season in third place in the American Division. The finals, however, looked a long way off. In Chicago's first series against the Americans, New York fans prevented the goal judge from turning on his indicator lamp and Alex Levinski's go-ahead goal did not register. (The referee allowed the goal.) Chicago advanced to play Toronto in the final series, and McLaughlin's "American dream team" defeated the Leafs in four games. Coach Stewart had done well, but like the only other Chicago coach to win the Cup before him (Tommy Gorman, 1933-34), he was fired for his trouble.

The success of the Detroit Red Wings of the 1930s can be summed up in three words: Lewis, Barry and Aurey. This line was not the most productive in the League, but for two brief seasons they were the toast of Motor City. The team was led by coach Jack Adams, who had earned his place in the Hall of Fame as a center in the PCHA and with Toronto in

CONTINUED ON PAGE 84

Thomas F. Lockhart had a long and illustrious association with amateur hockey in the United States. He was born March 21, 1892, and became involved with hockey in 1932 when he promoted amateur hockey at Madison Square Garden in New York.

The following year, he organized the Eastern Amateur Hockey League and in 1935 became its president. In 1937, Lockhart organized the Amateur Hockey Association of the United States and served as its first president. Between 1932 and 1952, he supervised the Metropolitan Amateur League, and at intervals, coached and managed the New York Rovers. For the final six years of that span he was business manager of New York Rangers. He died May 18, 1979, in New York. Elected 1965.

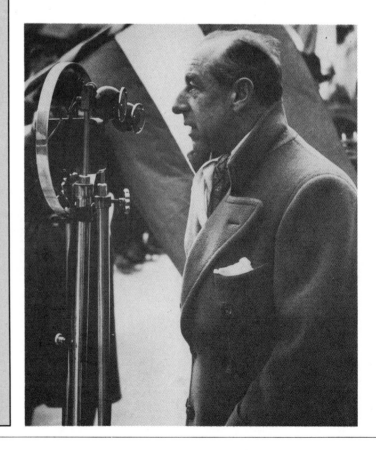

◁**M**ajor Frederic McLaughlin brought hockey to Chicago. In 1926, when the Patrick brothers, Lester and Frank, decided to sell six Western Canada League teams to interests in eastern Canada and the United States, McLaughlin was involved in the negotiations with Charles Adams. As a result, the Chicago Blackhawks were formed and named after the famous Blackhawk regiment, which he had commanded during World War I. McLaughlin became the organization's first president.

Major McLaughlin was born in Chicago on June 27, 1877, and died there on December 17, 1944. Elected 1963.

Sylvio Mantha enjoyed 14 seasons in the NHL as a hard-rock defenseman. During that span he played for nine first-place teams and three Stanley Cup winners. He joined the Montreal Canadiens in 1923-24, the first season they won the Cup in the NHL. Montreal won twice more with Mantha in the lineup, in 1930 and 1931.

Sylvio was born in Montreal on April 14, 1902, and learned his hockey there. Although he had played as a forward in amateur ranks, Mantha was moved back to defense after part of his first season with the Canadiens, remaining there for the balance of his career. He became a player-coach with Montreal in 1935 and then moved to the Boston Bruins, where he finished his playing days in 1937. For the next two years, Mantha acted as a linesman in the NHL and a referee in the American Hockey League. He died August 7, 1974. Elected 1960.

They said that he had color in his every motion, that his brilliance stood out in an era of brilliant hockey players. They were talking, of course, about Howarth William (Howie) Morenz, who was a runaway leader in a 1950 Canadian Press poll to select the outstanding hockey player of the half-century.

Morenz was born in Mitchell, Ontario, on September 21, 1902, and began his hockey career at nearby Stratford. He was signed to a pro contract by Leo Dandurand of the Montreal Canadiens and joined that club for the 1923-24 season. Morenz was an immediate million-dollar box office attraction. He had reckless speed and his headlong rushes set turnstiles clicking wherever the Canadiens played. He was nicknamed "the Babe Ruth of Hockey" by sportswriters in the United States.

Morenz performed in the NHL for 14 seasons, earning a variety of nicknames like the "Canadien Comet", the "Hurtling Habitant", the "Mitchell Meteor", and the "Stratford Streak." He had great stickhandling ability and a snapping shot. Morenz played with the Canadiens for 11 seasons before being traded to Chicago. He went to the New York Rangers midway through 1935-36 and came back to the Canadiens for the 1936-37 season. He broke his leg in a game on January 28, 1937, leading to his death on March 8, 1937.

During his career, Morenz scored 270 goals and won the Hart Trophy three times — 1928, 1931 and 1932. In 1929-30, he scored 40 goals in 44 games and in 1924-25 scored 30 goals in 30 games. He was twice named to the first all-star team and once to the second. Elected 1945.

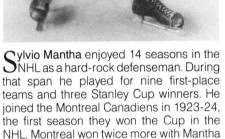

◁**P**aul Loicq was born in Brussels in 1890. He was elected president of the International Ice Hockey Federation in 1922 and served for 25 years, not only as an executive, but as a referee of international stature. It was during his term as IIHF president that international hockey made its greatest progress. Not only did the game's popularity increase across Europe, largely through his efforts, but hockey men agree that it was his influence that brought about acceptance of hockey as an official sport of the Winter Olympic Games.

Loicq was posthumously elected to the Hockey Hall of Fame and the Hall's official crest was presented to his widow by the president of the Belgian Olympic Committee. Elected 1961.

Herbert William "Buddy" O'Connor's ten-year NHL career with Montreal and the New York Rangers saw this centerman record 297 points, including 140 goals in 509 regular-season games. Throughout these years, O'Connor spent only 34 minutes in the penalty box.

A center, O'Connor was a small player at 5'7" and 145 lbs. Born in Montreal on June 21, 1916, he moved from the senior Montreal Royals to the Canadiens at the beginning of the 1941-42 season. His best year with Montreal was 1944-45, when he scored 21 goals and had 23 assists. He joined the Rangers for the 1947-48 season and had the best year of his career, finishing with 24 goals and 36 assists for 60 points in as many games en route to the Hart Trophy as MVP and Lady Byng as most gentlemanly player. Buddy O'Connor died August 24, 1977. Elected 1988.

James Norris was born December 10, 1879, in St. Catharines, Ontario, and spent his early years in Montreal.

He developed his enthusiasm for hockey when he played for the Montreal Victorias. Norris purchased the Chicago Shamrocks of the American Hockey Association in 1930 and three years later, with his son James D., bought Detroit's Olympia and its NHL franchise, the Falcons. They changed the team name to the Red Wings and immediately set out to capture the Stanley Cup. Two years later, in 1936, the Red Wings won, repeating in the following season. They won again in 1943 under the Norris banner.

James Norris was a firm believer in a strong farm system for his Red Wings, which kept the team competitive throughout the Norris years. At one time, Norris and his three children also owned Chicago Stadium and a majority interest in the Madison Square Garden Corporation, which owned the New York Rangers. James Norris died December 4, 1952. Elected 1958.

Harold (Harry) Oliver was born October 26, 1898, in Selkirk, Manitoba, and went on to greatness with the Boston Bruins and the New York Americans in an NHL career that spanned 11 seasons.

He moved to Calgary in 1920 to play in the Western Canada Hockey League, remaining there until 1926 when he was sold to the Boston Bruins. He played on a Stanley Cup winner in 1929, and was traded to the Americans in 1934, where he remained three more years.

During his pro career, Oliver scored 218 goals and had 144 assists. He died June 16, 1985, in Winnipeg. Elected 1967.

James Dougan Norris inherited two things from his father — great wealth and a passion for sports. The father-son combination acquired the Detroit Red Wings and the Olympia in 1933. In the next ten years Detroit won three Stanley Cups: 1936, 1937 and 1943.

In 1946, James D. and partner Arthur Wirtz assumed ownership of the Chicago Blackhawks. This team had finished last three straight seasons, but the partners built a valuable franchise, by following the same guidelines that had been successful in Detroit. The Hawks won a Stanley Cup in 1961. Norris died February 25, 1966. Elected 1962.

Although he was born and grew up in Exeter, Ontario, **Allan W. Pickard** spent his years as a hockey executive in western Canada.

During the late 1920s he served as coach, and president of the Regina Aces, a senior team. At that time he became an executive member of the Saskatchewan Amateur Hockey Association. Al Pickard took over as SAHA president in 1941 and served two terms. Pickard served as president of the Western Canada Senior League, governor of both Saskatchewan's and Western Canada's Junior Leagues, and president of the Canadian Amateur Hockey Association from 1947 to 1950. A life member of both the SAHA and CAHA, Al Pickard died April 7, 1975, in Exeter, Ontario. Elected 1958.

Born in Stoney Mountain, Manitoba, on January 7, 1916, **Walter (Babe) Pratt** played on the first Winnipeg playground championship team. By 1932, he was a member of the Elmwood Maple Leafs and led them to the Manitoba midget title. The following year, Elmwood won the juvenile crown. A Manitoba junior title with Kenora followed in 1934, but before he moved to Kenora, Pratt played on five league championship teams — in one year.

Pratt turned pro with Philadelphia, the Rangers' farm club, and moved up to New York in January, 1936. He played on a Stanley Cup winner with the Rangers in 1940 and with the league championship team of 1942. He was traded to Toronto in November, 1942, and won the Hart Trophy while with the Leafs in 1944.

In 1947, Pratt played with Hershey and, later, with New Westminster, British Columbia, and Tacoma, Washington, before retiring as a player. Elected 1966.

Joseph Lynn Patrick was a member of Hockey's "Royal Family", but he never took undue advantage of his nobility. His father, Lester, was named to the Hockey Hall of Fame in 1945 and his uncle, Frank, in 1958; others of the Patrick family have been associated with hockey for almost a century.

He was born February 3, 1912, in Victoria, British Columbia. Lynn's NHL debut was modest, but he progressed to twice lead the Rangers in scoring. He played for the Rangers' Stanley Cup-winning team of 1940 and was named a first all-star in 1942 and a second all-star in 1943. His NHL record includes 145 goals and 190 assists in 455 games, plus 10 goals in 44 playoff games.

He coached five seasons in Boston, his Bruins never missing the playoffs, and then spent the next ten years in the front office. In 1966 he became general manager of the St. Louis Blues and spent three brief stints as coach before retiring as a senior vice-president in 1977. He died January 26, 1980. Elected 1980.

As a Rhodes Scholar at Oxford during the 1930s, Clarence Campbell (center) took time off from his studies to play for the university hockey team. Here, he shows rather tentative form on an unidentified rink, perhaps on the European continent. In 1946, the lawyer/scholar/soldier was named president of the NHL, a position he held for 31 years.

the 1920s. The Wings came up out of the basement of the American Division in 1935, rising to the top of the League and two Stanley Cup championships before returning to the cellar in 1938.

The Great Depression took its toll on the NHL. With Ottawa, the Maroons, and Pittsburgh/Philadelphia folding, the NHL was left with only seven teams. The League, the players and the fans learned how to deal with tragedy as well. On December 12, 1933, in a game in Boston Gardens, Eddie Shore, the Bruins' star defenseman, brought down Toronto's Ace Bailey with a check from behind. Bailey was so badly injured that his death was reported in the morning papers. The report, as they say, was exaggerated, and to this day, some 55 years later, the Ace drops into the Hall of Fame to look over his scrapbooks. Ace's career came to an abrupt halt, however, and there were severe medical bills to be paid. League president Frank Calder mandated that a benefit game would be played for Ace, and on February 14 of the following year, the all-star game was born.

The Ace Bailey Benefit Game was a success, but the NHL All-Star Game didn't become an annual event until 1947. It took the tragic death of one of hockey's most exciting players to spark a second all-star benefit in 1937.

Howie Morenz was winding up his brilliant career with the Montreal Canadiens when his hockey playing days, and his life, were cut short. The Canadiens were in a race for first place when, on January 28, 1937, Earl Seibert tried to check the "Mitchell Meteor" as he closed in on Chicago goaltender Mike Karakas. Morenz's skate lodged in the end boards, and Seibert's full weight came down on Howie's backside. Morenz was hospitalized for a severe leg fracture and died

CONTINUED ON PAGE 88

Joseph (Joe) Primeau was both a great hockey player and a great coach. He was the only man to coach teams that won the Memorial Cup, Allan Cup and Stanley Cup at junior, senior and NHL levels of competition.

Joe was born in Lindsay, Ontario, on January 29, 1906. Conn Smythe signed Primeau to a professional contract in 1927 with the Toronto Maple Leafs, but he played much of the season with Ravinas and won the scoring title in the Canadian Pro League. Joe moved up to the Leafs in 1928 but finished the season with London and didn't arrive in the NHL to stay until 1929.

He became the center on Toronto's famous Kid Line with Charlie Conacher and Harvey Jackson on the wings, and although his linemates were more dazzling, Joe was the smooth-passing coordinator who made their exploits possible. He was a tenacious checker and an extremely clean player, often called "Gentleman Joe." He was also a strong penalty-killer.

Primeau retired as a player to go into business in 1937, but continued as a great coach for the next 23 years. Elected 1963.

For 40 years, Senator Donat Raymond was the spark behind ▷ professional hockey in Montreal. Although a keen hockey follower for several years, his first official connection with the game came in 1923 when he helped form the Canadian Arena Company. The firm built the Montreal Forum and, in 1937, acquired the Canadiens.

The Depression of the 1930s forced the Montreal Maroons to fold, and the Canadiens might have suffered a similar fate but for the faith and financial support of Senator Raymond, who absorbed the losses until fortunes took a turn for the better. He remained as company president until 1955 when he became chairman of the board. He held this office until his death on June 5, 1963. Elected 1958.

◁ **M**ilton Conrad Schmidt played center on one of the most potent forward units in the history of the NHL. This line, which combined Schmidt with Woody Dumart and Bobby Bauer, was dubbed the "Kraut Line" by Albert "Battleship" Leduc, who played in the NHL in the 1920s and 1930s.

Schmidt was born in Kitchener, Ontario, on March 5, 1918. With the exception of three years spent in the Royal Canadian Air Force in World War II, he played for Boston from 1936 until midway through the 1954-55 season, when he gave up playing to coach the Bruins. After seven seasons of coaching, Schmidt became the club's general manager.

As a player, Schmidt was a powerful, hard-hitting center who never gave up the puck without a fight. He stood six feet tall and weighed 185 pounds. During his NHL career, he scored 229 goals and a total of 575 points. He won the league scoring title in 1940 and the Hart Trophy as the MVP to his team in 1951. He played for Stanley Cup-winning teams in 1939 and 1941. He was voted to the league's first all-star team in 1940, 1947 and 1951, and to the second team in 1952.

During his years in the RCAF, Schmidt played for the Allan Cup-winning Ottawa Hurricanes. A strong skater, Schmidt was also a clever stickhandler and always dangerous around the net. Elected 1961.

No less than eight of the players and executives from the 1940 New York Rangers — the last Ranger team to win the Stanley Cup — are members of the Hockey Hall of Fame. The 1940 Rangers recorded one of the fastest starts in NHL history, playing their first 19 games without a loss. The team's goaltender, Dave Kerr, ended the season with an astonishing 1.60 goals-against average. The Rangers finished second to the Bruins in the standings, but ploughed over their arch-rivals from Boston, then the Toronto Maple Leafs, en route to the Cup.

◁ **D**avid (Sweeney) Schriner was a celebrated hockey player who divided his NHL career between two teams, the New York Americans and the Toronto Maple Leafs.

Schriner was born in Russia, on November 30, 1911. An outstanding leftwinger, Schriner turned pro in 1933-34 with Syracuse. The following season, he moved up to New York and won the Calder Trophy as the league's outstanding rookie, scoring 18 goals. He remained with the Americans until the season of 1938-39 when he was traded to Toronto in return for five players.

Schriner stayed in Toronto for the balance of his NHL career. Although he didn't play in 1943-44, Schriner scored 201 goals in 11 NHL campaigns. While with the Americans, he was twice scoring champion of the league, winning in 1936 with 45 points and 1937 with 46. As a member of the Maple Leafs, Schriner played on two Stanley Cup winners, scoring six goals in the Leafs' Cup win in 1942 and three in their victory of 1945. Sweeney was also named to the league's first all-star team in 1936 and the second team in 1937. Elected 1962.

THE NHL EMERGES

◁ **E**arl Walter Seibert played 15½ seasons in the NHL, and established himself as one of the game's all-time great defensemen. Earl was voted to NHL all-star teams in 10 consecutive seasons from 1935 to 1944. He was noted for his rushing ability and accounted for 89 goals and a total of 276 points in scheduled league games, adding another 11 goals and 8 assists in playoff competition.

Born in Kitchener, Ontario, on December 7, 1911, Earl began skating at an early age and was a consistent winner in the annual skating carnival in Kitchener. His speed and strong bodychecking as a junior player caught the eye of several clubs and he eventually turned pro in 1929 with the Springfield Indians, a farm club for the New York Rangers. He moved up to the Rangers in the 1931-32 season and almost immediately became a standout on defense. The Rangers traded him to Chicago in 1935-36 for Art Coulter, and ten years later he was traded to Detroit in exchange for three players.

Seibert's style of play was a great help to his goaltender. He was a shot-blocker, willingly dropping to the ice to stop shots before they reached the goal. Off the ice, Earl was a cheerful individual with an amazing fund of good humor. Earl's father, Oliver, was previously elected to the Hockey Hall of Fame, making them the first father-son combination so honored. Earl now lives in Agawam, Massachusetts. Elected 1963.

In the days when the NHL was filled with colorful players, **Edward (Eddie) Shore** took a back seat to no one. He had an explosive temper and hockey ability to match.

Eddie Shore was born in Ft. Qu'Appelle, Saskatchewan, on November 25, 1902, and moved up through amateur ranks to the Melville Millionaires in the season of 1923-24. From there, he graduated to the pros with the Regina Caps of the Western Canada League. The following season, he played with Edmonton.

Shore broke into the NHL in 1926 with the Boston Bruins and in subsequent seasons was to personify the most vigorous aspects of a hard, rough and fast game. His great talent was to take over the offense and set up plays, literally knocking down any opponent in his way. This, of course, brought him an abundance of penalties and he became involved in many hard-fought battles.

During his 13-year stay with the Bruins, Shore scored 105 goals and added 179 assists. He wound up his NHL career with the New York Americans in the 1939-40 season. Eddie Shore is the only defenseman to win the Hart Trophy four times — 1933, 1935, 1936, and 1938. He was also voted to the NHL all-star team on eight occasions. He played on Stanley Cup winners in 1929 and 1939. He died March 16, 1985. Elected 1945.

Joe Primeau, shown here in a 1932 trading card, centered Toronto's successful Kid Line.

Born January 7, 1903, in Toronto, **Regi-nald Joseph (Hooley) Smith** played his amateur hockey in that city and was a standout member of the Granites, winners of the Olympic hockey championship for Canada in 1924.

He turned professional the following year with Ottawa, who won the Stanley Cup in 1927. Ottawa dealt the 5′ 10″, 160 pounder to the Montreal Maroons before that next season, and once again his team was in the Cup final, losing to the Rangers.

With the Maroons, Smith combined with Nels Stewart and Babe Siebert to form the great "S-Line", combining great scoring power with aggressive play. This team won the Stanley Cup in 1935.

Smith was traded to Boston in 1936-37 and after one season joined the New York Americans, where he completed his career with his 200th goal in 1940-41. He died August 24, 1963, in Montreal. Elected 1972.

A great hockey player, with a heart as big as his massive body, **Albert (Babe) Siebert** was a broad-shouldered giant with cool, fearless eyes — a man who played with complete confidence.

The Babe was born in Plattsville, Ontario, on January 14, 1904, and played his minor hockey in Zurich, Ontario. He played for Kitchener in the Ontario Hockey Association junior league in 1922-23. Although still a junior, he moved up to play for the Niagara Falls seniors in 1924-25 and made the jump to the NHL the following season with the Montreal Maroons.

Siebert was an outstanding leftwinger, and combined with Nels Stewart and Hooley Smith to form the highly rated S-line, which played effectively for five seasons. This combination was broken with dramatic suddenness in 1932 with two trades; Stewart went to Boston and Siebert to the New York Rangers. Siebert was later traded to Boston himself and then returned to Montreal, this time to play for the Canadiens in 1936-37.

Late in his career, Babe Siebert's speed had gone, but he had developed into an outstanding defenseman. He was so good, in fact, that he was voted the Hart Trophy in 1937. Babe excelled at blocking out the opposition, using his weight and strength and balance to skate attackers off to the side. He was named to the first all-star team on defense in three consecutive seasons, beginning in 1936.

He drowned on August 25, 1939, in St. Joseph, Ontario. Elected 1964.

Conn Smythe is best remembered as the man who made professional hockey respectable. Smythe was born in Toronto on February 1, 1895, and first gained hockey prominence as captain of the University of Toronto Varsity team that won the 1915 Ontario championship. He coached the Varsity seniors to the 1927 Allan Cup, and this team played as the Varsity Grads and won the 1928 Olympic title as well.

He was hired by the newly established NHL New York Rangers, but was released after assembling the team that won the 1928 Stanley Cup playoffs. He then purchased the Toronto St. Pats and renamed the club the Maple Leafs.

By November, 1931, thanks to the perseverance of Smythe, Maple Leaf Gardens was constructed and became the team's home. He acted as managing director and later president of the Gardens, retiring in 1961 after his teams had won seven Stanley Cups.

The two things closest to his heart were his long association with the Ontario Society for Crippled Children and his personal supervision of the construction of the Hockey Hall of Fame. He died November 18, 1980, in Toronto. Elected 1958.

THE NHL EMERGES

within a few short weeks. It is often said that he died of a broken heart; this may well be true, but the late nights with the boys in a smoke-filled hospital room couldn't have helped.

Morenz was hockey's first real superstar. The people of Montreal and players on both the Canadiens and the Maroons clubs organized an all-star match for the benefit of his wife and young son. The stars of the two Montreal teams played at the Forum, and raised in excess of $25,000. A jersey from this second all-star game is on display at the Hockey Hall of Fame.

In 1939, Babe Siebert died in an off-season swimming accident. Siebert had made the rounds in the league, and had good friends in cities across the NHL circuit. Siebert was a grinder, and played hard for his money. He was not afraid to use his strength to force an issue when the situation called for it, and his teammates counted on him. His untimely death shocked the hockey world and another all-star benefit was staged. This game, held at the Montreal Forum in October 1939, raised $15,000 for the family.

World War II brought with it a serious challenge to the National Hockey League. The steady stream of players signing up for military service caused President Calder and the board of governors to suggest a suspension of operations for the duration of the war. The Canadian government asked the governors to reconsider. Prime Minister Mackenzie King believed that the distraction from the war provided by the NHL was just what people needed. He asked the NHL executives to "soldier on." King was correct and record crowds poured into the league's arenas.

Wartime hockey was on a par with many of the products available for public consumption during the conflict, though

When Nels Stewart, Babe Siebert and Hooley Smith played as the famed "S-Line" of the Montreal Maroons, they were considered to be the most feared trio in hockey. Centering this great line was **Nelson Robert Stewart**, who was born December 29, 1902, in Montreal.

Stewart was the top marksman of the three and his deadly accurate shot earned him the nickname "Old Poison" from goalies around the NHL. He scored 134 goals and added 56 assists during the five years the S-Line played as a unit.

A burly 200-pounder, he skated with short, toddling steps and used a stick with so flat a lie that he had to play the puck almost between his skates. But he was truly "Old Poison," collecting a total of 324 goals and 191 assists in 653 league games. He was the first player to score more than 300 goals in the NHL, and was the league's all-time goal-scoring leader for many years until surpassed by Maurice Richard.

Stewart learned his hockey in Toronto, where his family had moved when he was a boy. He grew up in the city's Balmy Beach district, where he became friends with his future linemate, Hooley Smith. He joined the Maroons for the 1925-26 season, scoring 34 goals in his rookie season. He topped that mark only once when he scored 39 in 1930. He was traded to Boston in 1932 and played three seasons with the Bruins before moving to the New York Americans. He remained with them until retiring in 1940, except for 1936-37 when he played part of the season in Boston.

Stewart won the Hart Trophy in 1926 and 1930 and played for a Stanley Cup winner in 1926. He died August 3, 1957, at his summer home near Toronto. Elected 1962.

In an era when great goaltenders were an important part of every NHL team, **Cecil "Tiny" Thompson** was one of the most consistent performers in the game. The tag of "Tiny" was something of a misnomer: he stood 5′ 10″ and weighed 170 pounds.

Thompson was born in Sandon, British Columbia, on May 31, 1905, and played his early hockey there.

The Boston Bruins purchased the contracts of Thompson and Cooney Weiland before the 1928-29 season, with Thompson taking over as the first-string goaltender from Hal Winkler. He remained with the Bruins for ten seasons. He played his final two NHL seasons with Detroit. His lifetime goals-against average in regular-season competition was 2.27; his playoff average was a remarkable 2.00. In addition to four Vezina Trophy triumphs, Thompson was selected to NHL all-star teams on four occasions.

His most memorable game was a marathon overtime session against Toronto in 1933. The game went into 104 minutes and 46 seconds of overtime before Toronto won, 1-0. Thompson died February 9, 1981. Elected 1959.

Lloyd **Turner** was "Mr. Hockey" to sports fans in Calgary and most of western Canada. He built teams, built leagues, built arenas and made hockey a lifetime career.

Turner was born in Elmvale, Ontario, in 1884. In Calgary, Turner had ice installed in an old roller-skating rink, and organized both a team and a league to play in this new facility. This new league produced the Calgary Tigers, unsuccessful challengers for the Stanley Cup in 1924.

Among Turner's many other accomplishments was the part he played in the resurgence of Allan Cup competition during the early 1930s. Perhaps most rewarding was his organization of Alberta's Indian tribes into tournament competition. He died April 7, 1976, in Calgary. Elected 1958.

Carl **Potter Voss** was a hockey player of above-average ability but he will be remembered for his enormous contribution to the development of referees and linesmen. Born January 6, 1907, in Chelsea, Massachusetts, he became the first Toronto Maple Leaf, signing a contract the day Conn Smythe purchased the Toronto St. Pats and changed the club's name. Voss later played with the New York Rangers and Americans and the Montreal Maroons as well as for Detroit, Ottawa, St. Louis and Chicago.

Carl Voss later became president of the U.S. Hockey League and in 1950 was named the first referee-in-chief of the NHL. As hockey developed, he also became referee-in-chief of other minor pro leagues which used officials provided by the NHL. During his career he conducted hundreds of officiating schools and was one of hockey's most effective and enthusiastic ambassadors. Elected 1974.

Goaltender Roy "Shrimp" Worters managed to ▷ vacate his net and end up under his own stick in this rare game action photo taken in the then brand new Maple Leaf Gardens. Worters, who always wore a peaked cap when he played, was a second team all-star in 1932.

everyone knew it could have been better. There were some outstanding evenings, and very entertaining players on the circuit, but the on-ice product was not hockey's finest.

The league responded to the slippage in the level of ability and speed with significant rule changes. Flooding the ice surface between periods to speed up the play became mandatory. The addition of the red line in 1943 enabled a team to pass the puck from anywhere in its end of the rink to the center of the ice. Before this, the puck had to be carried over both the defensive and offensive bluelines. A new era of breakaway speed in the NHL was about to begin.

In 1943, a native Montrealer burst to stardom and provided the spark that put the hockey world back on track. Maurice "the Rocket" Richard joined Toe Blake and Elmer Lach to propel the Canadiens to the top of the NHL. With 83 points on the season, Montreal was 25 ahead of second-place Detroit. The following year Richard scored 50 goals in 50 games, at a time when 25 goals was an all-star performance. A superstar was born, and hockey was launched into a new era where dynasties would become the rule, and the two Canadian teams would dominate possession of the Stanley Cup.

Arthur M. Wirtz, born January 23, 1901, was a Chicago native who joined forces with James Norris, Sr. in 1931. They formed the company that acquired the Detroit Red Wings hockey club and the stadium they played in, the Olympia. Both organizations were in receivership and could not continue operations without financial aid and management. Wirtz began his hockey affiliation with this investment and contributed substantially not just to the growth of hockey in the United States but to its survival.

In 1933, along with James Norris and James D. Norris, Wirtz acquired control of the Chicago Stadium Corporation, taking it out of receivership as well. One of the building's tenants was the Chicago Blackhawks hockey team, then owned by Major Frederic McLaughlin. The Norrises and Wirtz later acquired control of Madison Square Garden, St. Louis Arena and other facilities.

In 1954, two years after James Norris' death, Wirtz and James D. Norris bought the Chicago team from McLaughlin's estate. This purchase meant they had to divest themselves of their hockey interests in Detroit. Each lost approximately $2½ million while they rebuilt the Hawks from a losing team with attendance at an all-time low. The Hawks' franchise became one of the most successful in the National Hockey League and won a championship in 1961. In 1966, after the death of James D. Norris, Wirtz was primarily responsible for persuading the NHL to include St. Louis in its expansion plan. Wirtz sold the St. Louis arena to the Salomon family, owners of the new St. Louis Blues. Arthur Wirtz died July 21, 1983. Elected 1971.

One of the smallest goalies ever to play in the NHL, Roy "Shrimp" Worters was the first netminder to win the Hart Trophy as the NHL player most valuable to his team. Worters was only 5′ 2″ and seldom weighed more than 130 pounds, but he starred in the NHL for 12 seasons, often with teams that gave him minimal protection.

The Shrimp first played in the NHL for the Pittsburgh Pirates. He joined the New York Americans in 1928-29 and, except for part of the 1929-30 season when he played for the Montreal Canadiens, completed his pro career with that team.

He is credited with being the first goalie to use the back of his hands to divert shots to the corners. A gritty player, he finished his final season (1936-37) in a manner typifying his entire career. Worters played his last seven games with a severe hernia, defying anyone to sit him out of games. He died November 7, 1957, in Toronto. Elected 1969.

The Dynasty Years
1946-1966

The Dynasty Years (*clockwise from top left*)
The Lester Patrick Cup was awarded to the playoff champion of the Western Hockey League when that league functioned as one of the top minor-pro circuits in the game. The incomparable Rocket Richard wore the number 9 *sweater* for the Montreal Canadiens and finished with 544 goals. Toronto goaltender Johnnie Bower wore these *skates* through much of the 1960s, when the Leafs won four Stanley Cups. Jacques Plante designed and built the *mask* which became his trademark with Montreal and the New York Rangers. Dipping shots from the *curved sticks* used by Stan Mikita (right) and Bobby Hull (left) did much to popularize masks for goaltenders. The *puck* with which Bill Barilko scored the overtime Cup-winning goal in 1951 marked the young defenseman's last moment in the NHL.

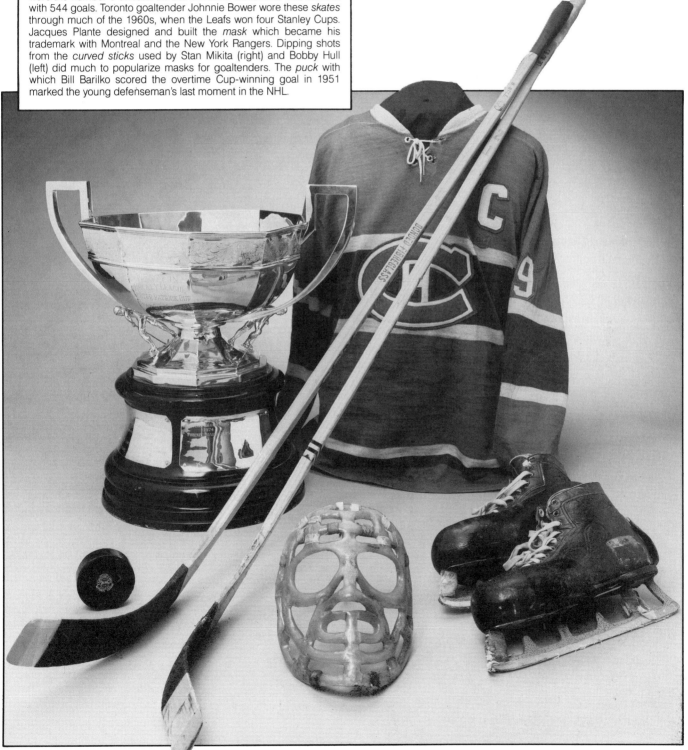

The National Hockey League enjoyed an extended period of franchise stability after World War II. Until the expansion of 1967, big-league hockey was a six-team affair, with an overnight train ride being the maximum distance between NHL cities. The clubs of this era — Boston, Chicago, Detroit, Montreal, the New York Rangers and Toronto — were felt to play the best and toughest hockey anywhere. With the help of print, radio and television, these teams came to occupy center stage in the imaginations of hockey fans throughout North America to the extent that almost all hockey fans today know them as the "Original Six," even though other NHL franchises had come and gone in the preceeding thirty years.

The post-war era began with Clarence Campbell succeeding Mervyn "Red" Dutton as League president. Campbell was a Rhodes scholar, soldier, prosecutor and former NHL referee. He would hold office for 31 years and, later in his career, oversee the growth of the NHL from six clubs to eighteen.

From 1946 to 1949, the NHL's six clubs played each other twelve times a season. In 1949, the regular season was increased from 60 to 70 games and the number of games played against each opponent increased to fourteen. With matchups against each team so frequent, rivalries were intense and players came to know each other's moves. The result was hockey that placed a premium on goal prevention. Defensemen defended, leaving the scoring to the forwards. Each club had its number-one goalie who played almost every minute of every game.

Competition for NHL jobs was fierce. With six teams each carrying no more than 19-man rosters, those 114 big-league jobs were precious and not given up without a fight. Careers tended to be longer

John Francis (Bunny) Ahearne was born in County Wexford, Ireland, in 1901, but lived most of his life in England. He opened a travel agency in London in 1928, and soon became involved in hockey. For more than 40 years he played a prominent, often dominant, role on the international scene.

Ahearne became secretary of the British Ice Hockey Association in 1933 and retained that position for 40 years. He eventually became an IIHF executive member and, in 1947, played an important role in negotiating the return of Canada and the United States to active membership. Elected an IIHF vice-president in 1955, he became president two years later and served in one of these two positions until retiring in 1975.

During the Ahearne years, the IIHF championship became a leading international sports event. International hockey had grown to 26 nations competing in three divisions by 1977. He understood the importance of television and negotiated sales of lucrative broadcast rights, providing security for the organization.

For more than two decades Bunny Ahearne ruled European, Olympic and other international ice hockey events. His personal contribution to international hockey is unparalleled. He died April 11, 1985. Elected 1977.

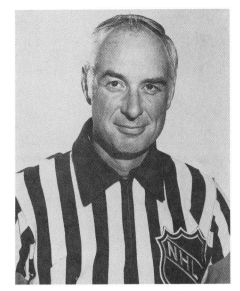

When he retired following the 1971-72 season, **John G. Ashley** was regarded as the top official in the NHL.

Born March 5, 1930, in Galt, Ontario, Ashley lived in Preston, Ontario, until he moved to Kitchener at age 21. His officiating career began in Kitchener minor hockey. After one season, he moved into the Ontario Hockey Association and signed an NHL contract in 1959, working his first season in the AHL and Eastern Pro Hockey League with spot assignments in the NHL.

During the next 12 seasons, he handled 17 games as a linesman and 605 games as a referee in regular-season play as well as working 59 Stanley Cup playoff matches. In 1971, he became the first man to referee the seventh game in each of three Stanley Cup playoff series that required that number of games. Elected 1981.

George Edward Armstrong was born in Skead, Ontario, on July 6, 1930, and grew up in the Sudbury area. He was born of a Scots father and a native Indian mother — a background that entitled him to claim Indian ancestry, which he has always done proudly.

Never very fast or maneuverable, Armstrong was a diligent positional player who became one of the Leafs' greatest assets, not only on the ice but in the dressing room where his leadership qualities enabled him to bring out the best in everyone with whom he associated. In 1,187 regular-season NHL games George scored 296 goals and 417 assists and was team captain when the Leafs won the Cup in 1962, 1963, 1964 and 1967. Elected 1975.

The combination of hockey and **Harold Edwin Ballard** was a natural. Born in Toronto in 1903, he helped his father manufacture the famous Ballard skates. It was a short step to participation in all aspects of amateur hockey and ultimately he achieved national recognition as coach and manager of the 1932 Allan-Cup-winning Toronto Nationals.

In 1961, Ballard became one of three principal owners and chief executive of Maple Leaf Gardens.

Always deeply conscious of the game's overall welfare, Harold Ballard has been a vigorous sponsor of amateur hockey at all levels and an active and respected participant in the affairs of the National Hockey League. He was a strong supporter of the first series with the Soviets and provided Maple Leaf Gardens without charge as a training camp for Team Canada in 1972. With no fanfare, he has also supported the handicapped and disadvantaged, supplying facilities without cost and often aiding with ideas and financing.

Flamboyant, often misunderstood by those who do not know him but liked and respected by those who do, Harold Ballard has given a half-century of dedicated support to hockey. Elected 1977.

◁ An outstanding athlete with rare skill and flair, **Andrew James (Andy) Bathgate** had an awesome shot but delighted in setting up goals for his linemates, as shown in his 624 assists in 1,069 NHL regular-season games. He also scored 349 regular-season goals, plus 21 goals and 14 assists in 54 playoff contests.

Bathgate enjoyed his greatest season in 1958-59 when he scored 40 goals, had 88 points and won the Hart Trophy as the league's MVP. In 1961-62 he tied Bobby Hull for most points in the season, but Hull was awarded the Ross Trophy on the basis of most goals scored. Andy was traded to Toronto in 1963-64, the principal man in a seven-player deal, and played on his only Stanley Cup winner. He was later acquired by Detroit and then by Pittsburgh in the 1967 expansion draft. After one season with the Penguins and two more with Vancouver of the Western League, he completed his NHL

career, returning to Pittsburgh in 1970-71. Bathgate was named twice to each of the NHL's first and second all-star teams against stiff competition from three other great rightwingers: Gordie Howe, Maurice Richard and Bernie Geoffrion. Elected 1978.

than in today's professional hockey, as players did their utmost to keep their spots in the NHL. Teams in minor professional leagues were affiliated with NHL clubs and provided a kind of long apprenticeship for players who understood that it might take years to get a chance to crack an NHL roster.

Television delivered the images and action of the game across Canada and into the United States. The players (still not wearing helmets) were widely recognized, both on the ice and off. Many of hockey's greatest stars — Richard, Howe, Hull, Mahovlich and others — were the top players in the League season after season and were destined for places in the Hall of Fame.

This era also saw the opening of the first permanent home for the Hockey Hall of Fame. The Hall had been founded in 1943 and opened its doors in a new facility on the grounds of the Canadian National Exhibition in Toronto in 1961. The building that housed the Hall was built as a result of co-operation between the NHL (whose member clubs funded construction), the City of Toronto (which provided the site) and the Canadian National Exhibition Association (which provided ongoing building maintenance).

Two of the Hall of Fame's honored members were directly involved in bringing the building to life. Conn Smythe, owner of the Toronto Maple Leafs, and Frank Selke, general manager of the Montreal Canadiens, arranged financing and supervised construction.

On-ice competition between the six clubs of the post-war NHL was fierce, but the "Original Six" teams weren't evenly matched. It was an era of dynasties, with the top teams a great deal stronger than the bottom. Montreal, Detroit and Toronto did most of the win-

CONTINUED ON PAGE 98

"Rarely has the career of an athlete been so exemplary. By his courage, his sense of discipline and honor, his lively intelligence and finesse, his magnificent team spirit, Beliveau has given new prestige to hockey," said Pierre Trudeau, Prime Minister of Canada, at Jean Beliveau Night, March 24, 1971, in the Montreal Forum.

" . . . It is hard, but I will play no more. I only hope I have made a contribution to a great game," Jean Beliveau stated as he announced his retirement from the NHL on June 9, 1971. Born August 31, 1931, in Trois-Rivières, Quebec, Jean Arthur Beliveau was to become a living legend. "Le Gros Bill", as he became known because of his 6'3", 205-pound frame, scored 507 goals during his 18 seasons in the NHL. His character would have won him respect even if he had scored but half that number. When he retired, Jean was named to an executive position with the Montreal Canadiens and was designated official spokesman of the organization. This was just an acknowledgement of the capacity he had been filling for a number of years, if not by words, then by actions.

He joined the Canadiens as a pro in the 1953-54 season, having played five NHL games as an amateur up from the Quebec Aces in two previous seasons — and from the first was a team leader, although he didn't officially become team captain until 1961. He still holds the record for most consecutive years in the Stanley Cup playoffs — 16 — and played 17 in all. His highest single goal-scoring season was 1955-56 when he not only won the Art Ross Trophy as scoring champion with 47 goals and 41 assists, but also won the Hart Trophy as the NHL's most valuable player. Three seasons later, he had a 45-goal effort. In 1963-64, Jean was again voted winner of the Hart Trophy and the following year won the Conn Smythe Trophy as the most valuable player in the Stanley Cup playoffs. In his final season, 1970-71, Jean collected 16 playoff assists and ended his playing career on a winning note as the Canadiens were upset winners of the Cup.

When Beliveau signed with the Canadiens, he received a five-year $100,000 contract, plus bonuses — a fantastic figure for that era — and became the game's most publicized rookie to that time. In addition to his 507 regular-season goals, Beliveau added 712 assists as well as recording 79 goals and 97 assists in 162 playoff games. He played on ten Stanley Cup championship teams.

Including playoffs, Jean played 1,287 NHL games. He was named six times to the NHL's first all-star team and four times to the second. Jean also scored 25 or more goals in 13 seasons, had 80 game-winning goals, three four-goal games and 18 three-goal games during his brilliant career. Elected 1972.

◁ **D**ouglas Wagner Bentley had all the attributes of a great hockey player. He had speed, scoring power, stamina, showmanship and was a fine back-checking leftwinger. All he lacked was size — his playing weight was 145 pounds — but his ability more than offset that.

In 1939 he moved up to start a 12-year stay with the Chicago Blackhawks of the NHL. For several seasons he was united with his brother Max and Bill Mosienko on one of the NHL's all-time great forward units, the Pony Line. All three scored more than 200 goals during their NHL careers, Doug getting 219 and winning a scoring title in 1942-43. He was also named to the first all-star team three times: in 1942-43, 1943-44 and 1946-47. A singular honor was bestowed on him in 1950 when a Chicago newspaper voted him the Half-Century Award as Chicago's best player up to that year.

One honor eluded Doug Bentley: he never played on a Stanley Cup winner. He died in Saskatoon on November 24, 1972. Elected 1964.

◁ **M**axwell Herbert (Max) Bentley was so frail-looking that he tried out with three NHL teams before getting a chance. At 145 pounds, he was hardly given a look at Boston, and when he tried out for Montreal, the doctor told him he had a heart condition and shouldn't play hockey. But Chicago finally took a chance on him and Max went on to become one of the all-time great playmaking and puck-handling centers.

At the height of his Chicago stardom, Max was the key figure in an amazing NHL trade. Toronto gave up five high-quality players for Bentley and an amateur player.

Max Bentley won the Hart Trophy in 1946, the Lady Byng Trophy in 1943 and the Art Ross Trophy in 1946 and 1947. He also was voted to the first all-star team in 1946. In 646 NHL games, Max scored 245 goals and had 299 assists for a total of 544 points. Elected 1966.

The hockey career of **Leo Joseph Boivin** spanned 1,150 games as a professional participant, beginning with a two-game stint in 1951-52.

Boivin is remembered as a rugged defenseman and as the premier bodychecker of his era. Many years later, Leo's checks are cited as the classic example of how to do it right. He also served as captain of the Boston Bruins from 1963 until he was traded to Detroit in 1966. At the time of his election to the Hall of Fame in 1986, Leo had an unbroken 34-year association with the game, serving as player, coach and scout. Elected 1986.

The Penticton Vees from British Columbia represented Canada at the IIHF World Championships in Krefeld, West Germany in 1955. The Vees won, defeating the Soviets who had won for the first time in 1954. This stamp, issued in 1955, celebrated Canada's role in international hockey.

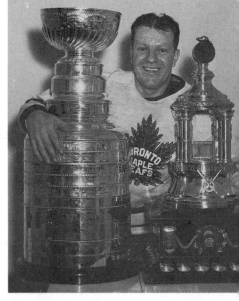

Born May 15, 1914, in Brandon, Manitoba, Walter Edward (Turk) Broda played for the International League champion Detroit Olympics in 1934-35 and shortly after was sold to the Toronto Maple Leafs for the then-record price of $8,000.

His pro career, all with the Leafs, spanned 16 seasons with two years lost to duty in the Canadian armed forces during World War II. He won the Vezina Trophy in 1940-41 and 1947-48 and shared it with Al Rollins in 1950-51 when Rollins played 39 games and Broda 31.

Broda earned 13 shutouts in 101 playoff games, posting a phenomenal 1.99 goals-against average. Broda also played on five Stanley Cup winners. He died in Toronto on October 17, 1972. Elected 1967.

When Emile Joseph Bouchard first reported to the Montreal Canadiens, he was young, eager and rough around the edges, but at 185 pounds he was one of the heaviest men on the roster. Butch was so keen, he rode a bicycle 50 miles to get to training camp and then proceeded to throw his weight around, much to the chagrin of some of the veterans.

Bouchard made the team that first season, 1941-42, and for 14 years was an outstanding defenseman.

Bouchard's contribution to the game goes far beyond his activity as a player. After his retirement from the NHL, he served as coach and president of junior teams. He also offered financial assistance to teams, both in hockey and other sports, and is a very popular figure in the Montreal area where he lives with his wife and family.

Emile Bouchard was born September 11, 1920. Elected 1966.

"When the competition got stiffer, I worked three times as hard. Competition drove me," said Johnny Bower, a remarkable hockey player and a remarkable man.

John William Bower was born November 8, 1924, in Prince Albert, Saskatchewan, the only boy in a family of nine. Johnny actually had two outstanding hockey careers: one in the minor pro leagues and one in the NHL. Drafted in 1945 by Cleveland, he bounced around the minors for 14 years, except for 1953-54 when he played for the New York Rangers. He won both the Les Cunningham Trophy as the American Hockey League's most valuable player and the Harry Holmes Trophy as the league's best goaltender on three occasions. He was the Western League's top goalie in his one season with Vancouver.

Drafted by Toronto Maple Leafs in 1958, he began his second career of 11 full NHL seasons. During his tenure with the Leafs the team won four Stanley Cups. He was named once to the NHL's first all-star team and played in five all-star games. He shared the Vezina Trophy in 1964-65 with Terry Sawchuk, and in 552 games, had a 2.52 goals-against average. Elected 1976.

Kids and collectors loved these colorful plastic hockey coins, which were found in food packages in the early 1960s. Each laminated color picture was inserted into a plastic disk colored to match the player's team. All the players depicted here are Hall of Famers.

Five-time all-star Milt Schmidt centered Boston's famed "Kraut Line" in the 1930s and 1940s. Schmidt played until the mid 1950s, retiring to become coach and later general manager of the Bruins.

King Clancy always wore the Maple Leaf proudly throughout his 56-year association with the Toronto hockey club. A bantam-weight rushing defenseman in the 1930s, Clancy remained a part of the Leafs' executive until his death in 1986.

Jean Beliveau was a hero in Quebec City where he was a scoring star for the Aces, the local entry in the Quebec Senior Hockey League. Beliveau did so well in Quebec that it was said he couldn't afford to turn pro despite two impressive tryouts with the Canadiens in 1951 and 1953. He finally joined the NHL fulltime for 1953-54 and was the league's MVP and top scorer in his third season. The Colisée, home of today's Quebec Nordiques, is still known as "the house that Beliveau built".

Gordie Howe's superb balance and legendary strength enabled him to control the puck or check an opponent at the limits of his considerable reach. Here he's bracketed by Vic Hadfield (11) and Arnie Brown of the Rangers.

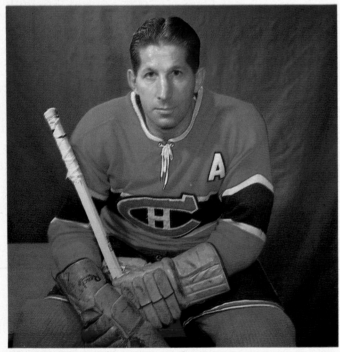

Elmer Lach won the Hart and Ross Trophies as NHL MVP and scoring leader in 1944-45, the same season in which his linemate, Rocket Richard, scored 50 goals in 50 games.

Toe Blake's scoring touch earned him the nickname of the "Lamplighter" during his 13 years with the Canadiens. Along with Lach and Richard, Blake was a part of Montreal's famous "Punch Line" in the late 1940s.

Maurice "Rocket" Richard was the NHL's most dazzling pure scorer in the late 1940s and 1950s. A 14-time all-star, the "Rock" was the NHL's top scorer on five occasions. His 626 goals include 82 in Stanley Cup play and a record six in overtime.

Montreal and Chicago had one of the NHL's finest rivalries in the 1960s. Here Jean Beliveau tries to set up in front of goaltender Denis DeJordy in this 1965 encounter. Hall of Famers Stan Mikita and Pierre Pilote are Beliveau's shadows.

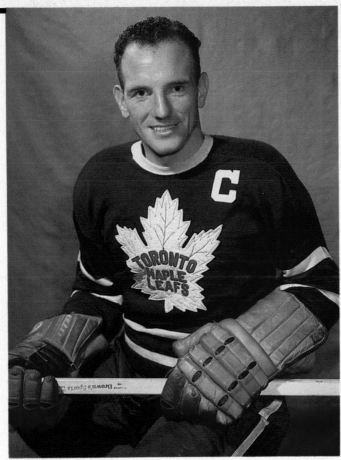

Teeder Kennedy was the kind of hard worker that Toronto manager Conn Smythe liked. A digger and hustler, Kennedy was a natural leader, becoming team captain in 1948. He won the Hart Trophy in 1954-55.

Bill Gadsby was a 20-year NHL defenseman who played for Chicago, the New York Rangers and Detroit. He was one of the league's top-scoring defenseman, earning seven all-star selections.

Words are being exchanged between the Leafs and Bruins as Allan Stanley (26) and Boston's Ted Green make their points. Stanley's defense partner, Tim Horton (7), looks on. With each of the six NHL teams playing its opponents 14 times a season, disputes were often carried over from one game to another.

Bernie Boom Boom Geoffrion was the NHL's second 50-goal scorer, equalling the Rocket's record in 1960-61. With 45 assists that season, Geoffrion was the league's top scorer and MVP.

Ted Lindsay was an ultra-tough left winger with a scoring touch who played much of his career on a line with Gordie Howe. Lindsay retired in 1960 but came back in 1964 to play one final season.

Frank Mahovlich was Toronto's only game-breaking superstar on the Cup-winning teams of the 1960s. Endowed with speed, size and a heavy shot, the "Big M" often found himself as depicted here — in all alone.

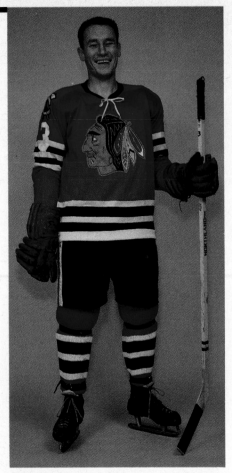

Pierre Pilote was selected as the NHL's top defenseman three consecutive seasons beginning in 1962-63. His 1964-65 point total of 59 broke Babe Pratt's 1944 scoring record for defensemen.

Photographer Frank Prazak climbed into the rafters to capture this aerial view of "Golden Jet" Bobby Hull during his record 54-goal season of 1965-66. Jacques Laperrière is Hull's checker as goaltender Gump Worsley looks for the pass in the slot.

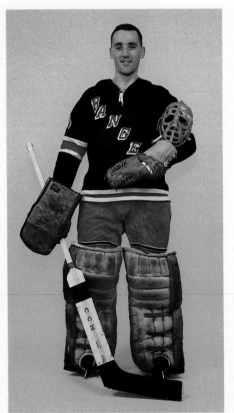

Jacques Plante's trademark mask traveled with him from Montreal to New York where he played two seasons beginning in 1964-65. Previously, Plante made good use of his own acrobatic skills and the Canadiens superb defense to win six Vezina Trophies.

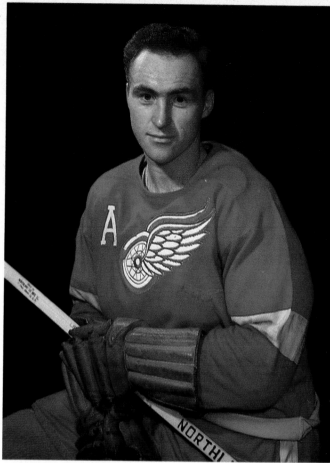

Red Kelly was Detroit's top defenseman during the Red Wings' domination of top spot in the NHL standings in the early 1950s. A part of four Cup teams in Detroit, Kelly was later traded to Toronto where he was converted to center and went on to win the Stanley Cup on four more occasions.

In an era of six teams and a handful of top goaltenders, Terry Sawchuk's name is near the top of any expert's list. The only man to record more than 100 shutouts in the NHL, Sawchuk registered five consecutive seasons in the early 1950s with a goal-against per game average of less than 2.00.

Norm Ullman (7) and Stan Mikita both reached the 1,000-point and 20-year plateaus in the NHL. Mikita played his entire career in Chicago while Ullman was part of the biggest deal of the 1960s, going from Detroit to Toronto with Paul Henderson and Floyd Smith for Frank Mahovlich, Garry Unger, Pete Stemkowski and the rights to Carl Brewer.

In 1966-67, 15-year New York Ranger veteran Harry Howell (at left) won the Norris Trophy as the NHL's top defenseman. In his acceptance speech he acknowledged that his win marked the end of one era and the beginning of the next. Beginning the following season, the award came to be dominated by Bobby Orr, (below, left) who won the Norris eight consecutive times, forever expanding the defenseman's offensive responsibilities in modern hockey. Orr was a three-time MVP and double winner of the scoring championship and playoff MVP awards before knee injuries ended his career. Orr, shown here at his first training camp with coach Harry Sinden, had yet to be assigned the number 4 sweater he made famous.

Born August 1, 1919, in Regina, Saskat-▷ chewan, **J.A. (Jack) Butterfield's** days as a player were cut short by an injury and he became a public relations man and trainer for the AHL New Haven Eagles, working for his uncle, Eddie Shore.

Butterfield was a dynamic and effective administrator of the game. Perhaps more than any other individual, he helped keep minor pro hockey alive during the years of National Hockey League expansion and competition for players from the World Hockey Association.

As president of the American Hockey League, a league that provided hundreds of players to the NHL, Butterfield spearheaded indemnification negotiations, twice rewrote the AHL constitution and bylaws, and several times revised player contract forms to stay abreast of a constantly changing hockey world. Elected 1980.

Frank Buckland was born May 23, 1902, in Gravenhurst, Ontario. His first involvement with hockey at the amateur level was in Toronto when he was coach, then manager, and later president of a junior club.

Buckland was elected to the Ontario Hockey Association executive and continued working in amateur hockey, becoming president of the OHA for a two-year term in 1955. In 1961, he was elected treasurer of the OHA and still held that office at the time of his election to the Hockey Hall of Fame in 1975.

The Canadian Amateur Hockey Association recognized his outstanding service in 1965 when it presented him with the CAHA Meritorious Award. The same year, the OHA presented Buckland with its Gold Stick Award and, in 1973, he was named a Life Member of the OHA. Buckland has made amateur hockey his life's work. Elected 1975.

Born July 9, 1905, in Fleming, Saskatche-▷ wan, **Clarence S. Campbell** was raised in western Canada. He graduated from the University of Alberta, then attended Oxford University as a Rhodes Scholar. Prior to W.W.II he refereed lacrosse and NHL hockey. Prior to succeeding Mervyn (Red) Dutton as NHL president in 1946, Campbell distinguished himself as a lawyer, then as a Canadian Army officer in World War II.

As president of the NHL Campbell established the NHL Pension Society in 1946 and successfully guided the league's expansion from six to twelve teams in 1967-68. In 1977 he retired after 31 years as NHL president. He died June 24, 1984. Elected 1966.

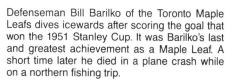

Defenseman Bill Barilko of the Toronto Maple Leafs dives icewards after scoring the goal that won the 1951 Stanley Cup. It was Barilko's last and greatest achievement as a Maple Leaf. A short time later he died in a plane crash while on a northern fishing trip.

ning. Chicago, the NHL's weakest club throughout the 1950s, became a contender in the 1960s by building an offense around Bobby Hull and Stan Mikita. Of the 21 seasons from 1946-47 to 1966-67, the Canadiens, Red Wings and Leafs won 20 Stanley Cups and finished first in the regular-season standings on an equal number of occasions. The "have-nots" appeared in the Stanley Cup finals on seven occasions, with the 1960-61 Chicago Blackhawks as the only winner.

The Dynasties

Toronto Maple Leafs, 1946-51
(Stanley Cup Champions, 1947, 1948, 1949, 1951)

The Toronto Maple Leafs of the 1940s and early 1950s played their best hockey in the Stanley Cup playoffs. The Leafs finished in first place in the regular season only in 1947-48, but won the Cup four times in five seasons from 1947 to 1951.

The Leafs were the first team in the NHL to win the Stanley Cup in three successive seasons. Their Cup wins were due in part to strong play by goaltender Turk Broda, who saved his best games for the playoffs. From 1946-47 to 1950-51, Broda's playoff goals-against average dropped each year from an excellent 2.24 in 1947 to only 1.12 in 1951. Broda stymied the NHL's top scoring unit, Detroit's "Production Line" of Sid Abel, Ted Lindsay and Gordie Howe, in the 1948 and 1949 finals as the Maple Leafs swept both series four games to none. In 1951 Toronto won again, defeating Montreal in five games with every contest decided in overtime. The photograph of Bill Barilko scoring the Cup-winning goal in the fifth game endures as one of the most vivid images of NHL hockey in the early 1950s. Barilko lost his life in a small airplane accident a few weeks after that game.

It didn't take **William L. (Bill) Chadwick** long to make his mark as an official in the NHL. The likeable American spent one year as linesman in the NHL in 1940, then moved up to referee hundreds of regular-season and Stanley Cup contests until he retired in 1955.

Born October 10, 1915, in New York City, Chadwick's playing days were launched with the Stock Exchange team in the Metropolitan League. While sitting out a game with injuries, he was asked to substitute for a referee who had failed to appear. He took an immediate liking to this aspect of the sport and worked many amateur games in the New York area, where he was spotted by an NHL observer.

As a referee, he found that he didn't know what to do with his hands, so he decided to use them to denote the reason for penalties. For a holding penalty, Chadwick grabbed his wrist and for a tripping penalty he slapped his shin. At first, observers thought he was showboating, but it quickly became apparent that he had added a new and desirable asset to the game, making it more understandable to players and fans alike. Elected 1964.

Sincerity was **Frank Dilio's** biggest asset. During his many years of service in the Quebec Amateur Hockey League and Junior Amateur Hockey Association, he maintained a broad outlook, realizing that amateur hockey's role was to provide boys with competition that might prepare them for the professional ranks. Hockey Hall of Fame members like Maurice ("The Rocket") Richard and Emile ("Butch") Bouchard, along with many other stars, emerged from these leagues while he was associated with them.

Born April 12, 1912, in Montreal, Frank Dilio joined the JAHA as secretary and moved up to become president by 1939. In 1943, he became registrar of the QAHA and added the duties of secretary in 1952. Elected 1964.

Only the second player in NHL history to play more than 20 seasons for one team, **Alex Delvecchio** played a total of 22 full seasons and parts of two others with the Detroit Red Wings before retiring on November 9, 1973. He was born December 4, 1931, in Fort William, Ontario, and graduated to the NHL from the junior Oshawa Generals. An affable, cigar-smoking player, Alex earned the nickname "Fats" early in his career, not because of obesity but for his round, pleasant face and warm, friendly smile.

An exceptionally clean player, Alex was a three-time winner of the Lady Byng Trophy for combining gentlemanly conduct with a high standard of play.

In his lengthy career, Alex was a member of many outstanding Detroit teams: Stanley Cup winners in 1952, 1954 and 1955 and Prince of Wales Trophy winners on six occasions when the trophy went to the team finishing first in NHL regular-season play. At the time of his retirement, Delvecchio ranked second to Gordie Howe in NHL records for games played, seasons played, most assists and most points. Elected 1977.

Born in Toronto on January 22, 1915, **William Ronald (Bill) Durnan** first achieved recognition as goalie for the Sudbury juniors in the 1934 Ontario Hockey Association finals.

His ambidextrous brilliance caught the eye of people in Montreal. With the Canadiens he was an instant sensation, winning the Vezina Trophy in 1944, his first season as a pro.

Bill won the Vezina Trophy six out of seven times, missing only in 1948 when Turk Broda of Toronto won the award. He was a six-time NHL first team all-star playing on four league championship teams and two Stanley Cup winners. In 1948-49, he established the modern NHL record for consecutive shutouts with four, playing 309 minutes and 21 seconds of shutout hockey. He played 383 scheduled games, allowing 901 goals for an average of 2.36 goals-against per game, with 34 shutouts. He died in Toronto on October 31, 1972. Elected 1963.

THE DYNASTY YEARS

After their first Cup win in 1947, Toronto manager Conn Smythe traded five players to Chicago to obtain Max Bentley in November 1947. Bentley had been the NHL's leading scorer the previous season playing with a Chicago team that was short on talent. His acquisition gave the Leafs another top centerman to go along with Teeder Kennedy and veteran star Syl Apps. Bentley enjoyed playing with a contending team and scored eleven points in nine games in the 1948 playoffs.

As the Leafs' team captain, Teeder Kennedy embodied the tough, team-first approach of Conn Smythe's Leafs. He wasn't a pretty skater, but played an effective, hard-working style that resulted in several 20-goal seasons.

These Toronto teams won four Stanley Cups without having a dominant player. The Leafs stressed team play, spreading the scoring evenly throughout the forward ranks. They relied on goaltending and defense to win low-scoring games. It was uncompromising hockey in the vision of Conn Smythe.

Detroit Red Wings, 1947-57
(Stanley Cup Champions, 1950, 1952, 1954, 1955)

The Detroit Red Wings' roster in the 1950s was filled with the names of several eventual Hall of Famers, but their crown jewel was a strong young rightwinger named Gordie Howe. Howe could do everything in hockey. He became not only the top scorer in the NHL, but also was very likely the League's strongest, fastest, smoothest-skating and, if he felt it was required, meanest player as well.

With Howe, the Red Wings finished in second place in 1947-48 and then recorded an unprecedented seven consecutive first-place finishes and four Stanley Cups.

Tough situations were almost commonplace to **William Alexander Gadsby.** Both on and off the ice, he faced them all the same way: head on.

Born August 8, 1927, in Calgary, Alberta, he spent 20 seasons in the NHL and proved himself to be a defenseman of outstanding ability.

In 1952, he was captain of the Chicago Blackhawks when struck by polio but beat this crippling disease and went on to become one of the few players to play 20 seasons in the NHL.

Gadsby graduated from Edmonton junior hockey, signed to play pro with Chicago and was sent to Kansas City for seasoning. He moved up to the Hawks early in 1946 and remained with them until he was traded to New York in 1954. Another trade took him to Detroit for the 1961-62 season and he played his last five seasons with the Wings. He returned to coach the Wings in 1968-69 and for two games of the 1969-70 schedule, when he was suddenly dismissed. Gadsby was an all-star five times, but never played on a Stanley Cup winner. Elected 1970.

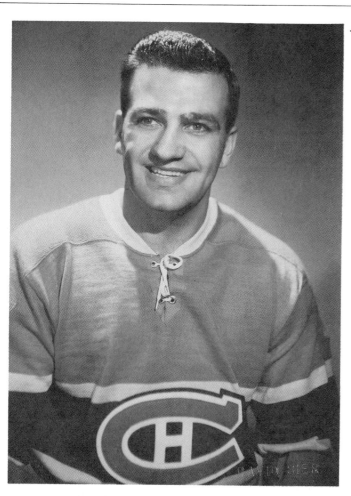

J oseph A. Bernard (Boom Boom) Geoffrion was born February 14, 1931, and stepped from the Montreal Nationals junior team to the Canadiens in 1951, scoring eight goals in 18 games. The 5′ 11″, 185-pounder went on to register 393 NHL goals before retiring in 1968.

Geoffrion blazed his name into the record book on several occasions. He won the Art Ross Trophy as scoring champion twice (1955 and 1961), the Hart Trophy as the most valuable player (1961) and the Calder Trophy as top rookie (1952). His career coincided with that of two of the game's greatest rightwingers, Gordie Howe and Maurice "The Rocket" Richard. He joined Richard as the second player to reach the 50-goal plateau in one season (1961), the year he achieved a personal high of 95 points.

Geoffrion turned to coaching, first with the Quebec Aces and then in the NHL with the Rangers, the newly formed Atlanta Flames and the Canadiens. Elected 1972.

Leafs captain Teeder Kennedy, missing several teeth, accepts the Stanley Cup from NHL President Clarence Campbell in 1949. At right is Leaf coach Hap Day, and, kneeling on the right, assistant captain Max Bentley. At left, owner Conn Smythe exudes the pride with which he infused the Toronto organization for more than three decades. A gentleman, Conn invariable wore spats.

Manager Jack Adams and coach Tommy Ivan built Detroit's offense around a new forward line that featured Howe on right wing, Ted Lindsay on left and Sid Abel at center. This "Production Line" quickly became hockey's top offensive unit and remained together for five seasons until Abel left Detroit to become the playing coach of the Chicago Blackhawks.

After Abel's departure, the center's spot on the Production Line was most frequently filled by Alex Delvecchio from Fort William, Ontario. Delvecchio combined size and skating ability in a way that made him the perfect setup man for his talented wingers.

Another Detroit all-star and Hall of Famer was defenseman Leonard "Red" Kelly. In an era in which the best skaters were usually forwards, Kelly was an exception capable of checking an opponent and rushing up the ice at top speed. Kelly was a vital part of the Wings' four Stanley Cup wins and, after being traded, would be part of another four-Cup hockey dynasty with the Leafs in the early 1960s.

Terry Sawchuk provided the Red Wings with splendid goaltending. Sawchuk, who could go down to block shots and then pop back to his feet like a rubber ball, played more than 20 seasons in the NHL and is the only goaltender in the League to register more than 100 shutouts.

General manager Jack Adams, who is a member of the Hall of Fame for his achievements as a player in the 1920s, was the architect of Detroit's great teams. Adams also coached the team from 1927 to 1947. His clubs made the playoffs for twenty consecutive seasons, beginning in 1938-39. He was an innovator, developing the first comprehensive farm system set up to develop talent for a single NHL club.

Tommy Ivan took over as coach of the Red Wings in 1947, finishing first in six

One of the magical names in hockey is **Glenn Henry Hall,** the veteran goalie who played 18 seasons in the NHL — four with Detroit, ten with Chicago and four with St. Louis. He was consistently one of the league's outstanding goaltenders and an all-star selection 11 times, finishing with a career goals-against average of 2.51.

Born October 3, 1931, in Humboldt, Saskatchewan, Hall led the NHL in shutouts in six seasons, including his rookie campaign when he won the Calder Trophy. He holds the NHL record for most consecutive games by a goaltender (502) and appeared in 906 league games. In playoff competition he holds goaltending records for most games (113) and most minutes played (6,899). His name appears on the Vezina Trophy three times.

Hall was the first player selected by the Blues in the NHL's expansion draft and posted goals-against averages of 2.50, 2.31 and 3.00 with St. Louis. He recorded 14 shutouts with the Blues and helped lead them to the Stanley Cup finals for three consecutive seasons. Until the final half of his last season Hall played without a mask. He played most of his career in the era when teams carried only one goalie, making his longevity a tribute to his durability. Elected 1975.

This vest pocket 1949 *NHL Record Book* came ▷ from the library of NHL president Clarence Campbell. This is the first edition of the *Record Book*, which was published annually. Bill Durnan, the Hall of Fame goaltender for the Montreal Canadiens, is depicted on the cover. Close examination of this photo reveals the identical gloves that enabled Durnan to catch pucks or handle his stick with either hand and leather biceps guards worn on top of his uniform.

Miles Gilbert (Tim) Horton was born January 12, 1930, in Cochrane, Ontario.

He became an NHL player to stay in 1952 when he joined the Toronto Maple Leafs. A defenseman who shot righthanded, he stood 5′ 10″, weighed 180 pounds and had strength few chose to challenge. He was to play almost 18 full seasons with Toronto, one each with the New York Rangers and Pittsburgh, and then two with Buffalo before a tragic accident ended his life on February 21, 1974.

He had a reputation as a peacemaker, flinging bodies out of piles during altercations and deterring over-eager opponents with a grasp known as the "Horton Bear Hug."

Tim played on four Stanley Cup winners with Toronto in the 1960s and was named six times to all-star teams: to the first team in 1964, 1968 and 1969, and to the second team in 1954, 1963 and 1967. He played 1,446 scheduled games with 115 goals, 403 assists and 1,611 penalty minutes. In 126 playoff games, Horton had 11 goals and 39 assists while drawing 183 minutes in penalties. Elected 1977.

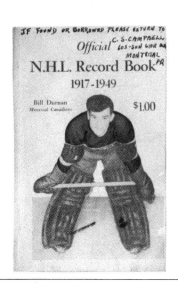

Douglas Norman Harvey was a superior athlete who excelled in many sports. Born December 19, 1924, in Montreal, Doug played baseball, football and hockey — all of them well.

Doug played 21 seasons of professional hockey, 14 of them with the Montreal Canadiens, where he played on six Stanley Cup championship teams. He won the Norris Trophy as top NHL defenseman seven times, virtually monopolizing this award from 1955 to 1962.

A left-handed shot, he stood 5′ 11″ and weighed 180 pounds. Harvey was an excellent blocker, had uncanny puck control and could set the pace of a game. Such was the calibre of this great defenseman that he was selected to NHL all-star teams on 11 occasions.

Although not a prolific goal scorer — 88 goals in regular-season play and eight in the playoffs — several of Harvey's goals came at crucial times for his team. Twice in key playoff games, an opposing forward stole the puck from him to score tying goals; minutes later, in each instance, he scored the winner. His passing ability is demonstrated by the 452 assists he recorded in regular-season play.

Doug Harvey is always mentioned when the greatest defensemen of all time are being compared. He seldom took himself seriously and often relieved dressing-room tension by a well-timed funny remark. He was traded to the New York Rangers in 1961-62 to become a playing-coach but did not at that time relish coaching responsibility and was eventually traded to Detroit. He was drafted by St. Louis, where he finished his playing career. Elected 1973.

At the age of 32, William (Bill) Hanley gave up the security of his family's business and cast his lot with the game of hockey. He went on to spend 27 years with the Ontario Hockey Association.

Born in Ireland on February 28, 1915, Bill grew up in Toronto and later moved to Dublin, Ontario. After service in the Royal Canadian Navy, Bill helped as a timekeeper for junior games at Maple Leaf Gardens in his spare time. Soon he was timekeeper for Leafs' games as well. George Panter, business manager of the OHA, asked Bill to assist him and, although the money wasn't good, Bill wanted to work in hockey full-time. He learned from three of the best — Panter himself, George Dudley and W.A. (Billy) Hewitt — and stayed on as secretary-manager of the OHA until his retirement in 1974. Elected 1986.

of seven seasons and winning the Stanley Cup three times. When Jim Norris, Jr., the son of the owner of the Red Wings, bought the Chicago Blackhawks in 1954, Ivan was hired as general manager and asked to build a farm system in the style of Jack Adams.

Montreal Canadiens, 1955-1960
(Stanley Cup Champions, 1956, 1957, 1958, 1959, 1960)

The Montreal Canadiens won the Stanley Cup an unequaled five straight times beginning in 1956. The team was so strong that with a break here and a bounce there, they could have won as many as eight Cups in a row. They won in 1953 and, the following season, lost in overtime of the seventh game of the finals against Detroit on a deflected screen shot. In 1955, they lost to Detroit again in seven games, but went into the playoffs without their top scorer, Maurice "Rocket" Richard, who had been suspended from post-season play, as a result of a outburst in Boston on March 13, 1955.

The frustration felt by Montreal hockey fans reached a flashpoint at the next game in the Forum on March 17. Smoke bombs resulted in the game being forfeited as disgruntled fans spilled out of the Forum. The damage and vandalism done that night in downtown Montreal became known as the "Richard Riot" and gave evidence to the passion aroused by the Rocket.

The suspension cost Richard the best opportunity in his career to win the NHL scoring championship. It was a factor in the Canadiens' regular-season finish two points behind Detroit and removed the club's leading scorer and the NHL's top playoff performer from a lineup that would still get to the seventh game of the finals before elimination.

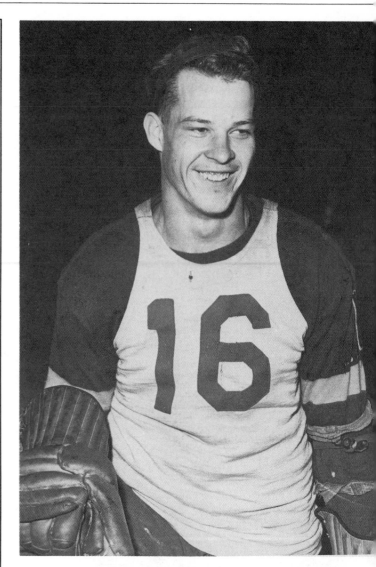

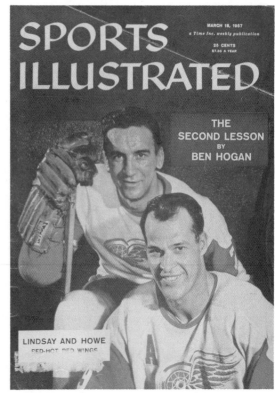

LINDSAY AND HOWE
RED-HOT RED WINGS

"**B**oth on and off the ice, **Gordie Howe's** conduct . . . has demonstrated a high quality of sportsmanship and competence which is an example to us all. He has earned the title: Mr. Hockey." Lester B. Pearson, former Prime Minister of Canada.

"Never in history . . . has there been such an obvious and dramatic loss by a single sport. There's no way hockey can ever repay you its debt of gratitude." Clarence Campbell, President of the NHL.

When Gordie Howe first retired from the NHL in 1971 after 25 glorious seasons, he said: "Say 'retired,' not 'quit.' I don't like the word quit." And that's one thing he never did during his brilliant career with the Detroit Red Wings, Houston Aeros and New England and Hartford Whalers. In all, he played 32 demanding big-league seasons in five different decades, establishing himself as one of sport's greatest-ever talents.

Gordon Howe was born March 31, 1928, in Floral, Saskatchewan, and played his last amateur game with the Saskatoon Lions juveniles. He played one year of minor pro with Omaha of the U.S. League before joining Detroit for the 1946-47 season. He had an effortless skating style and deceptive speed that, combined with his tremendous strength and ability to shoot with equal dexterity from either side, made him a difficult man to stop. Six feet tall, and 205 pounds, he was tough, but not in a bullying way.

Howe also earned numerous nicknames, such as "Mr. Elbows" from his opponents and "Power" from his teammates. He could also have been called "The Most" as he established more records than any other NHL player. Just a few from his impressive list are: most NHL seasons (26), games (1,767), goals (801) and assists (1,049). He also holds the record for most selections to NHL all-star teams with 21 (of which 12 were first team selections).

He retired in 1971, but came back to play seven more seasons, beginning in 1973-74 when he joined with his sons Mark and Marty to form an all-Howe family forward line for the WHA's Houston Aeros. In the WHA, Howe was an all-star, posting seasons of 96, 99, 100 and 102 points. When Hartford joined the NHL in 1979, Howe, then 51, played one last season in the NHL, appearing in the 1980 all-star game.

Gordie is a great ambassador for hockey off the ice, attending banquets, signing thousands of autographs and doing much little-publicized charity and community work. For excellence and durability, his career will probably never be matched. Elected 1972.

◁ Gordie Howe and Ted Lindsay were as tough and talented a pair of forwards as any in the NHL of the 1950s. Lindsay, who played ferocious hockey, was the NHL's top leftwinger and a nine-time all-star.

Henry Vernon (Harry) Howell appeared in more games than any defenseman in the history of major league hockey. He played 1,581 games, 1,411 in the NHL and 170 in the World Hockey Association. He turned pro in 1952 with the New York Rangers and retired in 1975.

Harry, was born December 28, 1932, in Hamilton, Ontario. He missed only 17 games in his first 16 years in New York, and his 1,160 games and 17 seasons were a team record for the Rangers. Harry stood 6′ 1″, weighed 200 pounds and was a lefthanded shot. His main regret was that he never played on a Stanley Cup winner.

He moved to an administrative post in 1976, when he joined the NHL's Cleveland Barons as assistant general manager. Harry later became general manager and was serving in that capacity when the Barons merged with Minnesota in 1978. Elected 1979.

George Hayes, the first NHL on-ice official to work in more than 1,000 games, was a colorful character who, despite his share of disputes with league executives, was universally regarded as the best linesman of his day.

A native of Montreal, Hayes moved to Ingersoll, Ontario, where he began officiating minor and high school games in 1936. By 1943-44 he was officiating in the AHL and OHA. He signed his first NHL contract for $2,000 in April 1946. From 1946-47 to 1964-65, Hayes worked 1,544 regular-season, 149 playoff and 11 All-Star games. Hall of Fame referee Red Storey characterized Hayes as, "the best and most colorful linesman ever to work in the league. He had the highest respect from fans, players and fellow officials." George Hayes died November 19, 1987. Elected 1988.

In 1955-56, Hall of Fame player Toe Blake took over as coach of the Canadiens. Blake had been a star with Montreal, playing left wing on the "Punch Line" with Elmer Lach and Rocket Richard. Coach Blake knew that for Montreal to win, Rocket Richard would have to harness his volatile temper.

Looking to the 1955-56 season, Canadiens' general manager Frank Selke, Sr., knew Richard had run out of chances with NHL president Clarence Campbell. His choice of Blake, whom Richard respected, was a vital ingredient in the formula that made the Montreal Canadiens unbeatable for five seasons in the NHL.

The Canadiens' array of stars didn't stop at the Rocket. Three other Montreal forwards — Bernie Geoffrion, Dickie Moore and Jean Beliveau — led the NHL in regular-season goals or points during the club's five years on top. They were all native Quebecers and born in 1931, forming the greatest one-year harvest of local talent ever to play in the NHL.

Two future members of the Hall of Fame joined the Canadiens in 1955. Henri Richard, one of the NHL's fastest skaters, and Claude Provost, a top checking forward, made important contributions throughout the Canadiens' five-year hold on the Cup.

The Montreal defense of the 1950s was anchored by Tom Johnson and Doug Harvey, who was selected to the NHL all-star team for eleven consecutive years beginning in 1952.

Jacques Plante, the Canadiens' goaltender, was an innovator at the position. He developed the first practical goaltender's face mask and changed the way the position was played by increasing the goaltender's puck-handling responsibilities. Though he left the Canadiens in the

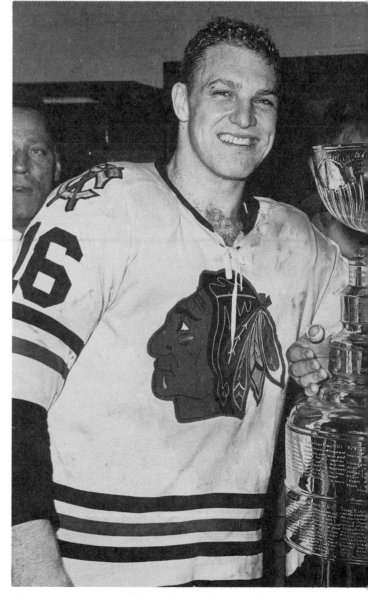

As early as age 10, **Robert Marvin (Bobby) Hull** was tagged as a sure-fire NHL player — and he didn't disappoint the experts. Born January 3, 1939, in Pointe Anne, Ontario, Hull progressed rapidly through minor hockey ranks and joined the Chicago Blackhawks.

Although he didn't invent the slapshot, Bobby's booming blaster made many goalies cower. He led the NHL in goals scored in seven seasons. Many tried to emulate his unerring accuracy with a slapshot. In 16 NHL seasons, Hull scored 610 goals and added 560 assists in regular-season play, and added 62 goals and 67 assists in Stanley Cup competition. His other NHL achievements were many: first to score more than 50 goals in a season (54 in 1965-66); winner of the Art Ross Trophy three times, the Lady Byng Trophy once, the Hart Trophy twice, and the Lester Patrick Trophy for contribution to hockey in the U.S. once. Bobby also dominated all-star selections, being named to the NHL first all-star team ten times and to the second team twice.

Hull was in the vanguard of players who helped launch the World Hockey Association. His signing by the Winnipeg Jets in 1972 gave the new league much-needed credibility. With Winnipeg, he added another 303 goals and 335 assists in 411 games, including 77 goals in 1974-75.

His blond good looks earned him the designation of the "Golden Jet" very early in his career and he was always a favorite with young fans because of his patient response to requests for autographs. Elected 1983.

A mixture of sports and politics dominated the life of **Fred John Hume**. Although he later devoted much of his drive and leadership to the professional game, amateur hockey was one of his keen interests. He worked to form the Western Hockey League and develop the New Westminster Royals Hockey Club.

Hume was born May 2, 1892, in New Westminster, British Columbia. At the age of 29 he ran for alderman and at age 38 became mayor of New Westminster. He later moved to Vancouver and became mayor of that city. He died February 17, 1967. Elected 1962.

George (Punch) Imlach was born March 15, 1918, and raised in Toronto. Even though he almost made the NHL as a player, it was as a coach and manager that he left his indelible mark on the game.

Imlach joined the Quebec Senior League's Quebec Aces and played four seasons, two as playing coach. At age 31, he reluctantly quit as a player and took on the job of general manager, later becoming a co-owner. He joined the NHL in 1958 as an assistant general manager of the Toronto Maple Leafs and took over as their coach as well as general manager during the 1958-59 season.

In his 11 seasons with Toronto, his teams made the playoffs ten times and won four Stanley Cups. After a season as a syndicated hockey columnist, he was named general manager and coach of the expansion Buffalo Sabres in May, 1970. Buffalo made the playoffs in their third season and went to the Stanley Cup finals in 1975. He left Buffalo in December, 1978, and rejoined Toronto in July, 1979, as general manager. Continuing heart problems led to the termination of his Toronto contract after the 1981-82 season. Imlach died on December 1, 1987. Elected 1984.

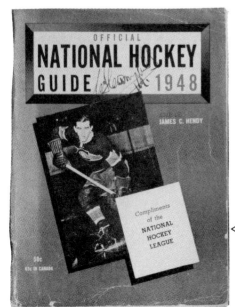

◁ James Hendy, a Hall of Fame member in the builders category, edited this edition of the *Official National Hockey Guide* in 1948. Hendy was a pioneer of statistical compilation in hockey. His slim volume is the grandfather of the *NHL Official Guide & Record Book* that is used by fans, scouts, general managers and reporters today.

early 1960s, Plante played in the NHL until he was over 40 before becoming a goaltending instructor and coach in North America and Europe.

Chicago Blackhawks 1960-67
(Stanley Cup Champions, 1961)

The Chicago Blackhawks were a bottom-rank team that was rebuilt by new ownership in the mid-1950s. From 1947 to 1958, the Blackhawks finished last nine times. With home crowds averaging less than 5,000 a game, the franchise was in trouble. Jim Norris, Jr., son of the owner of the Detroit Red Wings, bought the club in 1954. With Tommy Ivan as general manager and Dick Irvin as coach, the revitalized Blackhawks built a farm system of sponsored junior and minor pro clubs. The system paid off by the late 1950s as Bobby Hull and Stan Mikita joined the Blackhawks from the St. Catharines Teepees junior team.

In 1957 Dick Irvin retired as coach and Rudy Pilous, who had coached Hull and Mikita in St. Catharines, joined his all-star juniors in the NHL. The Blackhawks won the Stanley Cup in 1960-61, defeating Detroit in six games. This Cup win by the Blackhawks marked the only time between 1941 and 1969 that a team other than Montreal, Detroit or Toronto won the trophy.

Bobby Hull had speed, strength and the most powerful shot in hockey. In addition to the big slapshot, he could stickhandle and check. He was the NHL's top scorer in his third year, combining with Billy "Red" Hay and Murray Balfour on what was called the "Million-Dollar Line." He equalled Rocket Richard's and Bernie Geoffrion's NHL record of fifty goals in a season in 1962 and then surpassed it with 54 goals in 1966.

Center Stan Mikita was a digger who

Thomas N. (Tommy) Ivan never played professional hockey but he has a lengthy list of achievements as a coach and manager.

Born January 21, 1911, in Toronto, he first attracted attention as a coach of the Brantford, Ontario, junior team. Jack Adams brought him into the Detroit Red Wings' organization as a scout, then as a coach at Omaha and Indianapolis before moving him into the NHL with the Wings in the 1947-48 season. In Detroit, Ivan coached six straight NHL championship teams and three Stanley Cup winners. He left Detroit in 1955 to join the Chicago Blackhawks as general manager. After Chicago coach Dick Irvin fell ill, Ivan also coached for a season and a half.

The Hawks were losers both on the ice and at the gate and he helped rebuild them into one of the most successful organizations in the league. He also re-established a fine farm system. Under his tenure as general manager, the Hawks won their first Stanley Cup title in 23 years, in 1961, and their first East Division title in 1967.

Among the many highlights of his career, Tommy Ivan remembers coaching Gordie Howe in his first pro season; the Wings' eight-game sweep to a Stanley Cup triumph in 1952; and the six victorious years he coached teams in All-Star games. Elected 1974.

Thomas Christian Johnson was born in the small town of Baldur, Manitoba, on February 18, 1928. He didn't play hockey in a covered arena until he was 18, when he joined the junior Winnipeg Monarchs. Claimed by Montreal, he saw limited action the next year with the senior Royals and was sent to Buffalo for the 1947-48 season. His constant driving for victory plus his enthusiasm on the bench made him an instant favorite and he was called up to stay with Montreal the next season.

Johnson played 15 seasons in the NHL. In 978 games he had 51 goals and 213 assists. His best season was 1958-59, when he won the Norris Trophy as the NHL's premier defenseman.

He had the misfortune to suffer eye injuries twice, both accidentally inflicted by teammates. The second cut facial and eye muscles and threatened his sight. Because of his doubtful status as a player, he was left unprotected and claimed by the Boston Bruins. Shortly after, he was again injured, a skate severing a leg nerve, so he retired. Johnson played on six Stanley Cup winners. Elected 1970.

Born at Watrous, Saskatchewan, on June 20, 1914, **Gordon Juckes'** hockey career began as a player in minor hockey in Melville. He became president of the local club, and then president of the Saskatchewan Senior League. He was elected president of the Saskatchewan Amateur Hockey Association in 1953-54. Six years later he assumed the presidency of the CAHA. Appointed CAHA secretary-manager in 1960 (later the title changed to executive director), he served the CAHA until his retirement in 1978.

Juckes' contributions to hockey have been recognized in many ways: a AHAUS diploma in 1962; a diploma of honor from the International Ice Hockey Federation in 1967; the CAHA Meritorious Award in 1976; plus life membership in the SAHA. Elected 1979.

Leonard Patrick (Red) Kelly is the antithesis of that old saying "nice guys finish last." The friendly redhead flashed across NHL headlines for 20 seasons, winning much acclaim and countless friends.

Born in Simcoe, Ontario, on July 9, 1927, he graduated to the NHL at 19. He played with the Detroit Red Wings for 12½ seasons where he was a standout defenseman who was occasionally used as a forward. He was traded to the Toronto Maple Leafs, where he completed his playing career as a center. During that span Kelly was a four-time winner of the Lady Byng Trophy and the first winner of the Norris Trophy. In Detroit and Toronto, he played on eight Cup-winning teams.

With NHL expansion in 1967, Kelly accepted a coaching post with the Los Angeles Kings, guiding the team into the playoffs in the ensuing two seasons despite being hampered by what critics considered to be poor draft choices. He became coach of Pittsburgh in 1969 and Toronto in 1973. Elected 1969.

◁ Some of the most intense battles of the 1950s and '60s were waged between the Toronto Maple Leafs and the Detroit Red Wings. Here, Leafs captain George Armstrong and Detroit captain "Red" Kelly challenge one another in front of Terry Sawchuk, one of the last and greatest of the unmasked goaltenders. All three are members of the Hall of Fame, and all eventually played together with the Maple Leafs.

created scoring chances with hard work. Along with Hull, Mikita curved the blade of his stick, causing the puck to dip in flight. Despite the big banana curve, Mikita's backhand shot remained effective. In the Hawks' Cup-winning season, Mikita became part of the "Scooter Line" with Ken Wharram and Ab McDonald.

Hall of Fame member Pierre Pilote was Chicago's captain and one of the NHL's top defensemen. He played most of his career with Elmer "Moose" Vasko. Pilote, an eight-time all-star, set a scoring record for defensemen in 1965 with 59 points. Pilote was selected to the NHL all-star team eight consecutive times.

Chicago had hockey's most durable goaltender, Glenn Hall, who played in 502 consecutive NHL games. He played eighteen years in the NHL and was an eleven-time all-star.

Toronto Maple Leafs, 1961-67
(Stanley Cup Champions, 1962, 1963, 1964, 1967)

The Toronto Maple Leafs won four Stanley Cups in the 1960s when the NHL had four strong teams — Chicago, Detroit, Montreal and the Leafs. Toronto coach and general manager Punch Imlach combined veterans and young players to make a consistent winner. Though he was hard on his players, Imlach stood up for them, resisting pressure to make sweeping changes after the Leafs lost in 1965 and 1966. Imlach's old pros responded, winning the Cup in 1967. The players on the ice at the final buzzer averaged 38 years of age.

The Leafs stressed defense. Three of their defensemen — Red Kelly, Tim Horton and Allan Stanley — are in the Hall of Fame today. A fourth Bob Baun was a fine skater and checker who is remembered for playing through a painful leg injury (later revealed to be a broken bone)

If ever a player made it into the Hockey Hall of Fame on sheer hard work, it was **Theodore Samuel (Ted or Teeder) Kennedy.** Never a free skater, Kennedy made up for this deficiency with bulldog tenacity and a competitive spirit that made him one of the outstanding centers and leaders in the game's history. He sparked the Toronto Maple Leafs to five Stanley Cup triumphs during a 12-year stay in the NHL and in his final season, 1954-55, was awarded the Hart Trophy as the MVP to his team in the NHL.

Ted was born in Humberstone, Ontario, on December 12, 1925, and was originally slated to play for the Montreal Canadiens. He attended their training camp when he was 16 but was so homesick that he packed up and left. The next year, Leafs traded the rights to Frank Eddolls, then in the Royal Canadian Air Force, for Kennedy and he broke into the NHL at the age of 18. His first Stanley Cup team was the 1944-45 Leafs and he became a dogged leader of the club in its first triple triumph — 1947 through 1949. He succeeded Syl Apps as team captain in 1948 and led the team to another cup triumph in 1951. He came out of retirement in January, 1957, to help the injury-riddled Leafs but retired to stay at the end of the season.

Ted Kennedy is still remembered as one of the greatest face-off men in the game's history. In 696 league games, he scored 231 goals and collected 329 assists. Elected 1966.

En route to four Cup wins in the 1960s, Punch Imlach's Maple Leafs only finished first in regular-season play once. In 1962-63 they finished with 82 points, one more than second-place Chicago. The Leafs and Hawks met in the finals, with Toronto winning four games to two.

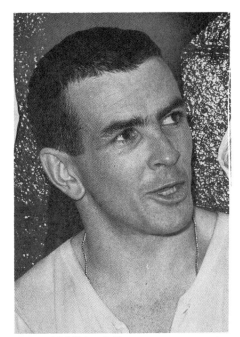

avid Michael Keon was an amazing athlete who spent 22 seasons in professional hockey — 18 in the NHL and four with the World Hockey Association. He played the impressive total of 1,296 regular-season games in the NHL, 301 in the WHA, and an additional 128 in the playoffs. In all of that time he picked up only 151 penalty minutes.

Born March 22, 1940, in Noranda, Quebec, Davey Keon became one of the most proficient checking centers in the history of the game. He joined the Toronto Maple Leafs for the 1960-61 season and won the Calder Trophy as the NHL's best rookie. In ensuing years, he also won the Lady Byng Trophy twice (in 1962 and 1963) and the Conn Smythe Trophy as most valuable playoff performer in 1967.

Keon was a member of four Stanley Cup championship teams, including three in a row starting in 1962.

After 15 seasons with Toronto of the NHL, Keon shifted to the World Hockey Association in 1975 and played for Minnesota, Indianapolis and New England over the next four seasons before returning to the NHL with the Hartford Whalers. Elected 1986.

Elmer James Lach brought great skills to the NHL. He had an unusual gift for playmaking, blinding speed, a high degree of courage, an intelligent approach to the game and a spirit of dogged determination.

Lach was born in Nokomis, Saskatchewan, on January 22, 1918. He turned professional in 1940 with the Montreal Canadiens and in the ensuing 13 seasons, posted an enviable record.

He played in 664 regular-season and 76 playoff games. In league play he amassed 215 goals and 408 assists, adding 19 goals and 45 assists in the playoffs. Elmer was selected to five all-star teams, making the first team in 1945 with a total of 80 points — 26 goals and 54 assists in a 50-game schedule. Lach was also voted winner of the Hart Trophy that season. Elected 1966.

Jacques Laperriere continued the Montreal Canadiens' tradition of recruiting big, mobile defensemen. Born November 22, 1941, in Rouyn, Quebec, he joined the NHL Canadiens late in 1962-63 and proved he was ready for the big leagues by winning the Calder Trophy as the NHL's top rookie in 1963-64.

The Canadiens won the Stanley Cup in 1965, Laperriere's second season, and went on to win it three times in the next four seasons.

He played his entire NHL career in Montreal, where he was part of six Stanley Cup winners. A serious knee injury forced him into retirement in 1974.

He remained involved in hockey with the Canadiens and, at the time of his election to the Hockey Hall of Fame, was an assistant coach with the team. Elected 1987.

in the 1964 finals against Detroit. He scored the overtime winner in game six and had a strong game in game seven before he submitted to x-rays that revealed the extent of his injury. Red Kelly, who had starred with Detroit in the early 1950s, was equally important to the Leafs in the 1960s. By 1965, he spent much of his playing time at center, but during the Leafs' first three Cups in the 1960s, he contributed from the defenseman's spot. Tim Horton was widely regarded as one of the strongest and toughest players in the NHL in the 1960s. He led the Leafs with 16 points in the 1962 playoffs. Allan Stanley was a ten-year NHLer when he joined the Leafs. At 6′ 2″, he was a big man who could rush with the puck. He earned three all-star selections during his years in Toronto.

Goaltender Johnny Bower joined the Leafs in 1958 after a long apprenticeship in the American Hockey League. He was the master of the poke-check. Beginning in 1965, Bower was part of an exceptionally experienced goaltending tandem, as Imlach had acquired Terry Sawchuk from Detroit.

The Leafs' most exciting forward was Frank Mahovlich, a six-time all-star and Hall of Famer who scored a club-record 48 goals in 1961. He had a huge stride and could dominate a game in superstar fashion. Chicago owner Jim Norris captured the headlines when he offered one million dollars, an unheard-of sum, for Mahovlich's contract. Mahovlich never played for Norris, but was later traded to Detroit and Montreal, where he excelled.

Dave Keon was rookie of the year with the Leafs in 1961, centering either Mahovlich and Bob Nevin or George Armstrong and Dick Duff. In 22 big-league seasons, he spent only 117 minutes

CONTINUED ON PAGE 116

Ted Lindsay was a remarkable hockey player and, although he will always be known as "Terrible Ted," he will also be remembered as one of the greatest leftwingers of all time. Christened Robert Blake Theodore Lindsay, he was born in Renfrew, Ontario, on July 29, 1925, but gained his early hockey prominence in Kirkland Lake, Ontario.

He joined Detroit later in 1944 and quickly established himself as a leader, both on and off the ice. Lindsay played on the great Production Line with Sid Abel and Gordie Howe. That line played a major role in the phenomenal success of the Wings between 1949 and 1955 when they won seven consecutive league titles and the Stanley Cup four times.

Ted played 13 seasons with Detroit before being traded to Chicago prior to the 1957-58 season. He retired in 1960 but made a remarkable comeback with Detroit in 1964-65 and was an inspiration in their winning the Prince of Wales Trophy. He retired again, this time to stay, with 379 goals in his 17 NHL seasons. Lindsay was named to the first all-star team eight times and to the second team once. Elected 1966.

Robert LeBel devoted many years to hockey, first as a player but mainly as an organizer and administrator.

Born September 21, 1905, in Quebec City, he was founder and first president of the Interprovincial Senior League from 1944 to 1947. LeBel presided over the Quebec Amateur Hockey League from 1955 to 1957, then he served as president of the Canadian Amateur Hockey Association from 1957 to 1959, and the International Ice Hockey Federation from 1960 to 1963. He was the first French-Canadian to hold the latter two offices.

In 1964, he was named a life member of both the QAHA and the CAHA. He is a former mayor of the city of Chambly, Quebec, where he now resides. Elected 1970.

The puck hangs in the twine behind Terry Sawchuk as Frank Mahovlich scores for Toronto in this 1962 photograph. The shadows cast by the players on the ice illustrate how arena lighting has improved with the advent of color television broadcasts. Red Wings in this photo are, from left to right, Vic Stasiuk, Marcel Pronovost, Warren Godfrey, Norm Ullman and Sawchuk. Leafs are Mahovlich, Allan Stanley (at the blue line), Red Kelly and Bob Nevin. All but Stasiuk, Godfrey and Nevin are Hall of Famers.

H arry Lumley was an outstanding netminder who spent 16 seasons in professional hockey. He was the Vezina Trophy winner in 1954; a first team all-star in 1954 and 1955; and backstopped a Stanley Cup winner in 1950.

Born November 11, 1926, in Owen Sound, Ontario, the easy-going youngster showed such talent that he was signed by the Detroit Red Wings at the age of 16. He played six full seasons with Detroit before being replaced by another phenomenon named Terry Sawchuk. After two seasons with Chicago he was traded to Toronto, where he was simply outstanding.

In 1953-54 with the Leafs, Lumley had 13 shutouts, a modern-era NHL record that held up until Tony Esposito recorded 15 in 1969-70. In 804 regular-season games he posted a very fine total of 71 shutouts — plus seven more in 76 playoff encounters. His goals-against record of 2.76 in regular-season action and 2.51 in the playoffs ranks with the best of any era.

Lumley completed his NHL career with the Boston Bruins, wrapping up a three-year stint in 1960. Elected 1980.

W hen a superstar retires from sport there is usually international publicity. But when **Frank Mahovlich** retired as a hockey player in November, 1978, he did it in much the same way as he had tried to live his life — quietly and privately.

Hailed as a superstar while still an amateur, Frank was an enigma to hockey fans. He won the Calder Trophy as top NHL rookie in 1958 and did just about everything a player should be expected to do — but there were fans and hockey experts alike who felt he could have been even greater. "The Big M," as he became known, played on six Stanley Cup winners, four with Toronto and two with Montreal. He was selected to the NHL first all-star team three times and to the second team on six occasions.

Born January 10, 1938, in Timmins, Ontario, Francis William Mahovlich played junior hockey with Toronto St. Michael's, where he won the Red Tilson Memorial Trophy as the OHA Junior A MVP. Beginning with his outstanding rookie season in the NHL, Mahovlich was an important and productive player for three NHL teams: Toronto, Detroit and Montreal. He played four seasons in the WHA in Toronto and Birmingham. During his three seasons with the Detroit Red Wings he was part of one of the league's top forward combinations with Alex Delvecchio and Gordie Howe.

His swooping style earned him 533 goals and 1,103 total points in 1,181 regular-season games, and his NHL playoff record included 51 goals and 118 points in 137 games. He was a member of Team Canada '72, playing in six of the eight contests against the Soviet nationals. Elected 1981.

Jean Beliveau's stickhandling finesse was once ▷ described as "impeccable stitchtaking". The great Canadiens centerman often found himself at close range with opposition goaltenders, and has said that he liked to "make them swim" as he applied his deceptive moves before slipping the puck past them. Here, Johnny Bower of the Maple Leafs appears to have thwarted Beliveau without swimming a stroke.

J ohn Mariucci was born on May 8, 1916, in Eveleth, Minnesota, often called the birthplace of hockey in the United States. As a professional, John played five National Hockey League seasons with the Chicago Blackhawks and was a solid defenseman. In 1952, he began the career that earned him the title "Godfather of Minnesota hockey". He encouraged high school hockey programs and recruited American players for the University of Minnesota. Previously, the team had been stocked mainly with Canadian players. The Minnesota high schools' program increased from a handful of teams in 1952 to over 150 teams playing in covered rinks within metropolitan Minnesota areas by 1980. Mariucci produced a dozen All-Americans while coaching at Minnesota and coached the U.S. Olympic club to a silver medal at Cortina in 1956.

In 1967, he returned to the NHL as assistant to the general manager of the Minnesota North Stars, a position he held at the time of his election to the Hall of Fame. He was a charter member of the U.S. Hockey Hall of Fame and won the Lester Patrick Award for his contribution to hockey in the United States.

Mariucci's belief that American boys could participate at all levels of hockey was avant-garde in his day, but the success of his programs over several decades proved him correct and earned him a place in the Hockey Hall of Fame. He died March 23, 1987. Elected 1985.

S tanley Mikita was born on May 20, 1940, in Czechoslovakia. In 1949, accompanied by his aunt and uncle, he came to Canada. Enrolled in public school in St. Catharines, Ontario, at first he had a difficult time adapting to both a new country and a new language. Perhaps his dogged perseverence then laid the framework for his entry into the NHL with the Chicago Blackhawks in 1958-59.

His determination in hockey led to impressive totals in both scoring and penalty minutes in Stan's early years. He played 20 full seasons in the NHL, plus parts of two others. Stan's intelligence made him a respected leader, and an integral part of the Chicago team that won the Stanley Cup in 1961, Chicago's only Cup win since 1938. Mikita was an NHL all-star on eight occasions, being picked to the first team six times.

As he gained more experience in the league, his penalty totals dropped to the extent that Mikita became the the first player to win the Ross, Hart and Lady Byng Trophies as top scorer, MVP and most gentlemanly player in the same season. He carried off this impressive triple win in two consecutive years — 1967 and 1968. He also won the scoring title in 1964 and 1965 and the Lester Patrick Trophy for outstanding contributions to hockey in the U.S. in 1976.

When Stan retired in 1980, he had played in 1,394 regular-season games, scored 541 goals and recorded 926 assists. In 155 playoff games he added 59 goals and 91 assists.

Mikita founded the American Impaired Hearing Association for hard of hearing youngsters. He stages an annual tournament involving several teams of hearing-impaired hockey players in Chicago. Elected 1983.

in the penalty box. He was a superior skater who was adept at avoiding opposing checkers. Keon was playoff MVP in 1967.

Another member of the Hall of Fame who played a part in the Leafs' 1964 Stanley Cup was right winger Andy Bathgate. Bathgate had been with the New York Rangers before being traded to the Leafs, where he played on a line with Frank Mahovlich. He had nine points in the 1964 playoffs and played on the only Stanley Cup winner of his career.

Montreal Canadiens, 1965-1969
(Stanley Cup Champions, 1965, 1966, 1968, 1969)

By the mid-1960s, only coach Toe Blake, Jean Beliveau, Henri Richard and Claude Provost remained from Montreal's five-Cup dynasty teams of the late 1950s.

Lorne "Gump" Worsley and Charlie Hodge shared goaltending duties for the Canadiens. Worsley was an established goaltender who, until he was acquired by Montreal in a trade with New York, had never played with a strong defense in front of him. As a member of the Canadiens, Worsley played on four Cup-winners, sharing the Vezina Trophy as top goaltender on two occasions. Charlie Hodge, who had been Montreal's second goaltender behind Jacques Plante, continued this role when the Canadiens acquired Worsley. An injury to Worsley gave him a chance to play regularly in 1964, and he responded with an all-star berth and the Vezina Trophy.

The Canadiens of the early 1960s were a small team that ran into trouble in the tough going of the playoffs. The addition of John Ferguson, a 25-year-old rookie left-winger, changed that. Ferguson was a capable hockey player and an on-ice policeman who took on any opposing players who menaced the smaller Cana-

In his early stages of hockey, **Richard Winston Moore** was a tough competitor. Born January 6, 1931, in Montreal, he was tagged "Digging Dickie" at an early age and, to his final game, his aggressive play merited praise from all who saw him in action.

In 1951-52 he was called up to the pro Canadiens and played with them until retiring in 1963.

Dickie came out of retirement twice, playing 38 games with Toronto in 1964-65 and 27 games with St. Louis in 1967-68.

Although plagued with injuries throughout his career — bad knees, shoulder separations, broken hands and wrists — he twice led the NHL in scoring. His first title, in 1958, was achieved despite a left wrist broken with three months left in the schedule. At his own request, a cast was placed on the wrist to enable him to grip his stick. He didn't miss a game, topping the league with 36 goals and 48 assists. The following year, he scored 96 points, breaking the existing record of 95 set by Gordie Howe in 1953. Elected 1974.

The Hon. **Hartland de Montarville Molson** was born in Montreal on May 29, 1907. Senator Molson became president and, later, chairman of the Canadian Arena Company and the Montreal Canadiens hockey club from 1957 to 1968. He joined the NHL finance committee and played a vital role in strengthening owner-player relations. He was also one of the six club owners who agreed to finance construction of the Hockey Hall of Fame building. Before retiring from the Canadiens, Senator Molson modernized the Forum, making it one of the largest arenas in the NHL, with excellent sight lines throughout. Elected 1973.

Bruce A. Norris was born February 19, 1924, in Chicago, and 31 years later became one of the youngest owners in pro sport when he took over as president of the Detroit Red Wings and the Olympia arena.

Bruce Norris carried out a $2.5 million expansion program that made the Olympia one of the finest arenas in the NHL; every seat in the building was padded. Although hockey was his favorite sport and enterprise, Bruce Norris had many other business interests. He died January 1, 1986. Elected 1969.

The Chicago Blackhawks had a great forward unit known as the "Pony Line" during the 1940s. It was composed of the Bentley brothers, Max and Doug, and right-winger **William (Bill) Mosienko**. During a 14-year stay in the NHL, Mosienko was a very productive scorer, accounting for 258 goals and 540 points in 711 games. He spent a total of 20 years in professional hockey, playing in 1,030 games, and in that time accumulated only 129 minutes in penalties.

He was born in Winnipeg, Manitoba, on November 2, 1921. In 1942, he joined the Blackhawks and remained with them through the 1954-55 season. Mosienko won the Lady Byng Trophy in 1945 and was twice named to the NHL's second all-star team — in 1945 and 1946. He also set an NHL record by scoring three goals in 21 seconds against the New York Rangers in New York on March 23, 1952. Elected 1965.

THE DYNASTY YEARS

diens' stars. With room to move, Montreal's scorers put the puck in the net and Ferguson found himself an important part of five Stanley Cup championships in just eight seasons.

Yvan Cournoyer, who joined the Canadiens in 1963, was the kind of small, skilled player who benefited from the arrival of John Ferguson. Cournoyer had several big scoring years to come after expansion, and was another candidate for the unofficial title of "Fastest Man in Hockey."

The Canadiens' defense was led by Jacques Laperriere, who won the Calder Trophy as rookie-of-the-year in 1964. His size, big reach and skating enabled him to cover a lot of the rink. Serious knee injuries shortened his career.

Toe Blake retired after winning the 1968 Stanley Cup, his eighth in 13 years as a coach.

Outside the Dynasties

With Detroit, Toronto and Montreal winning nineteen Stanley Cups from 1947 to 1967, many of the NHL's top players and future members of the Hall of Fame were denied the joy of being part of a Cup winner.

Leo Boivin began his career in 1952 with Toronto before a trade took him to the Bruins in 1954-55. A stocky defenseman, Boivin was an acknowledged master of the open-ice bodycheck. In a career of more than 1,100 games, he reached the Stanley Cup finals on three occasions.

Bill Gadsby was a twenty-year NHLer and eight-time all-star. Along with Red Kelly, he was the highest-scoring rearguard of the era, playing for Chicago, New York and Detroit.

Seventeen of Harry Howell's 24 seasons in big-league hockey were with the New York Rangers. He was an effortless skater

Murray Bert Olmstead broke into the NHL with the Chicago Blackhawks during the 1948-49 season, when he played nine games. He went on to play 13 seasons in the NHL, establishing a reputation as one of the game's hard-nosed players.

He was born on September 4, 1926, in Scepter, Saskatchewan. After playing the 1949-50 season in Chicago, he was traded to Detroit and then on to Montreal in 1950-51, where he became an integral cog in the Canadiens' machine that was to win the Stanley Cup in 1953, 1956, 1957 and 1958.

The talent-rich Canadiens left Olmstead unprotected after the 1958 season and the Toronto Maple Leafs claimed him in the intraleague draft. Bert played a major role in the Leafs' rebuilding process. He was with the Leafs' Stanley Cup team in 1962, retiring after that season when claimed by the New York Rangers in the draft.

In 848 regularly scheduled games, Olmstead scored 181 goals, assisted on 421 and collected 884 penalty minutes.

Bert later tried his hand at coaching — he was the first coach at Oakland after the 1967 NHL expansion — but later retired from hockey. He resides in Calgary. Elected 1985.

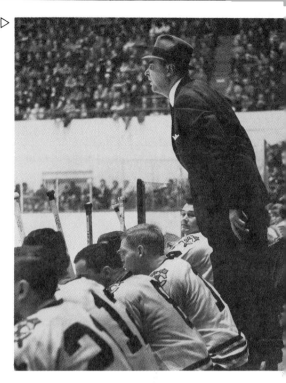

Matt Pavelich is the first linesman to be inducted into the Hockey Hall of Fame. Born in Park Hill Gold Mines, Ontario, on March 12, 1934, he began officiating bantam and midget games in nearby Sault Ste. Marie at the age of 14.

After impressing American Hockey League referee-in-chief Carl Voss with his performance in the AHL in 1955-56, Pavelich was ready for his NHL debut.

He set an NHL record for officials when he worked his 148th Stanley Cup playoff game, surpassing George Hayes' mark.

The brother of former Red Wing Marty Pavelich, Matt worked his 1,727th and final regular-season game on April 8, 1979. Elected 1987.

Rudy Pilous was playing junior hockey when Frank Boucher, the Rangers' coach, told him that he lacked the necessary skating speed to make the NHL, so he headed to St. Catharines where he was promised a job and a spot on the senior team. By 1942, he had set up a junior club in St. Catharines. His club made the playoffs the next three seasons, establishing St. Catharines on the hockey map. In 1946, he moved to Buffalo as a scout and promotions assistant. The next season, he went to Houston to help the faltering Huskies win the U.S. Hockey League title. Buffalo then sent him to the San Diego Skyhawks, who won the Pacific Coast championship in 1949. This success established Pilous' reputation both as a troubleshooter and as a promoter.

His teams won numerous laurels during his career: he managed and coached Memorial Cup winners in St. Catharines in 1954 and 1959; coached the Stanley Cup-winning Chicago Blackhawks in 1961; managed and coached the Western Hockey League champion Denver Invaders in 1964; and managed the World Hockey Association's Avco Cup-champion Winnipeg Jets in 1976 and 1978. Pilous later scouted for Detroit and Los Angeles of the NHL and was general manager of Toronto's NHL farm club in St. Catharines. Elected 1985.

Joseph Albert Pierre Paul Pilote left the NHL in 1969 having played in 976 games. In that span, Pierre recorded 559 points and 1,353 penalty minutes. He had also played on one Stanley Cup championship team, the Chicago Blackhawks of 1961, and in eight all-star games.

Born at Kenogami, Quebec, on December 11, 1931, he broke into the NHL with Chicago in 1956 after serving his pro apprenticeship in Buffalo. During his first five full seasons with Chicago, he never missed a game but was finally forced out in 1962 with a shoulder separation.

Pilote was voted to NHL all-star teams in eight consecutive years. He was also rated the NHL's outstanding defenseman and winner of the Norris Trophy in 1963, 1964 and 1965. Pilote played his final NHL season in Toronto. Elected 1975.

and a defenseman's defenseman. He was team captain, won the Norris Trophy and was selected an all-star in 1967, his 15th NHL season.

Billy Mosienko played 14 seasons with the Chicago Blackhawks. With brothers Doug and Max Bentley he was part of the "Pony Line," which was the NHL's top-scoring line in 1947. In 1952, Mosienko set the closest thing to an unbreakable record in the NHL: three goals in only 21 seconds.

Bill Quackenbush was a rushing defenseman and fine checker for Detroit and Boston. A five-time all-star, he played the entire 1948-49 season without drawing a penalty.

Center Norm Ullman joined the Red Wings in 1955 and went on to score more than 20 goals in 16 NHL seasons. He had his best year in 1965, when his 42 goals led all NHL scorers. In all, he played 22 big-league seasons.

Rule Changes

Rule changes designed to speed up play and increase skating room were made throughout the six-team era, starting with the addition of the center-ice red line in 1943-44.

In 1951, the goaltender's crease was enlarged from 3' x 7' to 4' x 8' and the face-off circles enlarged from a 10-foot to a 15-foot radius. In 1964 a new rule forbade any body contact on face-offs in an attempt to eliminate players checking one another without playing the puck.

The potent power play of the Montreal Canadiens in the 1950s led to a modification of the penalty rules in 1956-57. Prior to this time, a team assessed a two-minute penalty played a man short until the two minutes had expired, even if the opposing team scored several times with the man advantage. The new rule stated

Born in Shawinigan Falls, Quebec, on January 17, 1929, **Joseph Jacques Omer Plante** was a remarkable athlete, a goaltender who played with total dedication. Jacques' contributions as a player and innovator are substantial.

A product of the Montreal system, he made two brief but spectacular appearances with the Canadiens before becoming a regular in 1954-55. In 20 games he allowed 31 goals and had five shutouts; he also played in 12 playoff contests, allowing just 22 goals while recording three more shutouts. Plante played with Montreal until 1963, when he was traded to the New York Rangers.

He retired after two seasons in New York but, in 1968-69, was lured back into the NHL by an offer from the second-year expansion St. Louis Blues. Despite three seasons of inactivity and being 40 years of age, Plante combined with Glenn Hall to win the Vezina Trophy with the Blues. It was his seventh Vezina. After another season he was dealt to Toronto and continued to play strongly. The Leafs traded him to Boston near the end of the 1972-73 season, his last as an NHL player.

An extrovert, Jacques played his position with enthusiasm. His roving style excited fans everywhere. Throughout his career he was plagued with recurring asthma and, after missing 13 games due to a sinusitis operation, he began using a mask in practice. Although not the first to wear one, he was the first to adopt it permanently and it has become a standard part of every goaltender's equipment. Management opposed the mask but Plante refused to play without it. His subsequent brilliant play softened management's attitude and the rest is history.

An all-star seven times, he also won the Hart Trophy as MVP in 1962. In 837 scheduled games he earned 82 shutouts and posted a goals-against average of 2.37. He also played for six Stanley Cup winners with 15 shutouts in 112 playoff games. He died February 27, 1986, at his home in Switzerland. Elected 1978.

B orn December 15, 1925, in Montreal, Sam Pollock became involved in hockey at an early age. He managed a softball team composed mostly of Montreal Canadiens' hockey players, and also operated the Canadiens' midget hockey team. After six years in minor hockey, in 1947 he was directly employed by the Montreal Canadiens. Three years later he became their director of personnel, continuing in that capacity until 1964, when he was named a vice-president and general manager of the club.

During the 30 years prior to his election to the Hockey Hall of Fame he coached or managed many championship teams. These included the Montreal Junior Canadiens, Memorial Cup, 1950; the Hull-Ottawa Junior Canadiens, Memorial Cup, 1958; the Hull-Ottawa Canadiens, Eastern Pro League champs, 1961 and 1962; the Omaha Knights, Central Pro League champs, 1964; and the Montreal Canadiens, Stanley Cup champions nine times in 14 years. After retiring from the NHL, he has worked with Hockey Canada as part of its management group. Elected 1978.

J oseph René Marcel Pronovost played 20 seasons in the NHL, 15 with Detroit and five with Toronto. He was on seven championship teams and four Stanley Cup winners in Detroit, adding another Stanley Cup triumph with the Leafs in 1967.

A very competitive athlete, Marcel was a solid blueliner who combined stickhandling and graceful skating with natural incentive to give his best effort. He played a prominent role as a clubhouse leader with astute counselling to younger players.

Born at Lac la Tortue, Quebec, on June 15, 1930, Marcel joined Detroit for the 1950 NHL playoffs and was immediately on a Cup-winner.

Traded to Toronto in the 1965-66 season, he was a key man in an eight-player deal that helped bring the Leafs a Stanley Cup in the final year before expansion. He stayed with Toronto three more seasons, became a coach at Tulsa, Oklahoma, of the Central League and retired from playing after 1970-71. Elected 1978.

H ubert George (Bill) Quackenbush was an excellent checker and one of the most effective rushing defensemen in the game. He was named to five all-star teams, but in 774 NHL games he collected a mere 95 minutes in penalties.

Born March 2, 1922, in Toronto, Quackenbush played junior at Brantford under Tommy Ivan, who also coached him later as a pro at Detroit. Signed by the Wings, he was sent to Indianapolis for seasoning in 1942 and, after being called up, played only ten games before breaking his wrist. This prevented his playing on a Stanley Cup winner and also reduced his shooting power, but he became a puck-control artist and amassed 222 assists to go with his 62 goals. In 79 playoff games he scored twice, drawing 21 assists and eight penalty minutes.

Bill played 13 NHL seasons: six with Detroit and seven with Boston, where he was a defensive stalwart. His average of 0.12 penalty minutes per game is a record not approached by a defenseman before or since. Elected 1976.

Hockey cards were packaged with bubblegum rather than cigarettes by 1960. These four Hall of Famers had 20-year NHL careers. The Red Wings - Norm Ullman and Bill Gadsby, never played on a Stanley Cup winner. The Canadiens - Jean Beliveau and Henri Richard, won 21 Cups between them.

that a penalized player would be allowed to return to the ice if the opposing team scored during his two-minute penalty time. Substitutions were allowed on coincidental major penalties beginning in 1966-67. This new rule allowed teams to play with five skaters on the ice even if several players had received majors.

Television made itself felt in the NHL rule book as standardized signals were adopted for referees in 1946 and for linesmen in 1956. The ice surface was painted white to make the puck easier to follow in 1950 and a convention of wearing colored uniforms at home and white uniforms on the road was adopted in 1951.

Overseas

European hockey improved steadily during the 1950s. The Winter Olympics and the annual International Ice Hockey Federation (IIHF) championship tournament were international hockey's major events.

The World Championship and Olympics were closed to professional athletes, so NHL players weren't involved. The United States and the European countries were represented by national amateur teams while Canada sent the winner of the Allan Cup senior amateur championship. In the 1950s, these clubs usually won the World Championship and teams like the Lethbridge Maple Leafs, Edmonton Mercurys, Penticton Vees, Whitby Dunlops, Belleville McFarlands and Trail Smoke Eaters won World Championships or Olympic gold. All this changed in the mid-1950s.

The Soviet Union took up hockey in the late 1940s. The Soviets played a game called bandy, which was played with short curved sticks and a ball on frozen soccer fields. In 1954, the Soviets entered the annual world hockey championships, win-

Born August 11, 1920, in Sutherland, Saskatchewan, this great goaltender was christened **Claude Earl Rayner**, but early in his hockey career he picked up the nickname Chuck — and it stuck.

Rayner signed a professional contract with the Springfield Indians in 1939. After only a few games, he was sold to the New York Americans of the NHL, where he played 12 games that season. The following year, the New York club became the Brooklyn Americans, and Rayner played 36 games before joining the Royal Canadian Navy, serving until the end of World War II. When the Americans franchise folded, he became the property of the New York Rangers. He played with the Rangers until the end of the 1952-53 season, when he retired.

Although six-foot-one and weighing 205 pounds, Rayner was a very agile goalie. His goals-against average for 10 seasons in the NHL was 3.06, a very respectable figure considering that the Rangers made the playoffs only twice. Rayner retired to Kenora, Ontario. Elected 1973.

Kenneth Joseph Reardon's headlong, fearless style of play ▷ accounted for many injuries during his NHL career, but his dashing disregard for personal safety made him a favorite of fans around the league.

Reardon was born in Winnipeg, Manitoba, on April 1, 1921. He came to the Montreal Canadiens as a green 19-year-old, determined to succeed, and his fine record shows that he did. World War II interrupted his pro career, but Kenny played with the Ottawa Commandos, the army team that won the Allan Cup in 1943.

Reardon rejoined the Canadiens for the 1945-46 season and, for each of the next five seasons, was named to either the first or second all-star team in the NHL. He played on a Stanley Cup winner in 1946.

He retired in 1950 and became a successful executive in the Montreal organization. Elected 1966.

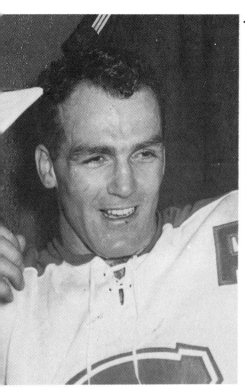

◁ Although relatively small in stature, Joseph **Henri Richard** achieved great success during an NHL career that spanned 20 years.

Born February 29, 1936, in Montreal, Henri followed in the footsteps of his older brother, the illustrious Maurice (The Rocket) Richard. Stamina and toughness became trademarks of this extremely clever center who stood only 5′ 7″ and weighed 160 pounds. Playing most of his career at a time when the NHL had an abundance of great centers, he was named an all-star four times.

Henri broke into the NHL in 1955-56 with Montreal and, in 1,256 regular-season games, scored 358 goals. He excelled as a playmaker, collecting 688 assists, and twice leading the league in that category. Richard was recognized for his sportsmanship. In 1974 he won the Masterton Trophy, awarded annually to the player best exemplifying perseverance, sportsmanship and dedication to hockey.

A fast, smooth skater, his acceleration often baffled opponents. His style was both artistic and delightful. He was a member of 11 Stanley Cup teams and in 180 playoff games he scored 49 goals and earned 80 assists. Elected 1979.

Whenever the name of Joseph Henri **Maurice Richard** is mentioned, it immediately conjures up a vision of flashing skates and brilliant goal-scoring. Maurice was know as "The Rocket" throughout an 18-year NHL career that saw him score 544 goals in 978 league games.

Maurice was born in Montreal on August 4, 1921, and played for the Verdun juniors and the Canadiens seniors before joining the NHL Canadiens in 1942-43. He scored five goals in his first 16 games, but a broken ankle sidelined him for the rest of the season. Although he was to miss only 12 games in the next six years, injuries followed The Rocket to the end of his playing days.

Richard was the first NHLer to score 50 goals in a season, reaching this total in 50 games in 1944-45. He also scored important goals, including 83 game-winners and 28 game-tying goals. In 133 playoff games he had 82 goals and 44 assists. On December 28, 1944, he spent the day moving into a new home, then went out and notched five goals and three assists. He was named to the NHL's first all-star team eight times and to the second team on six occasions.

A fiery-tempered player, Richard was once suspended from the playoffs for striking an official. This caused a riot that began in the Montreal Forum and spilled out into downtown Montreal, resulting in thousands of dollars of damage on the streets surrounding the arena. The game between the Canadiens and Red Wings was forfeited to Detroit. Despite his fury, Richard was dedicated to playing well. NHL President Clarence Campbell said of Richard: "We all have a lesson to learn from this man . . . Never . . . have I met a man with such singleness of purpose and so completely devoted to his profession." Elected 1961.

ning in that first year and finishing in the medals in seven of the next eight tournaments. From 1963 to 1971 the Soviets, coached by Hall of Fame member Anatoli Tarasov, finished first in nine consecutive championship tournaments. The Soviet players were constantly in motion, which demanded precision and superb conditioning. By the mid-1960s, the Soviet Nationals were acknowledged as one of the world's great hockey teams, but their showdown with NHLers wouldn't come until 1972.

Canada established its own national amateur team program under the direction of Father David Bauer. These teams were the best Canada had ever sent to the World Championships, but the Soviets, Czechs and Swedes were good and getting better. The Canadian Nationals finished third in 1966, 1967 and 1968.

The United States National Team won an upset gold medal at the 1960 Winter Olympics in Squaw Valley, California. Hot goaltending by Jack McCartan enabled the Americans to upset both Canada and the Soviet Union. The American team also finished third in 1962. American college hockey, which has grown into an important source of talent for both the U.S. National Team program and the NHL, established its foundations in the 1950s and 1960s.

While the NHL cruised through the first 20 years of the post-war era, North America grew up around it. Because cities as far away as California clamored for new teams in new sports, in 1967 the NHL responded, putting into motion the largest expansion in professional sports.

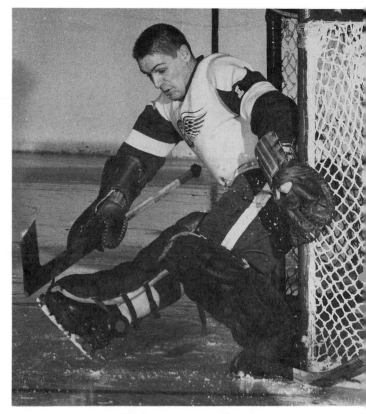

Terrance Gordon Sawchuk was one of the greatest goaltenders in hockey history. He played more seasons and more games, recording more shutouts than any other goalie. He played the position like a gymnast, peering out to spot the puck and dropping at lightning speed into a butterfly crouch that closed off the lower corners of the net.

Sawchuk appeared in 971 regular-season games during more than 20 seasons in the NHL — 734 with Detroit, 102 with Boston, 91 with Toronto, 36 with Los Angeles and 8 with New York. He allowed 2,401 goals against, for an average of 2.52 and registered 103 shutouts. Terry was the first player to win the rookie award in three professional leagues — the old U.S. Hockey League in 1948, the AHL in 1949 and the NHL in 1951.

Some of his greatest moments came in the 1952 Stanley Cup playoffs when he led Detroit to the Stanley Cup in the minimum eight games, collecting four shutouts and allowing only five goals against. He appeared in 106 Stanley Cup games, allowing 267 goals against for a 2.64 average, with 12 shutouts. Terry played for three Stanley Cup championship teams in Detroit and another with Toronto. He was a member of five NHL championship teams, all with the Red Wings. He won the Vezina Trophy three times with Detroit and shared the award with Johnny Bower in Toronto in 1967.

Sawchuk was named to the NHL's first all-star team three times and to the second team on four occasions. Born December 28, 1929, in Winnipeg, Sawchuk died May 31, 1970, in New York City. Elected 1971.

Born March 1, 1926, in Timmins, Ontario, Allan Herbert Stanley played three seasons with Providence of the American Hockey League before breaking into the NHL with the New York Rangers as part of a deal in which the Rangers gave up two NHL-roster players, four minor leaguers and a sizeable amount of cash. He later played for the Chicago Blackhawks, Boston Bruins and Toronto Maple Leafs (where he was on four Stanley Cup winners) before concluding his noteworthy career with the Philadelphia Flyers in 1969.

A prototype of the defensive defenseman, Stanley was never noted for his skating speed, but his exceptional anticipation of the unfolding play enabled him to remain in the NHL for more than two decades. Elected 1981.

Devotion and determination were the ingredients of the great success of Frank J. Selke, a man who served hockey as a coach, manager and executive for more than 60 years.

He was born May 7, 1893, in Kitchener, Ontario. By 1918, employment had brought him to Toronto where he became associated with Conn Smythe, and the friendship that grew between the two men flourished during the trying, early years of the Toronto Maple Leafs.

He left Toronto in 1946 after being Smythe's assistant general manager for three Stanley Cup teams. Selke went to Montreal and managed six more Cup champions, retiring after 18 years as general manager of the Canadiens. Although he figured prominently in the construction of Maple Leaf Gardens, Cincinnati Gardens, Rochester War Memorial and numerous other arenas, he probably derived the most satisfaction from the part he played in establishing the Hockey Hall of Fame. He died July 3, 1985, in Rigaud, Quebec. Elected 1960.

John Sherratt (Black Jack) Stewart probably earned his nickname because of his dark, handsome features, but many who played against him in the NHL might suggest that this outstanding defenseman's name was a tribute to his abilities as a punishing bodychecker.

He was born in Pilot Mound, Manitoba, on May 6, 1917, and signed a pro contract in 1938 with the Detroit Red Wings. The Wings sent him to Pittsburgh but recalled him for 33 games that season and he quickly established himself as a great defenseman.

In 1950 the Wings dealt him to Chicago where he finished his playing career at the end of the 1951-52 season. Stewart played on Cup-winning teams in 1943 and 1950, and was named to five NHL all-star teams.

Jack Stewart played in 565 NHL games, recording 115 scoring points. He died May 25, 1983, at his home near Detroit. Elected 1964.

◁ Born in Barrie, Ontario, on March 5, 1918, Roy Alvin (Red) Storey first burst onto the sports scene in football, where he was a standout until injuries curtailed his career.

Storey played junior hockey for Barrie and one senior season with the Montreal Royals. Red's first claim to sports immortality came in 1938 as a member of the Toronto Argonauts football team. He came off the bench to score three touchdowns in the final 13 minutes of the Grey Cup game, one of them on a 102-yard run, to lead the Argos to a 30-7 victory over the Winnipeg Blue Bombers.

It was as an NHL referee from 1951 to 1959 that he made his greatest contribution to sports. Storey was among the most colorful officials ever employed by the NHL. He refereed more than 2,000 hockey games at all levels. Looking back, he says his biggest thrill was "just being involved with a great bunch of guys." Elected 1967.

◁ **N**orman Victor Alexander Ullman — Norm to his friends — was born December 26, 1935, in Provost, Alberta. Twenty years later, he broke into the NHL with Detroit and spent the next 20 years plying his craft at center ice for the Red Wings and Toronto Maple Leafs.

A quiet man who shunned the limelight, Ullman was often underrated, but his natural talent ultimately gained him recognition as one of the NHL's premier centers. In his 20 NHL seasons, Norm scored 490 goals and assisted on another 739. He was voted to two all-star team berths despite formidable opposition. In 16 of his 20 seasons, he scored 20 or more goals and led the league with 42 goals in 1965.

Following his years in the NHL, Norm moved to the WHA for a final two seasons, in which he added another 47 goals and 83 assists before retiring in 1977. An excellent stickhandler, he was also a strong skater noted for durability and consistency. When he retired, Ullman ranked in the top ten in both goals and assists among NHL all-time scoring leaders. Elected 1982.

Lorne John Worsley played goal for three NHL teams — the New York Rangers, Montreal Canadiens and Minnesota North Stars — and, in a professional career that spanned 24 seasons, established an enviable record. Because of a physical resemblance to a popular comic strip personality, Worsley was nicknamed "Gump" early in his career, and it stuck.

His long career took him to teams in New Haven, St. Paul, Saskatoon, Vancouver, Providence, Springfield and Quebec in the minor leagues. At St. Paul, he won the Charles Gardiner Memorial Trophy as outstanding rookie of the U.S. League. In 1953, he won the Calder Trophy as the NHL's top rookie.

In the NHL, in addition to the Calder, Worsley was twice a Vezina Trophy winner — in 1966 with Charlie Hodge and 1968 with Rogatien Vachon. He also played for four Stanley Cup championship teams with Montreal in 1965, 1966, 1968 and 1969. His NHL goals-against average was 2.91 for 860 regular-season matches, including 43 shutouts. In 70 playoff games, his goals-against average was 2.82. He was born May 14, 1929, in Montreal. Elected 1980.

Despite the many physical risks of his business, **Frank Udvari** missed only two officiating assignments in 15 years. He refereed 718 regular-season and 70 playoff games in the NHL, 229 in the American Hockey League, seven in the Western League, 15 in the Eastern League and seven in the Central League, as well as serving as AHL referee-in-chief for many years.

Born January 2, 1924, in Yugoslavia, he moved with his parents to Canada at the age of seven, growing up in Kitchener. Only three years after refereeing his first minor-league game, Frank officiated his first games in the NHL, handling 12 matches in the 1951-52 season. He remained in the NHL as a referee through 1965-66, recognized as the best man on staff for a number of seasons. He has remained an active participant in the youth programs of his community. Elected 1973.

William Thayer Tutt was born March 2, 1912, in Coronado, California, but became associated with hockey in Colorado Springs, Colorado.

He became active in the Amateur Hockey Association of the United States through his acquaintance with Walter Brown of Boston. When the National Collegiate Athletic Association needed a site for its first national championship hockey tournament, Tutt offered his family-owned Broadmoor Arena at Colorado Springs. He underwrote the costs of the tournament for its first ten years, until the event was able to pay its own way. He helped organize American national ice hockey teams, and negotiated and financed the first series in the United States against visiting Soviet teams in 1959. He hosted the 1962 International Ice Hockey Federation world championships, served as IIHF president from 1966 to 1969, and later as an IIHF vice-president and council member.

In 1972, Tutt succeeded Tommy Lockhart as president of AHAUS. Elected 1978.

Post 1967 Expansion and the International Arena

Expansion and the International Arena *(clockwise from top left)*
Sweaters belonging to Soviet goaltender Vladislav Tretiak and Team Canada's Paul Henderson were worn in the epic Super Series of 1972. Beginning in 1976, the *Canada Cup* was staged as an open international tournament featuring the world's top players. The Philadelphia Flyers were the first expansion team to win the Stanley Cup, winning in 1974 and 1975 behind the superior goaltending of Hall of Famer Bernie Parent. Parent used this *goalie's stick*. Glenn "Chico" Resch's *mask* bore a map of Long Island as his team won the Cup in 1980. The Islanders won four straight Stanley Cups. Wayne Gretzky's hockey career started on these *baby skates*. Gretzky's pro career began in the World Hockey Association, which began play in 1972 using *blue pucks*. Bobby Orr used this almost tapeless *stick* to score the Cup-winning goal for Boston in 1970. Mario Lemieux used this fully-taped *stick* to record six points in the NHL's 1988 All-Star Game in St. Louis. Ken Dryden's white-red-and-blue *facemask* was almost a trademark of the Canadiens' dynasty team of the late 1970s.

The formal announcement of NHL expansion plans came on June 25, 1965, when League president Clarence Campbell announced that the NHL was expanding to what he referred to as "major-league cities in the United States and Canada." Ownership groups representing ten different cities applied for admission and, on February 8, 1966, the NHL awarded franchises to Los Angeles, Minnesota (Minneapolis-St. Paul), California (Oakland), Philadelphia, Pittsburgh and St. Louis. Beginning in 1967-68, these franchises would play in a new West Division.

On June 5, 1967, these new clubs formally received their NHL franchise charters, and the efforts of expansion architects Bill Jennings of the Rangers (a Hall of Fame member in the builders category) and David Molson of the Canadiens had paid off. What had been a cozy, six-team league for 25 seasons officially became a continent-spanning twelve-team operation.

While some NHL expansion was regarded as inevitable — good players were giving up their hockey careers because there were so few big-league roster spots in the six-team days — critics of the league's 1967 doubling felt it was too drastic a step and that the new clubs would be outclassed by their established rivals. Clarence Campbell and the league's governors acknowledged that the new clubs couldn't be as good on the ice as those from organizations with established player development systems, and so set up a 74-game schedule in which teams played 50 of 74 games against clubs in their own division. In the playoffs, the two divisions would only play each other in the Stanley Cup finals. The West Division winners would be awarded the new Clarence Campbell Bowl; the East

The 1967-68 NHL expansion brought the game to new markets and a new look to the game.

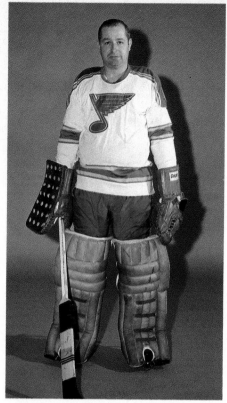

Glenn Hall joined the new St. Louis Blues in the NHL's 1967 expansion. Hall would win a Vezina Trophy in his first year in St. Louis.

Johnny Bucyk played 21 seasons in Boston and saw his club rise from perennial last-place finisher to Stanley Cup champion. Bucyk had 51 goals and 116 points in 1970-71.

Defenseman Tim Horton played 18 seasons in Toronto, earning four all-star berths before trades took him to the Rangers, Pittsburgh and Buffalo. He was killed in a highway accident late in February of 1974.

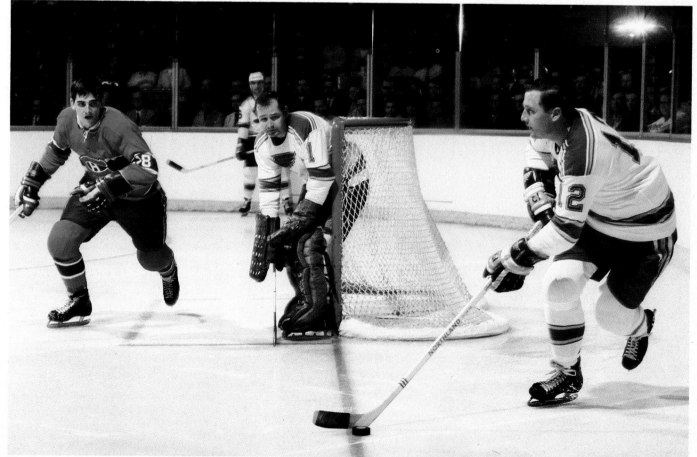

St. Louis reached the Stanley Cup final in the first three seasons following expansion. With Glenn Hall and, later, Jacques Plante in goal and steady veterans like Hall of Famer Dickie Moore (18), the Blues were competitive with all but the best of the established six teams. A young Serge Savard looks on for the Canadiens.

Jacques Lemaire, here checking Toronto's Jim McKenny, evolved from sniper to checker to playmaker in his 12 years with the Canadiens.

Ken Dryden came up from the minors to lead the Canadiens to an upset Stanley Cup win in 1971. The big goaltender was a winner, as his Canadiens won the Cup in six of his eight seasons in the nets.

Stan Mikita played 22 seasons for the Chicago Blackhawks from 1959 to 1979. A four-time scoring champion, Mikita recorded 1,617 points and scored an even 600 goals, including playoff competition.

Boston's Ted Green is a second goaltender in this 1967 contest between the Bruins and Canadiens. Yvan Cournoyer is looking to deflect the shot on its way in. Cournoyer had four 40-goal seasons, finishing with 863 points in 968 regular season games.

Rod Gilbert overcame a debilitating injury in junior hockey to score more than 406 goals in sixteen seasons with the New York Rangers. A right winger, Gilbert combined with Vic Hadfield and Jean Ratelle to form the Rangers successful G-A-G (Goal-A-Game) line in the 1970s.

Boston's big centerman, Phil Esposito, won the Art Ross Trophy as the NHL's top scorer on five occasions. His 76 goals and 76 assists in 1970-71 set a single-season scoring record that has since been surpassed only by Wayne Gretzky and Mario Lemieux.

Gump Worsley joined the Minnesota North Stars late in the 1969-70 season where he finished his 21-year NHL career in 1974. Despite playing for many seasons with clubs near the bottom of the standings, Worsley's cumulative goals-against per game average was only 2.90.

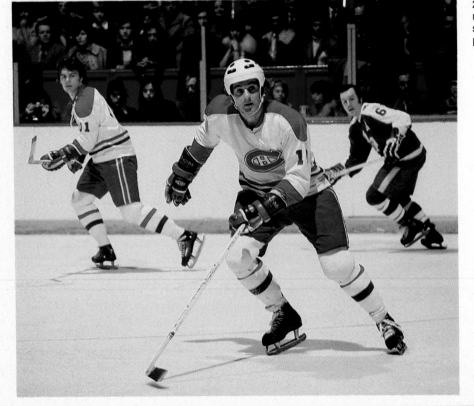

Guy Lafleur was junior hockey's top scorer with the Quebec Remparts in 1970 and 1971 before joining the Montreal Canadiens. He blossomed in his fourth season in Montreal, recording the first of six consecutive 50-goal seasons.

Dave Keon played 22 seasons of big-league hockey, including 15 with the Leafs, four in the WHA and three with Hartford when that former-WHA franchise joined the NHL in 1979-80.

Alex Delvecchio played 22 full seasons with Detroit, winding up his career in 1973 with 456 goals in 1,549 regular-season games.

The Philadelphia Flyers inaugurated a new era in the NHL with impressive Stanley Cup victories in 1974 and 1975. The expansion Flyers won with a style that took the "Big, Bad Bruins" approach one step further. During these successful seasons goaltender Bernie Parent's goals-against per game average hovered around the 2.00 mark in regular-season and Stanley Cup play.

Bobby Hull, Chicago's handsome leftwinger with the devastating shot, led the NHL in goal scoring on seven occasions. His decision to sign with the WHA and the Winnipeg Jets did much to make the new league a credible alternative to the established NHL.

Gordie Howe soldiered on into his 50s in the WHA where, in 1974, he was an effective member of an all-star team that played eight games against the Soviets. Howe had two 100-point seasons in the WHA playing with his sons Mark and Marty for the Houston Aeros and New England Whalers. The three Howes returned to the NHL with Hartford in 1979.

Jacques Laperrière was a vital part of an effective Montreal defense corps that enabled the Canadiens to win the first two Stanley Cups after expansion in 1967. A serious leg injury ended his career in 1974.

The Super Series, the Summit Series and the Showdown were all unofficial names for the first meeting of a team of NHL all-stars (Team Canada) and the Soviet Nationals in September of 1972. The NHLers prevailed, but required three consecutive one-goal wins in Moscow to win the series four games to three, with one tie. In this photo, Hall of Famer Brad Park is checked by Soviet captain Boris Mikhailov. Gary Bergman is ready to come to Park's aid, as Soviet Yuri Blinov sweeps in looking for the puck.

Gerry Cheevers was the "money" goaltender for the Boston Bruins in the 1970s.

Tony Esposito recorded 15 shutouts and won the Vezina and Calder Trophies in 1969-70.

Sam Pollock quietly built an enduring dynasty for the Canadiens in Montreal during the 1960s and 70s. He also lent his expertise to Hockey Canada, participating in the selection of players for the first Canada Cup tournament in 1976. This version of Team Canada was led by Bobby Orr, who was named tournament MVP, and Bobby Clarke (below), who worked hard in every game, including this final overtime win against the Czech Nationals.

John Paul Bucyk brings outstanding credentials to the Hockey Hall of Fame. When he retired as a player after the 1977-78 season, he left behind a record of 1,540 games, 556 goals and 813 assists for a total of 1,369 points in an NHL career that spanned 23 years.

He also is remembered as a winner of the Lady Byng Trophy in 1971 and 1974, a member of Stanley Cup winning teams in Boston in 1970 and 1972, and as a first all-star in 1970-71 and second all-star in 1967-68. He scored 51 goals during the 1970-71 season.

Born May 12, 1935, in Edmonton, the stocky leftwinger played two pro seasons with Edmonton of the Western Hockey League where he set records as a rookie, then graduated to the Detroit Red Wings for another two years before moving on to the Boston Bruins in a trade for Terry Sawchuk prior to the 1957-58 season. He stayed and starred in Boston for another 21 years. Elected 1981.

Gerald Michael (Gerry) Cheevers once asked a Boston hockey writer, "Do you think I'll ever win the Vezina Trophy?" The writer replied, "No." To which Cheevers retorted, "Do you think it matters to me?" The answer again was "No." Winning an individual trophy wasn't Cheevers' prime objective. The bottom line for the Bruins' goalie was winning games.

He played goal well enough for the Bruins to win Stanley Cups in 1970 and 1972 and reach the finals in 1977 and 1978. Harry Sinden, who coached the team in 1970 and became general manager in 1972, said, "Certainly we had Bobby Orr and Phil Esposito, but I'm sure we couldn't have won the Cups without Gerry Cheevers."

In the midst of his fine career with Boston, he left the club to play 3½ seasons with Cleveland in the WHA. In 1974 he was the outstanding player for the WHA's Team Canada in their series against the Soviets. He returned to Boston in 1976, retiring as an active player at the end of the 1979-80 season because his knees had worn out. He was named coach of the Bruins in July 1980 and compiled a record of 204-126-46 in his 4½ seasons as coach. Elected 1985.

winners the existing Prince of Wales Trophy.

In addition, the new franchises participated in an expansion draft in which they could select players from the rosters of the "original six". The established clubs entered this draft with protected lists of only eleven skaters and one goaltender. In 1968 and 1969, to further force-feed the new clubs' improvement, only 12 skaters and two goaltenders could be protected. Many well-known NHL players, including a number of future Hall of Famers, found themselves in new uniforms.

Andy Bathgate was drafted by Pittsburgh from Detroit while Bert Olmstead was drafted by California. Young goaltender Bernie Parent moved from Boston to Phildelphia while veterans Terry Sawchuk and Glenn Hall moved to Los Angeles and St. Louis, respectively. The new St. Louis Blues, who reached the Stanley Cup Finals in each of their first three seasons, added ex-Montreal veterans Dickie Moore and Doug Harvey. In 1968-69, they obtained Jacques Plante to play a two-goalie system with Glenn Hall.

The Montreal Canadiens won the first two post-expansion Stanley Cups, defeating the Blues in four straight games in 1968 and 1969. Glenn Hall, who kept the Blues close in each game of the 1968 final, won the Conn Smythe Trophy as playoff MVP. After the 1968 win, Montreal coach Toe Blake, a Hall of Fame member as a player, retired with eight Stanley Cups to his credit in 13 seasons as Montreal's coach. In 1969, three Hall of Fame members, Phil Esposito, Bobby Hull and Gordie Howe, became the first NHLers to score more than 100 points in a single season, with Esposito recording 126 points and Hull 58 goals.

Despite the Canadiens' Cup wins, the NHL's old order was bound to change

No hockey player worked harder than **Robert Earle (Bobby) Clarke**, the tenacious center who played 15 seasons with the Philadelphia Flyers. Beginning in 1969-70, his first season in the NHL, Clarke gave his coaches, teammates and fans full value, playing his regular shift, killing penalties and working the powerplay.

Despite a life-long love of the sport, a hockey career must have seemed only a remote possibility to Bobby Clarke when, as a 15-year-old, he learned he had diabetes. Born in Flin Flon, Manitoba, on August 13, 1949, he played junior hockey in his home town, leading the Western Canada Junior Hockey League in assists and points in his final two seasons.

The Flyers drafted him 17th overall and he immediately excelled in the NHL. His point totals steadily climbed until in 1972-73, his fourth campaign in the NHL, he became the first expansion-team player to record a 100-point season. Though just 23, his team leadership was recognized as coach Fred Shero named him team captain that same year. He won his first of three Hart Trophies as MVP to his team that season.

He was essential to the Flyers' two Stanley Cup championship teams in 1973-74 and 1974-75.

Clarke became general manager of the Flyers at the start of the 1984-85 season. Elected 1987.

For 15 NHL seasons "The Roadrunner," **Yvan Serge Cournoyer**, terrorized opposition defenses with blazing speed and superb puck-handling skills. Although small — 5'7", 178 pounds — Yvan broke into the NHL to stay with the Montreal Canadiens in 1964-65.

He was used sparingly at first, but in time proved he could hold his own against much bigger players. Before a recurring back injury ended his career in 1979, he scored 428 goals in 968 regular-season games. He also added 64 more in 147 playoff contests, en route to 10 Stanley Cup triumphs.

The speedy rightwinger was born in Drummondville, Quebec, on November 22, 1943. Used mainly on power plays at first, Cournoyer established a reputation for durability and was named to the League's second all-star team on four occasions.

A truly clean player, Cournoyer was penalized a total of only 255 minutes throughout his career, an average of only 17 minutes per season. Elected 1982.

Kenneth Wayne Dryden is a big man — 6'4" and 205 pounds — so he covered a lot of the net during his days as a goalie with the Montreal Canadiens. "He's a damn octopus," is the way Phil Esposito described this native of Hamilton, Ontario. But Ken had other attributes: he was an articulate scholar-athlete who starred as a student at Cornell University, then worked his way through law school with his earnings with the Canadiens.

He debuted in the NHL at the end of the 1970-71 season, sparking the Canadiens to an upset Stanley Cup victory while winning the Conn Smythe Trophy as MVP in the playoffs. He won the Calder Trophy as NHL rookie of the year in 1972. In his seven-plus seasons with the Canadiens he had 46 shutouts and a 2.24 goals-against average, and played every game in helping Montreal win six Stanley Cups, including four in succession from 1976 to 1979. Ken was named to five NHL all-star teams and won or shared the Vezina Trophy on five occasions. His forte was his consistency.

Dryden retired in 1979 at the age of 31 at the peak of his career, when he was earning $200,000 annually. "It was a decision I had to make," he said calmly, "it seemed the time to do it." It was expected that he would enter law or politics following his retirement, but instead he took his wife and two children to England, settled down in a brownstone house in Cambridge and wrote a book based on his hockey experiences. In 1982 he returned to Toronto, where he served as Commissioner of Youth for the Province of Ontario. Elected 1983.

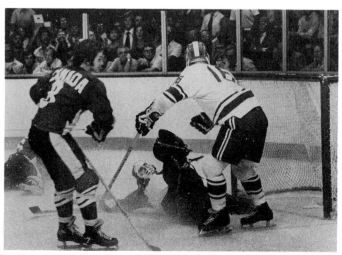

The now-legendary Summit of 1972 saw the best NHL players take on the Soviet national team for the first time. The results were staggering to North American hockey fans. The Soviets were better skaters and passers than we were; they were better conditioned. Even so, the free-spirited Canadians prevailed, narrowly winning the eight-game series on Paul Henderson's goal in the last minute of the final game in Moscow. Here, Vladimir Petrov beats Ken Dryden during the first game at the Montreal Forum. The Soviets won the game 7-3.

EXPANSION AND THE INTERNATIONAL ARENA

after the 1967 expansion. The most visible sign of a shift in hockey power was not the emergence of one of the "second six" teams that joined the NHL in 1967, but the ascendancy of Boston's "Big, Bad Bruins" to a Stanley Cup championship in 1970. Boston was the definitive "have-not" team of the 1960s, missing the playoffs in the eight consecutive seasons prior to expansion. With the signing of junior superstar Bobby Orr, and the acquisition of Phil Esposito from Chicago, the Bruins emerged as a boisterous, crowd-pleasing team. They eliminated New York and Chicago before sweeping St. Louis to bring Boston its first Cup since 1941. Orr scored the winner in overtime in game four against St. Louis.

Bobby Orr's hockey achievements rank him as one of the game's all-time greatest players. His mobility, acceleration and puck-handling skills redefined the defenseman's role in the NHL. He perfected a quick-changing game, grabbing the puck and, rather than just clearing it out or pushing it forward, going all-out on offense. From 1970 to 1975 Orr finished first, second or third in the NHL scoring race. His damaged knees made continued play impossible, but during Orr's decade in the NHL, three MVP, two playoff MVP, two scoring crowns, eight Norris Trophies as top defenseman, and two Cups testified to his dominance of the league.

The Vancouver Canucks and Buffalo Sabres were added to the NHL for the 1970-71 season. Both played in the East Division as Chicago shifted to the West. The season was extended to 78 games and the playoff format amended so that West and East Division clubs would meet in the semi-finals. This allowed strong teams playing in the same division to meet in the final. Buffalo's first draft

Tony Esposito, a standout goaltender, was one of the first players of the modern era to reach the NHL after an apprenticeship in American college hockey.

Born in Sault Ste. Marie, Ontario, on April 23, 1943, Esposito played part of the 1968-69 season with Montreal before being drafted by the Chicago Blackhawks. He became a workhorse for Chicago, appearing in 873 games in the next 15 seasons. He won or shared the Vezina Trophy three times and was a five-time all-star selection. His first full season with Chicago saw him win the Vezina and the Calder as top rookie as he posted 15 shutouts and a 2.17 goals-against average in 63 games. Two seasons later, he lowered his goals-against average to 1.76.

He was appointed vice-president and general manager of the Pittsburgh Penguins in 1988. Elected 1988.

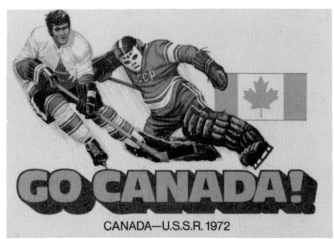

GO CANADA!

CANADA—U.S.S.R. 1972

Pre-printed postcards made supporting Team Canada an easy task in 1972

Emile P. Francis became known as "The Cat" during his 14 years as a player but it is his work as coach, manager and executive that has made him one of the most respected individuals in the game.

Born September 13, 1926, in North Battleford, Saskatchewan, he played for 12 pro teams before retiring in 1960 to coach the Rangers-sponsored junior team in Guelph, Ontario. Two seasons later, he became assistant general manager of the Rangers, and was soon appointed general manager. Throughout the next ten seasons he served three terms as coach while retaining the GM's post.

He joined the St. Louis Blues in April, 1976, as executive vice-president, general manager and coach, and it seemed "The Cat" needed his nine lives to handle it all.

He was named president and general manager of the Hartford Whalers in May 1983.

Francis is a strong supporter of youth hockey programs. He was a founder of the New York Junior League and a supporter of the St. Louis Metro Junior B League. He also developed support for the Amateur Hockey Association of the United States. Elected 1982.

Phillip **Anthony Esposito** was born February 20, 1942, in Sault Ste. Marie, Ontario, and did not seriously take up skating until he was almost a teenager. He never became a great skater, but strength, enthusiasm and an uncanny scoring eye carried him through an exceptional career in the NHL.

He was the first player to crack the 100-point barrier, in 1968-69, and totalled at least 55 goals in five consecutive seasons; upon his retirement in 1981, only Wayne Gretzky had surpassed his single-season mark of 76 goals, set in 1970-71. He also left a marvelous legacy of scoring statistics: 1,590 points on 717 goals and 873 assists in 1,282 games over 18 seasons.

Phil grew up in "The Soo," an area where Chicago sponsored minor hockey, so he filtered into the Blackhawks' system and spent two years in the minors before making it to the NHL in 1963. Chicago traded him to Boston in a six-player deal in 1967. Shortly after his joining the Bruins, Boston ended its 29-year drought with Stanley Cup victories in 1970 and 1972. During 8½ seasons in Boston, Espo won five NHL scoring titles and finished second twice. He was also named to the NHL's first all-star team six times and to the second team twice. He won the Hart Trophy as the league's MVP twice, the Pearson Trophy twice as the player selected most valuable by his playing peers and, in 1978, was recipient of the Lester Patrick Trophy for contribution to hockey in the U.S.

He was traded to the New York Rangers in 1975-76 and finished his pro career in Madison Square Garden, retiring just before his 39th birthday. Esposito was also the individual leader and top point-scorer for Team Canada (7 goals, 6 assists) in 1972's remarkable "Super Series" against the Soviet national team.

He was named vice-president and general manager of the Rangers in July 1986. Elected 1984.

choice, Gil Perreault, was selected rookie of the year in his club's inaugural NHL season.

The Bruins, with Orr, Esposito, Gerry Cheevers, John Bucyk and others, appeared set to establish an old-style NHL dynasty that was highly favored to win the Cup in 1971. Their regular-season campaign was a record-breaker, as Boston finished with 121 points and only 14 losses. The club scored 399 goals, 108 more than its closest competitor.

Phil Esposito scored an unheard of 76 goals in 78 games. He finished with 152 points, a mark since surpassed only by Wayne Gretzky and Mario Lemieux. In the first round of the 1971 playoffs, Ken Dryden, a virtually untested goal-tender called up by the Canadiens from their Nova Scotia farm club, frustrated Boston's scoring machine as the Canadiens upset Boston in seven games, out-scoring them 28-26 on the series.

The Canadiens needed six games to defeat Minnesota in the semi-finals and then won the Cup with a seven-game triumph over Chicago. Tony Esposito and Dryden matched each other throughout the series, but two goals by Henri Richard in the third period of the final game won the Cup for the Canadiens. Dryden, who would later become the first player selected to the Hall of Fame whose NHL career began after the 1967 expansion, won the Conn Smythe Trophy as playoff MVP. Hall of Famer Jean Beliveau retired a champion with his tenth Stanley Cup.

Two Quebec-born players were taken at the top of the 1971 Amateur Draft — Guy Lafleur by Montreal and Marcel Dionne by Detroit.

The Bruins were regular-season and Stanley Cup champions again in 1971-72. A record four teams — Boston, New York and Montreal in the East along with Chi-

Rodrique Gabriel Gilbert overcame almost insurmountable odds to become successful in his chosen profession — as one of the top rightwingers in the NHL.

Born July 1, 1941, in Montreal, he progressed through minor hockey to star as a junior in Guelph, Ontario. During a junior game he skated over a piece of debris on the ice and suffered a broken back. He nearly lost his left leg during two operations to correct the damage.

During almost 16 full seasons with the New York Rangers he set or equalled 20 team scoring records and, when he retired in 1977, Rod trailed only one other rightwinger (Gordie Howe) in total points. He had 406 goals and 615 assists in 1,065 regular-season NHL games, plus 34 goals and 33 assists in 79 playoff encounters. In 1976, he was awarded the Masterton Trophy as the player "who best exemplified the qualities of perseverance, sportsmanship and dedication to hockey." This, too, was a tribute to Gilbert's courage in coming back from his original injury. Elected 1982.

Charles Hay will be remembered in sports history as the man who brought the best teams of Canada and the Soviet Union together in the first "World Series" of hockey. The retired oil company executive co-ordinated the negotiations that culminated in the Team Canada-Soviet Nationals hockey series in September, 1972.

In December, 1968, he attended a meeting with representatives of the NHL, the CAHA and Canadian business and government to set up Hockey Canada. He later became president of the organization, created to operate a Canadian hockey team for international competition.

Born in Kingston, Ontario, in 1902, he moved to Saskatoon in 1913. Charles Hay died October 24, 1973. Elected 1974.

E dward (Eddie) Giacomin was on born June 6, 1939. He joined the New York Rangers in 1965 when that franchise was rebuilding. In his second NHL season, he led the Rangers into the playoffs, earned a first team all-star selection and posted nine shutouts. He went on to become one of the NHL's best and most durable goaltenders, playing in almost every game. He became a fan favorite in Madison Square Garden, making acrobatic saves and leaving his crease to retrieve the puck and pass it up to his forwards. The Rangers of this era were surprisingly strong in the playoffs, upsetting Boston in 1973 and Montreal in 1972 and 1974.

He was traded to Detroit in 1975-76 and played for the Red Wings until he retired in 1978. In 13 NHL seasons, Giacomin recorded a 2.82 goals-against average. Elected 1987.

The best of '72: Tony Esposito (Vezina Trophy), Jean Ratelle (Lady Byng Trophy), Bobby Orr (Hart Memorial Trophy and Norris Trophy), and Ken Dryden (Calder Memorial Trophy). If the NHL had awarded a trophy for wide lapels, these four might well have added additional silverware to their winnings.

cago in the West — finished with more than 100 points. Esposito and Orr topped all scorers, followed by the Rangers' high scoring Goal-A-Game line of Jean Ratelle, Vic Hadfield and Rod Gilbert.

Other developments in the game took the spotlight away from the NHL in 1972-73. A rival major professional league — the World Hockey Association — opened for business. WHA operators saw themselves as an alternative to the NHL and did their utmost to sign junior prospects, top minor leaguers and big-name NHLers. Hockey salaries rose as NHL teams were forced to match offers from the new league. Wayne Gretzky, Mark Messier, John Tonelli, Rob Ramage, Rick Vaive, Craig Hartsburg and other NHL stars of the 1980s started their pro careers as teenagers in the WHA.

Many Hall of Famers continued or extended their careers in the WHA. Bobby Hull was a top attraction in the NHL when he jumped to the WHA's Winnipeg Jets. Gerry Cheevers, Bernie Parent, Dave Keon, Norm Ullman and Frank Mahovlich played in the WHA, as did Gordie Howe, who came out of retirement to join his two teenaged sons, Mark and Marty, on a forward line with the Houston Aeros.

The WHA lasted seven seasons, finishing in 1978-79. During those years, New England, Winnipeg, Houston and Quebec won the championship Avco Cup. Thirty-two teams played in 24 cities, and although the quality of play in the WHA wasn't a match for the NHL in the league's first few seasons, by the late 1970s WHA teams would have been competitive.

The WHA was a showcase for European players in North America. In their quest for new talent, WHA clubs signed numerous Czech, Swedish and Finnish

William Mitchell Jennings began his association with hockey in 1959. He acted as counsel for the Graham-Paige Corporation when it acquired a controlling interest in the Madison Square Garden Corporation, which in turn owned the New York Rangers hockey club. He became president of the Rangers and its governor in the National Hockey League in 1962.

He still held both offices at the time of his election to the Hockey Hall of Fame. Throughout Jennings' association with the league, he was an ardent advocate of expansion and one of its principal architects. In addition to his successful leadership of the Rangers, Bill Jennings worked for recognition of American participation in hockey. In 1966 he established the Lester Patrick Award for persons who have rendered "outstanding service to hockey in the United States." For his own distinguished services, Jennings was given this award in 1971.

Jennings was born December 14, 1920. He died in August 1981, in New York. Elected 1975.

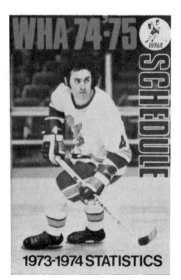

The World Hockey Association, which began play in 1972, was the first rival league to compete with the NHL for players and fan interest since the Pacific Coast and Western Canada loops of the 1920s. WHA rosters mixed veteran ex-NHLers, career minor pros, Europeans and young junior stars. Mike Walton, pictured on the cover of the WHA's 1974-75 schedule, led the league with 117 points in 1973-74.

Guy Damien Lafleur was the NHL's most exciting scorer in the second half of the 1970s. He was widely heralded as a junior hockey sensation, scoring 209 points in his final season with Quebec City, where comparisons to another favorite son, Jean Beliveau, were inevitable. When the Canadiens claimed him first overall in the 1971 Amateur Draft, it was apparent to hockey fans and reporters that Montreal had landed another superstar in the Morenz-Richard-Beliveau mold.

Lafleur's promise was fulfilled in 1974-75 when he embarked on his first of six consecutive 50-goal seasons. During these years, he earned first team all-star status on right wing, won the Art Ross Trophy as scoring champion three times and the Hart Trophy as MVP twice. The Canadiens won four consecutive Stanley Cups from 1976 to 1979. Through it all, Lafleur was the NHL's most compelling player, combining superior speed with a hard, accurate shot and a dazzling array of improvisational moves. At the time of his retirement early in the 1984-85 season, Lafleur had recorded 518 goals and 728 assists in 961 career games. In playoff competition he had 57 goals and 76 assists in 124 games. Elected 1988.

Jacques Gerard Lemaire was a remarkable hockey player. The definition of a two-way hockey player, Lemaire was an integral part of eight Stanley Cup championships with the Montreal Canadiens. In 145 Stanley Cup games, he scored 61 goals and earned 78 assists for 139 points.

Born September 7, 1945, in LaSalle, Quebec, Lemaire joined the Montreal club in 1967 and played his entire NHL career with the Canadiens, retiring in 1979. In 853 regular season games, Lemaire scored 366 goals and added 469 assists for 835 points. His penalty total was a mere 217 minutes.

It was not until his NHL retirement when he went to Switzerland as a playing coach that Lemaire's true contribution to the Canadiens became apparent. Some say it was not coincidental that Montreal's dominance of the NHL and Stanley Cup play waned after he retired. He returned to the Canadiens in the 1983-84 season as a member of the coaching staff, taking over as head coach midway through the schedule. Elected 1984.

players. Winnipeg, with nine Scandinavians on its 1976-77 roster, iced a line of Ulf Nilsson, Anders Hedberg and Bobby Hull that was one of the best forward combinations in hockey. Richard Farda and Vaclav Nedomansky defected from Czechoslovakia to play for the Toronto Toros/Birmingham Bulls.

Clandestine NHL - WHA meetings aimed at bringing the two leagues together began in 1973. Hall of Fame member Bill Jennings, who had been instrumental in negotiating the NHL's 1967 expansion, led the NHL delegation that met with WHA owners. An accommodation between the leagues was reached after the 1978-79 season, and Edmonton, Hartford, Quebec and Winnipeg joined the NHL.

The launch of a new major league wasn't the biggest hockey event of 1972. Instead it was the first encounter between a team of NHL stars, patriotically called Team Canada, and the Soviet National hockey team that captivated the hockey world. Since first winning the IIHF World Championship in 1954, the Soviets had dominated international hockey, winning every year since 1963, but they had never played top North American professionals.

Charles Hay, a member of the Hall of Fame, and Alan Eagleson, executive director of the NHL Players' Association, negotiated the details of the eight-game September series. Team Canada, coached by Harry Sinden, was made up of the best NHL players who were Canadian citizens. Excluded were Bobby Hull, who had signed with the WHA, and Bobby Orr, who was unable to play because of recurring knee injuries.

The results of the series are well documented. Though an easy triumph for Team Canada was widely predicted, the

Born July 29, 1914, in Charlottetown, Prince Edward Island, **John Calverley (Jake) Milford** was an excellent junior player, turning down NHL offers from both Detroit and New York to play three years in England and later with Cleveland of the American League. Jake once made hockey history: Eddie Shore traded him from Springfield to Buffalo of the AHL — for two sets of used Art Ross goal nets!

Milford was a coach in the Rangers' system for 14 years, grooming future stars and winning championships. He became general manager of the Los Angeles Kings in late 1973 and guided that club to three strong second-place finishes behind the Montreal Canadiens. Milford became general manager of the Vancouver Canucks in 1977, and made moves that strengthened the club enough to make the Stanley Cup finals in 1982.

Long noted as a shrewd and objective judge of talent and an astute dealer at the trading table, Jake Milford developed many fine players, coaches and managers. He died December 24, 1984, in Vancouver. Elected 1984.

Robert Gordon Orr played in twelve seasons in the NHL but his achievements rank alongside those of the greatest superstars in the game. The outstanding NHL rookie in 1967, despite a knee injury that plagued him throughout his career, he was also named to the league's second all-star team.

Bobby held a monopoly on the Norris Trophy as the premier defenseman in the league and rated first all-star team honors each of the next eight seasons. Orr also won the league's MVP honors three times, and — unheard of for a defenseman — twice won the scoring championship. He was the outstanding player in the playoffs in 1970 and 1972. He also won the Lou Marsh Trophy as Canada'a top male athlete, and the Lester Patrick Trophy for contributions to hockey in the United States.

Born March 20, 1948, in Parry Sound, Ontario, he was marked for stardom long before his junior days at Oshawa. At 18, he broke into the NHL with Boston and became the keystone of a rebuilding program that saw Boston win two Stanley Cups with Orr on defense. He was the dominant player in the NHL, controlling the pace of every game in which he played. His knees were badly damaged, however, and repeated surgery reduced his playing time and, eventually, his effectiveness.

In 1976 he became a free agent and signed with Chicago. In that year he also played for Canada in the inaugural Canada Cup series and was voted the outstanding player of the event. That was his last great performance on the ice. After a sixth knee operation and sitting out all of the 1977-78 season, Orr attempted a comeback but his knees were not up to the task and after six games he retired as a player on November 8, 1978.

In 657 scheduled games Orr scored 270 goals and collected 645 assists. He changed the nature of the defenseman's role in modern hockey, making the position a glamorous one and moving the rearguard up into offensive play. Elected 1979.

Bernard Marcel (Bernie) Parent allowed 20 goals in his first game in the nets — mind you, he was only 11 — but, as frustrated playing opponents were to find out, he quickly honed his skills and became the best in the NHL.

Bernie was born April 3, 1945, in Montreal. He perfected his craft, partly by watching the great Jacques Plante on televised games, and teamed with Doug Favell to backstop Niagara Falls to the Memorial Cup in 1965. Turning pro in 1965, he played 57 NHL games with Boston before being claimed by Philadelphia in the 1967 expansion draft. He left the Flyers to play 65 games with Toronto of the NHL and 63 with Philadelphia of the WHA, coming back to the Spectrum to stay in 1973.

The Philadelphia franchise was building a defensive powerhouse and Parent backstopped the Flyers to two Stanley Cup triumphs in 1974 and 1975.

Parent won the Conn Smythe Trophy as the outstanding player in the playoffs each of those two years; he also shared the Vezina Trophy with Tony Esposito in 1974 and won it outright in 1975. First team all-star honors the same two seasons came almost automatically. An eye injury prematurely ended his career in 1979. In 608 NHL regular-season games, Parent posted a fine 2.55 goals-against average, recording 55 shutouts. In 71 playoff games, he had six shutouts and an even better 2.43 goals-against mark. Elected 1984.

Soviets were the stronger team in the Canadian portion of the series, winning two and tying one of the first four games. By the time the series shifted to Moscow, North American fans had been won over by the Soviet style of swirling, constant motion and admired the stars of the Soviet team: Vladislav Tretiak, Boris Mikhailov, Valeri Kharlamov, Aleksander Yakushev and others. In the Soviet Union, Team Canada lost game five and then reeled off three straight one-goal wins to capture the series four games to three with one game tied. Toronto's Paul Henderson scored the game-winning goal in each of the last three games.

Many on the Team Canada roster have since been inducted into the Hockey Hall of Fame. Coach Harry Sinden, Ken Dryden, Bobby Clarke, Yvan Cournoyer, Phil Esposito, Rod Gilbert, Frank Mahovlich, Stan Mikita, Jean Ratelle and Serge Savard — stars on their NHL clubs — were part of one of the greatest team efforts in hockey.

The 1972-73 NHL season saw the Atlanta Flames and New York Islanders join the league. Atlanta played in the West Division; New York in the East. Montreal won the East and the Stanley Cup while Chicago again finished first in the West. Two players from the expansion Philadelphia Flyers — Bobby Clarke and Rick MacLeish — finished second and fourth in the scoring race. Parity between the "original" and "second" sixes was approaching. The New York Islanders, who finished with a dismal 30 points in their first campaign, used their first overall draft selection to lay the foundation for a dynasty by picking defenseman Denis Potvin.

By 1975 the NHL had been irrevocably altered. Not only was there a rival league (the WHA) and a rival hockey power (the

Douglas Bradford Park earned all-star honors seven times in his 17-year career as an outstanding defenseman with the New York Rangers (1968-69 to 1975-76), Boston Bruins (1975-76 to 1982-83) and Detroit Red Wings (1983-84 and 1984-85). A mobile skater with a big shot, Park graduated from the Toronto Marlboros as the Rangers' first choice in the 1966 Amateur Draft. After a brief stint with Buffalo in the AHL, he joined the Rangers for 54 games in his rookie season. His best offensive years came in New York in 1973-74, when he had 25 goals and 57 assists for 82 points, and in Boston in 1977-78, when he scored 22 goals and 57 assists for 79 points. Park was a member of the 1972 Team Canada that defeated the Soviet Nationals 4-3-1 in the first confrontation between NHL and Soviet teams. Elected 1988.

Joseph Gilbert Yvan Jean Ratelle ended a 20-year NHL career in May, 1981, as the league's sixth-leading scorer with 1,267 points: 491 goals and 776 assists. In 1,281 games, this classy center collected only 276 penalty minutes.

Ratelle spent 13 of his 20 seasons with the New York Rangers, many of them centering the very productive "G-A-G" or "Goal-A-Game Line" with Rod Gilbert and Vic Hadfield. Ratelle and Gilbert were hockey playmates going back to their youth and over the course of approximately 30 years, Gilbert said he never saw Ratelle fight on or off the ice, and never heard him use profanity.

Jean Ratelle won the Lady Byng Trophy for gentlemanly play in 1972 and 1976, the Lester B. Pearson Award in 1972 as the outstanding NHL player as selected by the players, and the Bill Masterton Trophy in 1971 for exemplifying the qualities of perseverance, sportsmanship and dedication to hockey.

Jean Ratelle didn't make his mark in the NHL until he had almost five pro seasons under his belt. His early years saw him travel up and down from New York to Kitchener-Waterloo of the Eastern Pro League and Baltimore of the American Hockey League. He came up to the Rangers to stay in 1964. Elected 1985.

Dedication to the team concept was a trademark of **Serge Aubrey Savard** throughout his hockey career. He played 14 seasons in the NHL with the Montreal Canadiens and two more with the Winnipeg Jets, totalling 1,040 regular-season games and 130 in the playoffs.

In 14 seasons with Montreal, including two as team captain, the Canadiens won the Stanley Cup eight times. He was a member of the 1972 Team Canada club, which defeated the Soviet Nationals in the first series between the Soviets and the NHL's best. He was the only team member not to play in a losing game in the series.

Savard retired from the Canadiens in 1981 but was persuaded to join Winnipeg, a team that had failed to make the playoffs in its first two seasons in the NHL. With Savard in the lineup, the Jets earned 80 points in 1982, posting the largest single-season improvement in the league and qualifying for post-season play.

Savard was named managing director of the Montreal Canadiens in 1983. Elected 1986.

Soviet Union), but an expansion club (the Philadelphia Flyers) had won the Stanley Cup for two consecutive seasons. The Flyers built on the organized application of muscle that had worked for Boston in the early 1970s. They did what they had to do to win, taking a record number of penalties en route.

Goaltender Bernie Parent and center Bobby Clarke, both members of the Hall of Fame, were important cogs in the Flyers' machine, as were Bill Barber, Reggie Leach and Rick MacLeish. Clarke won the Hart Trophy as League MVP in 1975; Parent won the Vezina Trophy for lowest goals-against average and the Conn Smythe Trophy as playoff MVP in 1974 and 1975.

The league expanded again in 1974-75, adding franchises in Washington and Kansas City. The East and West Divisions were replaced by two conferences each made up of two divisions. These divisions were named after pioneer builders and members of the Hockey Hall of Fame. The Prince of Wales Conference consisted of the Charles F. Adams and James Norris divisions. The Clarence Campbell Conference was made up of the Lester Patrick and Conn Smythe divisions. The schedule was increased to 80 games and twelve teams advanced to the playoffs.

In Buffalo, a "French Connection" line of Gil Perreault, René Robert and Rick Martin combined for 131 goals and 291 points as Buffalo finished first in the Adams Division and reached the Stanley Cup finals.

In Montreal, Guy Lafleur, 1971's first overall draft choice, emerged as a superstar in 1974-75. "The Flower's" goal production jumped from 21 to 53 and the Canadiens finally had an heir to Beliveau, Richard and Morenz.

Toronto defenseman Borje Salming

Harry J. Sinden never played in the National Hockey League, but he stepped into the Boston Bruins' organization with an impressive coaching record in minor pro hockey. Born September 14, 1932, in Collins Bay, Ontario, Harry was a fine senior amateur player. He captained the Whitby Dunlops to the Allan Cup championship in 1957, and the team won the World Amateur title in 1958.

Under Sinden's guidance, the Boston Bruins made the NHL playoffs for the first time in nine seasons in 1968. Two years later, the Bruins won their first Stanley Cup since 1941.

He went into private business the next season, but returned to hockey in 1972 to coach Team Canada in its memorable series against the Soviet Union. Harry molded a powerful unit of NHL stars that faltered, then came back to win "The Series" four games to three, with one tie. He returned to the Boston organization early in the 1972-73 season and, at the time of his election to the Hall of Fame, was general manager of the Bruins. Elected 1983.

Ed Snider was instrumental in bringing the Flyers to Philadelphia as part of the NHL expansion of 1967. A native of Washington, D.C., he came to Philadelphia in 1964 as vice-president of the Philadelphia Eagles NFL franchise and was soon part of the group that obtained an NHL franchise and began construction of a new arena — The Spectrum — in 1966. Under Snider's leadership, the Flyers built a team that stressed heart and total commitment from every member of the organization. In 1973-74 they became the first expansion franchise to break the 100-point barrier in regular-season play and then went on to win the first of two consecutive Stanley Cups.

In addition to success on the ice, under Ed Snider's chairmanship the Flyers became a model sports franchise popular with their fans while contributing much to community life in the Delaware Valley. Elected 1988.

Anatoli Vladimirovitch Tarasov is regarded as the architect of the Soviet Union's hockey power. A product of Soviet hockey himself, Tarasov coached his country's national team to nine straight world amateur championships and three consecutive Olympic titles before he retired after his team's gold medal win at Sapporo in 1972.

In the late 1940s and early 1950s he played for the Soviet teams that became challengers for the world amateur championship. After retiring as a player, he became assistant to head coach Arkadi Cherneshev, and then head coach himself. Under his coaching, the Soviet national team was soon capable of beating Canada's senior amateur champions.

Tarasov was a strong believer in conditioning and has written many books on hockey. He also supervised the Soviet Golden Puck tournament for boys; more than 1,000,000 youngsters were registered for the competition. In 1987 he served as a coaching consultant to the NHL's Vancouver Canucks. Elected 1974.

became the first European player named to an NHL All-Star team in 1974-75. Salming, one of the first European players to play regularly in the NHL, earned six consecutive all-star selections from 1975 to 1980.

The Lafleur-led Canadiens took the Stanley Cup back from the Flyers in 1975-76, sweeping the defending champions in a four-game final. Coached by Scotty Bowman, these Montreal teams of the late 1970s went on to win four consecutive Cups, averaging more than 125 points per season. Lafleur reeled off six consecutive 50-goal seasons, first playing on a line with Steve Shutt and Peter Mahovlich and later combining with Shutt and Hall of Fame member Jacques Lemaire. The Habs had three of the NHL's top defensemen in the prime of their careers in Guy Lapointe, Larry Robinson and Hall of Famer and current Canadiens managing director Serge Savard. With Ken Dryden in goal and two of the league's top defensive forwards — Bob Gainey and Doug Jarvis — these Montreal teams could defend as well as they could score.

In regaining the Cup in 1976, Montreal won 12 of 13 playoff games. Their most difficult test came in the semi-finals against a talented young New York Islanders club that featured Bryan Trottier, the NHL's rookie-of-the-year.

Eight NHL clubs played exhibition games against Soviet club teams over Christmas and New Year of 1975-76. Montreal and Philadelphia played Central Red Army, the club that featured most of the top players from the Soviet national team. The game in Montreal was played on New Year's Eve and is considered by many to be one of the most exciting ever played. The Canadiens outshot Red Army 38-13, but the Soviets got the last two goals as the game ended in a 3-3 tie. In

William Wadsworth (Bill) Wirtz, born October 5, 1929, grew up in a hockey environment. His father, Arthur M. Wirtz, was a partner in the group that acquired the Detroit franchise in 1933 and converted it into a hockey dynasty. When his father and James D. Norris acquired the Chicago Blackhawks in 1952, he joined the organization.

A year later he became a vice-president and in 1966 he joined the NHL Board of Governors. The Blackhawks enjoyed a resurgence and won the Stanley Cup in 1961. Bill became club president in 1966, the same year Chicago won its first league title.

Beginning in the early 1970s, Bill's efforts to make expansion a success were recognized by his peers who elected him to several two-year terms as Chairman of the NHL Board of Governors. As chairman he made a strong contribution to successful collective bargaining negotiations with the NHL Players' Association. Elected 1976.

Enamelled metal collector pins have become the international hockey fan's alternative currency. The NHL Challenge Cup was a three-game series between the NHL's All-Stars and the Soviet Nationals that replaced the regular NHL All-Star Game in February of 1979. Played in New York, the two teams split games one and two before the Soviets shocked the NHLers with a 6-0 shutout in game three. In recent Olympic and World Junior play, Canadian teams have worn five maple leaves. Though Canada finished out of the medals at the Calgary Winter Olympics, 1988 saw Canada win the World Junior, Izvestia and Spengler Cup tournaments.

◁ J ohn A. Ziegler, Jr. was born in Grosse Pointe, Michigan, on February 9, 1934. A graduate of the University of Michigan, Ziegler began to do legal work for Olympia Stadium, the Detroit Red Wings and Bruce Norris in 1959. In 1966, he joined the NHL Board of Governors as an Alternate Governor for the Red Wings.

He was elected NHL president and chief executive officer in September, 1977, the fourth person to hold this office since 1917. One of his first accomplishments was to negotiate a settlement with the World Hockey Association. As a result the NHL expanded in 1979, adding four former WHA cities — Edmonton, Hartford, Quebec and Winnipeg.

During his tenure with the NHL, Ziegler forged a working relationship with the Players' Association that is unparalleled in professional sport. Ziegler had participated in owner-player negotiations since 1966 and after 1977 served as co-chairman of the NHL owners' negotiating committee. During this period, the collective bargaining agreement between the league and the players' association was renegotiated and significantly amended.

An ardent sports fan, Ziegler played amateur hockey in the Detroit area from 1949 to 1969. Elected 1987.

American hockey's finest moment was the upset ▷ gold-medal win at the 1980 Winter Olympics, in Lake Placid, New York. Team USA, made up almost entirely of collegiate players, upset the defending world champion Soviets, demonstrating that U.S. college hockey could produce players competitive at the top levels of the game. Ken Morrow, the tall, dark-haired player just to the left of center in this photo, went directly from an olympic title to four consecutive Stanley cups with the New York Islanders.

EXPANSION AND THE INTERNATIONAL ARENA

Philadelphia, the Flyers bumped the Soviets and when veteran defenseman Ed Van Impe checked Valery Kharlamov to the ice, the Soviet players were pulled off the ice and retired to their dressing room. They returned to finish the game, which the Flyers won 4-1. Games between NHLers and the Soviets excited hockey fans as much in 1975 as they had in 1972.

A new international hockey tournament named the Canada Cup was staged in September 1976. Organized by Alan Eagleson in his role of chief international hockey negotiator for Hockey Canada, the tournament featured national teams from hockey's top six nations: Canada, Czechoslovakia, Finland, the Soviet Union, Sweden and the U.S. It was an open tournament staged before the start of the 1976-77 campaign, so NHLers played for their appropriate national teams. Team Canada and Team USA were entirely staffed by NHL and WHA players; the Swedes and Finns added a number of players with North American professional experience. Canada won this first tournament with Darryl Sittler scoring on Czech goaltender Vladimir Dzurilla in overtime. The Soviets would win the second Canada Cup in 1981.

The 1976 Canada Cup was the dramatic finale to Bobby Orr's magnificent NHL career. He was the tournament MVP and, despite limited mobility, controlled play when he was on the ice. After the Canada Cup, he joined the Chicago Blackhawks but was only able to play in 26 games before retiring in November 1978. At its next meeting, the selection committee of the Hockey Hall of Fame waived its customary waiting period and inducted Orr into the Hall in September 1979.

In September 1977, the torch was passed in the NHL's offices as John A. Ziegler, Jr., succeeded Clarence Campbell as president of the National Hockey League. Campbell, who had been inducted into the builders' category of the Hockey Hall of Fame in 1966, had held office for 31 years.

Franchise shifts continued in the late 1970s. The California Seals became the Cleveland Barons and the Kansas City Scouts became the Colorado Rockies in time for the 1976-77 season. In 1978-79, the Cleveland and Minnesota franchises merged with the resulting team based in Minnesota and continuing as the North Stars. In 1979-80 four WHA franchises — Edmonton, New England (now called Hartford), Quebec and Winnipeg — made the NHL a 21-team league.

American college hockey had become an increasingly important source of talent for the NHL throughout the 1970s, but it took what has since become known as the "Miracle on Ice" during the 1980 Winter Olympics to demonstrate how good college players had become. The Soviets were heavily favored to win the gold medal and had beaten the U.S. by a lopsided score in a pre-Olympic exhibition game. In front of a partisan crowd in Lake Placid, the American team played an emotional, opportunistic and egoless game that earned them a 4-3 win over the Soviets. The U.S. went on to capture the gold medal with a win over Finland.

Hockey enjoyed a surge of popularity in the U.S. as college and Olympic programs became a high-profile way to earn a chance to play professionally. U.S. Olympic team coach Herb Brooks and several players (including Ken Morrow, Dave Silk and Neal Broten) went directly to NHL teams after their Olympic victory. In the 1988 NHL entry draft, 104 out of 252 players selected were U.S. college or high school players.

The Canadiens couldn't maintain their hold on the Stanley Cup into the 1980s, losing in seven games to the Minnesota

North Stars. The New York Islanders won the Cup, defeating the Flyers in a six-game final. The Islanders had been built into a powerhouse virtually overnight by general manager Bill Torrey and coach Al Arbour. The club had finished with more than 100 points in only its fourth NHL season. In 1979-80, the year of their first Cup win, the Isles had been in the NHL for only eight seasons.

The Islanders had been built through the draft. Their first pick in 1973 was Denis Potvin. In 1974, they took Clark Gillies and Bryan Trottier; 1976, Ken Morrow; 1977, Mike Bossy and John Tonelli; and in 1979, Duane Sutter and Tomas Jonsson. When the puzzle was almost complete, Torrey traded for veteran Butch Goring from Los Angeles and, with Billy Smith as number one goalie, a four-year Long Island lock on the Stanley Cup was underway.

Bossy was the sharpshooter who put the Isles over the top. His sniping turned hard work in the corners and along the boards into goals. Selected 15th overall in 1977, Bossy scored a record 53 goals as a rookie. He went on to nine straight 50-goal seasons and scored 60 or more on four occasions. His deflection of a point shot by Paul Coffey gave Canada an overtime win over the Soviets in the semifinal of the 1984 Canada Cup.

Franchises continued to shift in the 1980s. In 1980-81 the Atlanta Flames moved to Calgary. Colorado moved to New Jersey for 1982-83. The resulting shift of clubs between divisions left the NHL with a six-team Patrick and three five-team divisions. In 1981-82, the league realigned along geographical lines and adopted an unbalanced schedule so teams played their divisional rivals seven or eight times a season. The first two rounds of the playoffs determined a division champion, increasing interest in divisional play. Eventually, as clubs drafted and traded in an effort to win their own divisions en route to the Cup, the style of hockey played in the Adams, Norris, Smythe and Patrick divisions evolved separately, in effect turning the NHL into four mini-leagues.

A record-equaling fifth consecutive Stanley Cup proved to be as elusive for the Islanders in 1984 as it had been for the Canadiens four years earlier. In 1984, the Edmonton Oilers defeated the Islanders in a five-game final. Though Edmonton had been swept by the Islanders in the previous final, the dizzying scoring exploits of center Wayne Gretzky made an eventual Edmonton Cup triumph seem inevitable. Gretzky had been the first NHLer to record more than 160 points in a season in 1980-81, his second year in the League. In 1981-82, he finished with 212 points and scored 92 goals, surpassing Phil Esposito's 1971 NHL record of 76. In the next five seasons he won the Art Ross Trophy as the NHL's leading scorer, outdistancing the player finishing second by more than 70 points each season.

The Oilers set a new single season scoring mark with 417 goals in 1981-82, raising this total to 446 in their first Cup-winning season. Club president, G.M. and coach Glen Sather had more than Gretzky to work with in building the Oilers. Mark Messier, Glenn Anderson, Jari Kurri and Paul Coffey were 100-point scorers in the mid-1980s. Grant Fuhr was a top goaltender who thrived on lots of work.

With all of this talent, and two four-year Cup dynasties immediately preceeding the Oilers' rise to the top of the NHL, Sather's team set out to demonstrate its durability as the best club in the league. They won in 1984 and 1985, but were denied a third consecutive Cup when upset by the Calgary Flames in a seven-game Smythe Division final in 1986.

The Montreal Canadiens, rebuilt under the management of Ronald Corey and Serge Savard in the mid-1980s, won the Stanley Cup in 1986, combining as many as ten rookies with veterans like Guy Carbonneau, Bob Gainey, Rick Green, Mats Naslund and Larry Robinson. Rookie goaltender Patrick Roy, echoing Ken Dryden's walk-on performance in 1971, won the Conn Smythe Trophy as playoff MVP.

In 1986-87, the Oilers came right back, finishing first overall in the regular season. With a stirring seven-game win over Philadelphia, the Oilers won their third Cup in four appearances in the finals.

The NHL All-Stars split a two-game exhibition series against the Soviet Nationals in February of 1987. This series, called Rendez-Vous 87, was played in Quebec City and replaced the NHL All-Star Game for that year only. Organized by Marcel Aubut of the Nordiques, and set against the backdrop of Quebec's famous Winter Carnival, Rendez-Vous was a week-long hockey festival. The Hockey Hall of Fame moved to Quebec for Rendez-Vous and displayed photos and artifacts to more than 250,000 hockey fans.

A fourth Canada Cup tournament was played in the fall of 1987. Team Canada and the Soviet Nationals met in the three-game final. All three games ended 6-5, with the teams splitting a pair of overtime victories in games one and two. In the third and deciding contest, the Soviets scored four times in the first period, but Team Canada, getting goals from Rick Tocchet, Brian Propp, Larry Murphy, Brent Sutter and Dale Hawerchuk, took a 5-4 lead into the third period. Alexander Semak tied the game for the Soviets with eight minutes to play, but with time winding down, Wayne Gretzky led a rush into the Soviet end,

feathered a pass to Pittsburgh's Mario Lemieux and, with a snap of his wrists the puck was past goaltender Sergei Mylnikov and another international hockey candidate for "best game ever" was in the books.

Edmonton won its fourth Stanley Cup in five seasons in 1987 - 88. Though finishing behind Calgary and Montreal in the regular season, the now-veteran Oilers, led by Conn Smythe Trophy winner Wayne Gretzky, dominated post-season play. Pittsburgh's Mario Lemieux won the Hart and Ross Trophies, scoring 70 goals, and the New Jersey Devils won their first playoff encounters, reaching the Wales Conference final.

The Player Selection Committee of the Hockey Hall of Fame faces the pleasant but difficult task of evaluating the contributions of the elite players of modern hockey. Some, like Marcel Dionne, Gilbert Perreault, Denis Potvin and Lanny McDonald, have combined performance, longevity and leadership. Mike Bossy and Darryl Sittler set scoring records. International stars like Vladislav Tretiak, Valery Kharlomov and Viacheslav Fetisov made magnificent contributions to the game.

As for the stars at the top of their games in the late 1980s — Gretzky, Mario Lemieux, Peter Stastny, Grant Fuhr, Dale Hawerchuk, Igor Larionov, Pat LaFontaine, Mark Messier, Steve Yzerman, Luc Robitaille and others — how will their careers measure against the benchmarks set by Hall of Famers from different eras? Can they give as much to hockey as Frank Nighbor, Eddie Shore, or Teeder Kennedy?

Some of them already have, all of them can and others whose names aren't listed here probably will.

The determining factor hasn't changed from the thought expressed by Jean Beliveau: "It's the heart that counts."

Statistics/Index

Leagues

Years of
operation

AAHA	1907-1917	Alberta Amateur Hockey Association
AHA	1893-98	Amateur Hockey Association
CAHL	1899-1905	Canadian Amateur Hockey League
ECAHA	1906-1908	Eastern Canada Amateur Hockey Association
ECHA	1909	Eastern Canada Hockey Association
FAHL	1904-1907	Federal Amateur Hockey League
IHL	1904-1908	International (Pro) Hockey League

PLAYERS

Page	Last Name	First Name	Born	Died	Clubs
62	Abel	Sid	Feb. 22, 1918		Det. 1938-52, Chi. 1952-54
12	Adams	Jack	June 14, 1895	May 1, 1968	Calumet (NMSL) 1914-15*, Peterboro (OHA) 1915*, Sarnia (OHA) 1916*, Tor. 1917-19, 1922-26, Van. (PCHA) 1919-22, Ott. 1926-27
64	Apps	Syl	Jan. 18, 1915		Toronto 1936-48
93	Armstrong	George	July 6, 1930		Toronto 1949-71
65	Bailey	Ace	July 3, 1903		Toronto 1926-34
13	Bain	Donald	Feb. 14, 1874	Aug. 15, 1962	Wpg. (MHL) 1896-1902
14	Baker	Hobey	Jan. 15, 1892	Dec. 21, 1918	St. Pauls 1908-09*, Princeton U. 1910-14*, St. Nicholas 1914-15*
65	Barry	Marty	Dec. 8, 1905	Aug. 20, 1969	Gurney (MRIL) 1922-23*, St. Michaels (MRIL) 1923-25*, St. Anthony (MRIL) 1925-27*, NYA 1927-28, Bos. 1929-35, Det. 1935-39, Mtl. 1939-40
93	Bathgate	Andy	Aug. 28, 1932		NYR 1952-63, Tor. 1964-65, Det. 1966-67, Pit. 1967-71, Van. 1974-75
94	Beliveau	Jean	Aug. 31, 1931		Montreal 1950-71
94	Bentley	Doug	Sept. 3, 1916	Nov. 24, 1972	Chi. 1939-52, NYR 1953-54
94	Bentley	Max	Mar. 1, 1920	Jan. 19, 1984	Chi. 1940-47, Tor. 1948-53, NYR 1953-54
65	Blake	Toe	Aug. 21, 1912		Maroons 1932-35, Montreal 1936-48
94	Boivin	Leo	Aug. 2, 1932		Tor. 1951-55, Bos. 1955-66, Det. 1966-68, Pitt. 1968-69, Minn. 1969-70
15	Boon	Richard	Jan. 10, 1878	May 3, 1961	Monarchs 1897-98*, Mtl. AAA Jrs. 1899*, Mtl. (CAHL/FAHL) 1899-1905
96	Bouchard	Emile	Sept. 11, 1920		Montreal 1941-56
67	Boucher	Frank	Oct. 7, 1901	Dec. 12, 1977	Ott. 1921-22, Van. Maroons (PCHA/WCHL) 1922-26, NYR 1926-38, 1943-44
67	Boucher	George	Aug. 18, 1896	Oct. 17, 1960	Ott. (NHA) 1915-17, Ott. 1917-29, Maroons 1929-31, Chi. 1931-32
15	Bowie	Russell	Aug. 24, 1880	Apr. 8, 1959	Mtl. Victorias (CHAL/ECAHA) 1899-1908
16	Broadbent	Punch	July 13, 1892	Mar. 6, 1971	Ott. (NHA) 1912-15, Ott. 1918-24, 1927-28, Maroons 1924-27, NYA 1928-29
129	Bucyk	John	May 12, 1935		Det. 1955-57, Bos. 1957-78
69	Burch	Billy	Nov. 20, 1900	Nov. 30, 1950	Hamilton 1922-25, NYA 1925-1932, Bos. 1932-33, Chi. 1933
17	Cameron	Harry	Feb. 6, 1890	Oct. 20, 1953	Tor. (NHA) 1912-16, Mtl. (NHA) 1917, Tor. 1917-18, 1919-20, 1920-23, Ott. 1918-19, Mtl. 1919-20, Sask. (WCHL) 1923-26
69	Clancy	King	Feb. 26, 1903	Nov. 10, 1986	Ott. 1921-30, Tor. 1930-37
70	Clapper	Dit	Feb. 9, 1907	Jan. 21, 1978	Boston 1927-47
129	Clarke	Bobby	Aug. 13, 1949		Philadelphia 1969-84
19	Cleghorn	Sprague	1890	July 11, 1956	NY Crescents 1910*, Renfrew (NHA) 1911, Wanderers (NHA) 1912-17, Ott. 1919-21, Tor. 1921, Mtl. 1922-25, Bos. 1926-28
70	Colville	Neil	Aug. 4, 1914	Dec. 26, 1987	New York Rangers 1935-49
71	Conacher	Charlie	Dec. 10, 1909	Dec. 30, 1967	Tor. 1929-38, Det. 1938-39, NYA 1939-41
71	Cook	Bill	Oct. 8, 1895	Apr. 6, 1986	Sask. (WCHL/WHL) 1922-26, NYR 1926-37
72	Coulter	Art	May 31, 1909		Chi. 1931-36, NYR 1936-42
131	Cournoyer	Yvan	Nov. 22, 1943		Montreal 1963-79
72	Cowley	Bill	June 12, 1912		St.L. 1934-35, Bos. 1935-47
19	Crawford	Rusty	Nov. 7, 1885	Dec. 19, 1971	Que. (NHA) 1913-17, Ott. 1917, Tor. 1918-19, Sask. (WCHL) 1922, Cgy. (WCHL) 1923-25, Van. (WHL) 1926
19	Darragh	Jack	Dec. 4, 1890	June 25, 1924	Ott. (NHA) 1911-17, Ott. 1917-21, 1922-24
20	Davidson	Scotty	1890	June 6, 1915	Tor. (NHA) 1913-14
73	Day	Hap	June 1, 1901		Tor. 1924-37, NYA 1937-38
99	Delvecchio	Alex	Dec.4, 1931		Detroit 1950-74
21	Denneny	Cy	Dec. 23, 1891	Sept. 9, 1970	Shamrocks (NHA) 1914-15, Tor. (NHA) 1915-16, Ott. (NHA) 1916-17, Ott. 1917-28, Bos. 1928-29
73	Drillon	Gordie	Oct. 23, 1914	Sept. 22, 1986	Tor. 1936-42, Mtl. 1942-43
21	Drinkwater	Graham	Feb. 22, 1875	Sept. 27, 1946	Mtl. Victorias (AHA/CAHL) 1893-99
20	Dunderdale	Tommy	May 6, 1887	Dec. 15, 1960	Wpg. (MHL) 1907-08, Tor. (NHA) 1910, Que. (NHA) 1911, Vic. (PCHA) 1912-15, 1919-23, Ptld. (PCHA) 1916-18, Sask. (WCHL) 1923-24, Edm. (WCHL) 1924
74	Dutton	Red	July 23, 1898	Mar. 15, 1987	Cgy. (WCHL) 1921-26, Maroons 1926-30, NYA 1930-36
22	Dye	Babe	May 13, 1898	Jan. 2, 1962	Tor. 1919-20, 1930-31, Hamilton 1920, Tor. 1920-26, Chi. 1926-28, NYA 1928-29
133	Esposito	Phil	Feb. 20, 1942		Chi. 1963-67, Bos. 1967-76, NYR 1976-81
23	Farrell	Arthur	1877	Feb. 7, 1909	Mtl. Shamrocks (AHA/CAHL), 1897-1901
23	Foyston	Frank	Feb. 19, 1891	Jan. 19, 1966	Tor. (NHA) 1913-16, Seattle (PCHA) 1916-24, Vic. (WCHL/WHL) 1924-26, Det. 1926-28

MHL 1905 Manitoba (Senior) Hockey League
MNSHL 1891-1904 Manitoba and Northwestern Senior
MRIL c.1905 Mount Royal Intermediate League
MSHL 1906 Manitoba Senior Hockey League
NHA 1910-1917 National Hockey Association
NHL 1918- National Hockey League
NMSL 1915 Northern Michigan Senior League
OHA 1890-1917 Ontario Hockey Association
OPHL 1908-11 Ontario Professional Hockey League
PCHA 1912-24 Pacific Coast Hockey Association
WCHL 1922-25 Western Canada Hockey League

WHA 1973-79 World Hockey Association
WHL 1926 Western Hockey League
WpgHL 1911-12 Winnipeg Hockey League
WSHL 1913-15 Winnipeg Senior Hockey League

ABBREVIATIONS: * no statistics available. For Players — GP games played; G goals; A assists; Pts. total points; PIM penalty minutes. For Goaltenders — GP games played; Mins. minutes played; GA goals against; GAPG goals against per 60 minutes played; SO shutouts.

NOTES: Dates listed as "Years of Operation" refer to the hockey season that ends in that calendar year; e.g. 1918 refers to the 1917-18 hockey season. In most cases, dates listed in this table are an accurate indication of the years in which each league was active, but in the case of some of early regional circuits, leagues continued to operate using the same name long after the NHL emerged as the sport's elite league. The dates listed in this table designate the period in which each league could be considered to be part of "big-time" hockey.

REGULAR SEASON					PLAYOFFS					
GP	G	A	Pts.	PIM	GP	G	A	Pts.	PIM	
613	189	283	472	376	96	28	30	58	77	Abel helped lead the Wings to three Stanley Cups and five League titles.
243	134	51	185	409	28	15	1	16	46	Only man to have his name engraved on the Cup as player, coach and GM.
423	201	231	432	56	69	25	28	53	16	Apps captured the Lady Byng and Calder Trophies during his 10-year career.
1187	296	417	713	721	110	26	34	60	88	Captain of the Leafs for 10 years, Army led his troops to 4 Cup victories.
313	111	82	193	472	21	3	4	7	12	This famous Ace was the first Maple Leaf to lead the NHL in scoring.
*	*	*	*	*	11	10	*	10	0	Manitoba's finest athlete, excelling in different sports for 35 years.
*	*	*	*	*	*	*	*	*	0	The name "Hobey Baker" is synonymous with amateur hockey in the USA.
509	195	192	387	205	43	15	18	33	34	The missing piece in the Stanley Cup puzzle for Detroit in 1935-36-37.
1080	350	630	980	626	54	21	14	35	56	Always a classy playmaker, Bathgate led the NHL in assists 4 times.
1125	507	712	1219	1029	162	79	97	176	211	Beliveau was the catalyst on 10 Stanley-Cup-winning Montreal teams.
566	219	324	543	217	23	9	8	17	12	Twice led the NHL in goals, capturing the Art Ross in 1942-43.
646	244	300	544	192	52	18	27	45	14	Winner of the Hart, Art Ross and Lady Byng Trophies in a 12-year career.
578	235	292	527	272	57	25	37	62	23	Toe won 2 Stanley Cups as a player and added an amazing 8 more as a coach.
1150	72	250	322	1192	54	3	10	13	59	Though just 5'7", Boivin was the NHL's hardest hitting defenseman.
42	10	*	10	*	7	0	*	0	*	"Dickie" was noted for his speed and his development of the poke check.
781	49	144	193	863	113	11	21	32	121	Secretary of defense for 15 seasons, "Butch" was a 4 time all-star.
672	218	295	513	150	69	21	20	41	18	Frank was known as "Raffles" for his gentlemanly on-ice behavior.
472	141	62	203	739	46	12	4	16	85	Started at forward, he became one of the game's finest rushing defensemen.
80	234	*	234	*	4	1	*	1	*	Scored 8 goals in a game once, 7 goals twice, and 5 goals on 11 occasions.
359	174	44	218	507	47	15	1	16	76	Holds the consecutive game scoring record, with goals in 16 straight games.
1540	556	813	1369	497	124	41	62	103	42	The "Chief" holds Bruin records for games, goals, assists and points.
392	144	49	193	302	2	0	0	0	0	Born in Yonkers, Burch gave the Amerks a home-bred flavor.
313	169	52	221	213	29	9	0	9	34	A colorful figure on the ice, he dazzled opponents with his curving shot.
593	137	143	280	904	61	9	8	17	80	Wore his crown for more than 60 years as player, referee and executive.
833	228	246	474	462	86	13	17	30	50	Dit skated into the Hall of Fame in 1945, while still an active player.
1144	358	852	1210	1453	136	42	77	119	152	Bob still carries the Flyer banner as club general manager.
456	163	39	202	489	41	6	9	15	49	Perhaps the roughest and toughest defensive specialist of his era.
464	99	166	265	213	46	7	19	26	33	Nickamed "Frosty" for his cool on-ice demeanor, he was a 3-time all-star.
460	225	173	398	516	49	17	18	35	53	The Bomber led the NHL in goals 5 times, winning the Art Ross Trophy twice.
569	311	185	496	526	50	15	12	27	76	Cook scored the winner in overtime to give the Rangers the Cup in 1928.
465	30	82	112	563	49	4	5	9	61	This 4-time all-star played on the last Ranger Cup-winner in 1940.
968	428	435	863	255	147	64	63	127	47	"The Roadrunner" sped through his career, winning 8 Stanley Cup rings.
549	195	353	548	174	64	13	33	46	22	A flashy centerman and one of the best playmakers of his era in the NHL.
248	111	24	135	1856	15	6	2	8	10	"Rusty" in nickname only, he was a smooth skater and tireless backchecker.
250	195	*	195	*	30	20	*	20	*	One of the finest team players and clutch scorers in hockey's early years.
40	42	*	42	*	4	3	*	3	0	He played only 2 seasons, establishing himself as an accurate sharpshooter.
582	86	116	202	601	53	4	7	11	54	Though not a prolific scorer, Hap was the consummate team player.
1549	456	825	1281	383	121	35	69	104	29	A pure gentleman on and off the ice, Alex won the Lady Byng three times.
368	281	69	358	210	43	19	3	22	39	"The Cornwall Colt" was renowned for his crafty, pinpoint shooting.
311	155	139	294	56	50	26	15	41	10	The last Maple Leaf to capture the Art Ross Trophy as NHL scoring leader.
37	30	*	30	*	4	2	*	2	*	An outstanding all-round athlete, his team won 4 consecutive Stanley Cups.
291	228	61	289	503	10	6	1	7	3	He scored more goals than any player in the history of PCHA.
572	71	92	163	1181	27	2	1	3	46	An accomplished player, coach, manager and executive in his lengthy career.
270	202	41	243	190	15	9	2	11	18	Led the league in goals 3 times, twice capturing the Art Ross Trophy.
1282	717	873	1590	910	130	61	76	137	137	Espo led the NHL in goals 6 consecutive seasons, winning 5 scoring titles.
26	29	*	29	*	8	132	*	13	*	Authored what is believed to be the first book on hockey in 1900.
359	242	68	310	170	47	39	7	46	31	He played on three different Cup-winning teams in a 16-year career.

Page	Last Name	First Name	Born	Died	Clubs
24	Frederickson	Frank	June 11, 1895	May 28, 1979	Vic. (PCHA/WCHL/WHL) 1921-26, Det. 1926-27, Bos. 1927-28, Pitt. 1928-30, Det. 1930-31
100	Gadsby	Bill	Aug. 8, 1927		Chi. 1946-55, NYR 1955-61, Det. 1961-66
25	Gardiner	Herb	May 8, 1891	Jan. 11, 1972	Cgy. (WCHL) 1921-26, Mtl. 1926-28, Chi. 1928-29, Mtl. 1928-29
25	Gardner	Jimmy	May 21, 1881	Nov. 7, 1940	Mtl. (CAHL) 1901-03, Wanderers (FAHL/ECHA/NHA) 1904, 1909-11, Calumet (IHL) 1905-06*, Pitt. (IHL) 1907*, Shamrocks (ECAHA) 1908, New West. (PCHA) 1911-13, Mtl. (NHA) 1914-15
101	Geoffrion	Bernie	Feb. 14, 1931		Mtl. 1950-64, NYR 1966-68
25	Gerard	Eddie	Feb. 22, 1890	Dec. 8, 1937	Ott. Vics (FAHL) 1908, Ott. (NHA) 1914-23, Tor. 1922
134	Gilbert	Rod	July 1, 1941		New York Rangers 1960-78
26	Gilmour	Billy	Mar. 21, 1885	Mar. 13, 1959	Ott. (CAHL/FAHL/ECAHA) 1903-05, 1909, Victorias (ECAHA) 1908, Ott. (NHA) 1916
26	Goheen	Moose	Feb. 9, 1894	Nov. 13, 1979	St. Paul Athletic Club 1914-28*
75	Goodfellow	Ebbie	Apr. 9, 1906	Sept. 10, 1955	Detroit 1929-43
27	Grant	Mike	Jan. 1874	Aug. 19, 1955	Mtl. Victorias (AHA/CAHL) 1894-1900, Shamrocks (CAHL) 1901, Victorias (CAHL) 1902
27	Green	Wilfred	July 17, 1896	Apr. 19, 1960	Hamilton 1923-25, NYA 1925-27
28	Griffis	Si	Sept. 22, 1883	July 9, 1950	Rat Portage (MNSHL) 1903-05, Kenora (MSHL) 1907, Van. (PCHA) 1912-19
29	Hall	Joe	May 3, 1882	Apr. 5, 1919	Wpg. (MSHL) 1904, Que. (ECAHA/NHA) 1906, 1911-17, Brandon (MHL) 1907, Mtl. (ECAHA) 1908, Wanderers (ECHA) 1909, Shamrocks (ECHA) 1908-09, Mtl. 1918-19
103	Harvey	Doug	Dec. 19, 1924		Mtl. 1947-61, NYR 1961-64, Det. 1966-67, St.L. 1967-68
75	Hay	George	Jan. 10, 1898	July 14, 1975	Wpg. (MHL) 1915-16, Regina (MHL) 1917-18, Regina (WCHL) 1921-25, Portland (WHL) 1925-26, Chi. 1926-27, Det. 1927-34
77	Hextall	Bryan	July 31, 1913	July 24, 1984	New York Rangers 1936-48
32	Hooper	Tom	Nov. 24, 1883	Mar. 23, 1960	Rat Portage (MNSHL) 1905, Kenora (MSHL) 1907, Wanderers (ECAHA) 1908, Mtl. (ECAHA) 1908
77	Horner	Red	May 28, 1909		Toronto 1928-40
103	Horton	Tim	Jan. 12, 1930	Feb. 21, 1974	Tor. 1949-70, NYR 1970-71, Pitt. 1971-72, Buf. 1972-74
104	Howe	Gordie	Mar. 31, 1928		Det. 1946-70, Hous. (WHA) 1973-77, New Eng. (WHA) 1977-79, Hart. 1979-80
78	Howe	Syd	Sept. 28, 1911	May 20, 1976	Ott. 1929-30, 1932-34, Phi. 1930-31, Tor. 1931-32, St.L. 1934-35, Det. 1935-46
105	Howell	Harry	Dec. 28, 1932		NYR 1952-69, Oak.-Cal. 1969-71, L.A. 1971-73, NY-NJ (WHA) 1973-74, San Diego (WHA) 1974-75, Cgy. (WHA) 1975-76
106	Hull	Bobby	Jan. 3, 1939		Chi. 1957-72, Wpg. (WHA) 1972-79, Wpg. 1979-80, Hart. 1979-80
33	Hyland	Harry	Jan. 2, 1889	Aug. 8, 1969	Shamrocks (ECHA) 1909, Wanderers (NHA) 1910-11, 1913-18, New West. (PCHA) 1912, Ott. 1918
33	Irvin	Dick	July 19, 1892	May 16, 1957	Portland (PCHA) 1916-17, 1925-26, Regina (WCHL) 1921-25, Chi. 1926-29
78	Jackson	Busher	Jan. 19, 1911	June 25, 1966	Tor. 1929-39, NYA 1939-41, Bos. 1941-44
79	Johnson	Ching	Dec. 7, 1897	June 16, 1969	NYR 1926-37, NYA 1937-38
34	Johnson	Ernie	Feb. 26, 1886	Mar. 25, 1963	Mtl. (CAHL) 1904-05, Wanderers (ECAHA/ECHA/NHA) 1906-11, New West, (PCHA) 1911-14, Portland (PCHA) 1914-18, Vic. (PCHA) 1918-22
109	Johnson	Tom	Feb. 18, 1928		Mtl. 1947-63, Bos. 1963-64
79	Joliat	Aurel	Aug. 29, 1901	June 2, 1986	Montreal Canadiens 1922-38
34	Keats	Duke	Mar. 1, 1895	Jan. 16, 1971	Tor. (NHA) 1916-17, Edm. (WCHL-WHL) 1921-26, Det. 1926-27, Chi. 1927-29
109	Kelly	Red	July 9, 1927		Det. 1947-60, Tor. 1960-67
110	Kennedy	Ted	Dec. 12, 1925		Toronto 1942-57
111	Keon	Dave	Mar. 22, 1940		Tor. 1960-75, Minn. (WHA) 1975-76, 1976-77, Ind. (WHA) 1975-76, New Eng. (WHA) 1977-79, Hart. 1979-82
111	Lach	Elmer	Jan. 22, 1918		Montreal Canadiens 1940-54
137	Lafleur	Guy	Sept. 20, 1951		Montreal 1972-85
35	Lalonde	Newsy	Oct. 31, 1887	Nov. 21, 1970	Cornwall (FAHL) 1905, Portage (MHL) 1908, Tor. (OPHL) 1908-09, Mtl. (NHA) 1910, 1913-17, Renfrew (NHA) 1910, Van. (PCHA) 1912, Mtl. 1917-22, Sask. (WCHL) 1923-26, NYA 1926
111	Laperriere	Jacques	Nov. 22, 1941		Montreal Canadiens 1962-74
37	Laviolette	Jack	July 27, 1879	Jan. 10, 1960	Nationals (FAHL) 1904, Shamrocks (ECAHA/ECHA) 1908-09, Mtl. (NHA) 1910-17, Mtl. 1918
137	Lemaire	Jacques	Sept. 7, 1945		Montreal Canadiens 1967-79
112	Lindsay	Ted	July 29, 1925		Det. 1944-57, 1964-65, Chi. 1957-60
38	MacKay	Mickey	May 21, 1894	May 21, 1940	Van. (PCHA/WCHL/WHL) 1914-26, Chi. 1926-28, Pitt. 1928-29, Bos. 1929-30
114	Mahovlich	Frank	Jan. 10, 1938		Tor. 1956-68, Det. 1968-71, Mtl. 1971-74, Tor. (WHA) 1974-76, Birmingham (WHA) 1976-78
38	Malone	Joe	Feb. 28, 1890	May 15, 1969	Que. (ECHA) 1909, Waterloo (OPHL) 1910, Que. (NHA) 1911-17, Mtl. 1917-19, 1923-24, Que. 1920, Hamilton 1921-22

REGULAR SEASON					PLAYOFFS					
GP	G	A	Pts.	PIM	GP	G	A	Pts.	PIM	
328	170	96	266	418	28	12	11	23	54	Joined Victoria after helping Winnipeg Falcons win Olympic Gold in 1920.
1248	130	437	567	1539	67	4	23	27	92	Always a blue-line stalwart, he never sipped from the Silver Cup.
231	43	27	70	99	18	3	2	5	14	Despite not arriving in the NHL until the age of 35, he was MVP in 1926-27.
110	63	4	67	71	9	2	0	2	0	After shifting franchises much of his career, he became a referee in 1917.
863	393	429	822	689	132	58	60	118	88	"Boom-Boom" was the 2nd player in NHL history to score 50 goals in a season.
201	93	30	123	106	35	9	1	10	52	Gerard played professional football in Ottawa before joing the Senators.
1065	406	615	1021	508	79	34	33	67	43	Gilbert overcame two serious back injuries to play 18 seasons in New York.
32	26	*	26	0	9	7	0	7	*	One of the famous Gilmour Brothers, Billy played on four Cup-winning sides.
*	*	*	*	*	*	*	*	*	*	He was nicknamed "Moose" for his ability to play through injuries.
554	134	190	324	516	45	8	8	16	65	This 3-time all-star helped the Wings win 2 Stanley Cups in the 1930s.
55	10	*	10	*	8	0	*	0	*	Known for his end-to-end rushes with the Victorias.
107	33	8	41	151	*	*	*	*	*	"Shorty" came up big helping the Hamilton Tigers win the Allan Cup in 1919.
115	39	26	65	147	18	6	1	7	9	Blueline partner of Art Ross in the east and Frank Patrick in the west.
198	105	*	105	*	22	9	*	9	*	It was Hall's death that led to the cancellation of the 1919 Cup Series.
1113	88	452	540	1216	137	8	64	72	152	Virtually owned the Norris Trophy in his career, winning the honour 7 times.
372	178	108	286	123	13	4	4	8	14	Hay made up for a lack of size with uncanny stick-handling ability.
447	188	175	363	221	37	8	9	17	19	Led the NHL in goals twice and played on the last Ranger Cup winners.
11	12	*	12	*	10	6	*	6	*	A steady playoff performer, he was on two Stanley-Cup-winning teams.
490	42	110	152	1264	71	7	10	17	166	One tough blueliner, he led the NHL in penalties 8 consecutive seasons.
1446	115	403	518	1611	126	11	39	50	83	A classic stay-at-home defenseman, he played an amazing 24 seasons.
2186	975	1383	2358	2084	235	96	135	231	335	"Mr. Hockey" holds NHL marks for goals, points and games played.
691	237	291	528	214	70	17	27	44	10	He anchored the offense that brought three Stanley Cups to Detroit.
1581	101	360	461	1356	45	4	3	7	44	A 24-year veteran, he captured the Norris Trophy in 1967.
1474	913	895	1808	823	176	105	104	209	140	The Golden Jet scored 50 or more goals nine times in his NHL-WHA career.
157	199	*	199	44	3	3	*	3	*	Small in stature, big in talent, he once scored 8 goals in a single game.
250	153	62	215	229	8	4	0	4	8	Best remembered as a coach, he once led both the PCHA and NHL in goals.
636	241	234	475	437	71	18	12	30	53	Member of the famous "Kid Line", he won the Art Ross Trophy in 1931-32.
435	38	48	86	808	60	5	2	7	161	"Ching" was known to rattle a few bones as a hard-hitting blueliner.
270	123	37	160	255	21	20	0	20	9	"Moose" earned his name for playing through even the most severe injuries.
978	51	213	264	960	111	8	15	23	109	Tom teamed with Doug Harvey to solidify the Habs' defense and win 6 Cups.
654	270	190	460	757	54	14	19	33	89	One of the most colorful characters to ever wear the rouge, blanc et bleu.
254	184	86	270	470	6	2	3	5	13	"Duke" scored eight goals in a single game in 1922.
1316	281	542	823	327	164	33	59	92	51	One of only three players to win at least 2 Cups with two different teams.
696	231	329	560	432	78	29	31	60	32	The soul of the Leafs, "Teeder" led them to 5 Stanley Cup wins.
1597	498	779	1277	137	128	45	59	104	14	One of the classiest gentlemen to skate in the NHL and WHA.
664	215	408	623	478	76	19	45	64	36	Twice a recipient of the Art Ross Trophy, he carted home the Hart in 1945.
961	518	728	1246	381	124	57	76	133	67	Speed and style characterized the "Flower's" 14-year career.
334	446	50	496	301	41	49	1	50	25	Regarded as the dominant player of hockey's first quarter century.
691	40	242	282	674	88	9	22	31	101	Jacques led a Habs defense that carried 5 Cups back to Montreal.
178	58	*	58	*	14	1	*	1	*	He gave the "Flying Frenchmen" their flight with his spectacular rushes.
853	366	469	835	217	145	61	78	139	63	He won eight Stanley Cup rings in his 11-year career.
1068	379	472	851	1808	133	47	49	96	194	Lindsay gave the "Production Line" its muscle with his hard-nosed play.
399	242	111	353	313	49	18	11	29	53	A polished stickhandler and playmaker, known for his gentlemanly play.
1418	622	713	1335	1131	146	55	68	123	165	"Big M" used his graceful stride and booming shot to be a 9-time all-star.
271	342	18	360	35	15	23	1	24	0	Earned the handle "Phantom Joe" because of his slick and polished style.

Page	Last Name	First Name	Born	Died	Clubs
81	**Mantha**	**Sylvio**	Apr. 14, 1902	Aug. 7, 1974	Mtl. 1923-36, Bos. 1936-37
39	**Marshall**	**Jack**	Mar. 14, 1877	Aug. 7, 1965	Wpg. (MNSHL) 1901, Mtl. (CAHL) 1902-03, Wanderers (FAHL/NHA) 1904-05, 1910-12, 1916-17, Shamrocks (ECAHA) 1908-09, Tor. (NHA) 1913-15
39	**Maxwell**	**Fred**	May 9, 1890	Sept. 11, 1975	Wpg. Monarchs (MSHL) 1914-16*, Wpg. Falcons (MSHL) 1918-25*
39	**McGee**	**Frank**	1890	Sept. 16, 1916	Ott. (CAHL/FAHL/ECAHA) 1903-06
40	**McGimsie**	**Billy**	June 7, 1880	Oct. 28, 1968	Rat Portage (MNSHL/MSHL) 1903-05, Kenora (MSHL) 1907
40	**McNamara**	**George**	Aug. 26, 1886	Mar. 10, 1952	Shamrocks (ECHA/NHA) 1908-09, 1915, Waterloo (OPHL) 1911, Tecumsehs (NHA) 1913, Ontarios (NHA) 1914, Tor. Blueshirts (NHA) 1914, 1916, 228th Bttn. (NHA) 1917
115	**Mikita**	**Stan**	May 20, 1940		Chicago 1958-80
116	**Moore**	**Dickie**	Jan. 6, 1931		Mtl. 1951-63, Tor. 1964-65, St.L. 1967-68
81	**Morenz**	**Howie**	June 21, 1902	Mar. 8, 1937	Mtl. 1923-34, 1936-37, Chi. 1934-35, NYR 1935-36
117	**Mosienko**	**Bill**	Nov. 2, 1921		Chicago 1941-55
41	**Nighbor**	**Frank**	Jan. 26, 1893	Apr. 13, 1966	Tor. (NHA) 1913, Van. (PCHA) 1913-15, Ott. (NHA) 1915-17, Ott. 1917-29, Tor. 1929-30
42	**Noble**	**Reg**	June 23, 1895	Jan. 19, 1962	Tor. (NHA) 1916-17, Mtl. (NHA) 1916-17, Tor. 1917-25, Maroons 1925-27, 1932-33, Det. 1927-33
82	**O'Connor**	**Buddy**	June 21, 1916	Aug. 24, 1977	Mtl. 1941-47, NYR 1948-51
82	**Oliver**	**Harry**	Oct. 26, 1898	June 16, 1985	Cgy. (WCHL/WHL) 1922-26, Bos. 1926-34, NYA 1934-37
118	**Olmstead**	**Bert**	Sept. 4, 1926		Chi. 1948-51, Mtl. 1951-58, Tor. 1958-62
139	**Orr**	**Bobby**	Mar. 20, 1948		Bos. 1966-76, Chi. 1976-79
140	**Park**	**Brad**	July 6, 1948		NYR 1969-75, Bos. 1975-83, Det. 1984-85
44	**Patrick**	**Lester**	Dec. 30, 1883	June 1, 1960	Brandon 1904, Westmount (CAHL) 1905, Wanderers (ECAHA) 1906-07, Edm. (AAHA) 1908, Renfew (NHA) 1910, Vic. (PCHA) 1912-15, 1919-26, Spokane (PCHA) 1917, Seattle (PCHA) 1918, NYR 1926
82	**Patrick**	**Lynn**	Feb. 3, 1912	Jan. 26, 1980	New York Rangers 1934-46
45	**Phillips**	**Tom**	May 22, 1883	Nov. 30, 1923	Mtl. (CAHL) 1903, Tor. (OHA) 1904, Rat Portage (MHL) 1905, Kenora (MHL) 1907, Ott. (ECAHA) 1908, Edm. (AAHA) 1909, Van. (PCHA) 1912
119	**Pilote**	**Pierre**	Dec. 11, 1931		Chi. 1955-68, Tor. 1968-69
45	**Pitre**	**Didier**	Sept. 1, 1883	July 29, 1934	Nationals (FAHL) 1904-05, Shamrocks (ECAHA) 1908, Edm. (AAHA) 1908, Mtl. (NHA) 1910-13, 1915-17, Van. (PCHA) 1914, Mtl. 1917-23
83	**Pratt**	**Babe**	Jan. 7, 1916		NYR 1935-42, Tor. 1942-46, Bos. 1946-47
84	**Primeau**	**Joe**	Jan. 29, 1906		Toronto 1927-36
121	**Pronovost**	**Marcel**	June 15, 1930		Det. 1950-65, Tor. 1965-70
46	**Pulford**	**Harvey**	1875	Oct. 31, 1940	Ott. (AHA/CAHL/FAHL/ECAHA) 1894-1908
121	**Quackenbush**	**Bill**	Mar. 2, 1922		Det. 1942-49, Bos. 1949-56
46	**Rankin**	**Frank**	Apr. 1, 1889	July 23, 1932	Stratford (OHA) 1906-09*, Eatons (EAA) 1910-12*, St. Michaels (OHA) 1912-14*
141	**Ratelle**	**Jean**	Oct. 3, 1940		NYR 1960-76, Bos. 1976-81
123	**Reardon**	**Ken**	Apr. 1, 1921		Montreal 1941-50
123	**Richard**	**Henri**	Feb. 29, 1936		Montreal 1955-75
123	**Richard**	**Maurice**	Aug. 4, 1921		Montreal 1942-60
47	**Richardson**	**George**	1887	Feb. 9, 1916	14th Regiment 1906-12*, Queen's Univ. 1908-09*
47	**Roberts**	**Gordie**	Sept. 5, 1891	Sept 2, 1966	Ott. (NHA) 1910, Wanderers (NHA) 1911-16, Van. (PCHA) 1916-17, 1919-20, Seattle (PCHA) 1917-18
49	**Ross**	**Art**	Jan 13, 1886	Aug. 5, 1964	Westmount (CAHL) 1905, Brandon (WHL) 1907, Kenora (MHL) 1907, Wanderers (ECAHA/ECHA/NHA) 1908-09, 1910-14, 1917-18, Haileybury (NHA) 1909-10, Ott. (NHA) 1914-17, Wanderers 1918-19
50	**Russell**	**Blair**	Sept. 17, 1880	Dec. 7, 1961	Victorias (CAHL/ECAHA) 1900-08
50	**Russell**	**Ernie**	Oct. 21, 1883	Feb. 23, 1963	Mtl. (CAHL) 1905, Wanderers (ECAHA/NHA) 1906-1908, 1910-14
50	**Ruttan**	**Jack**	Apr. 5, 1889	Jan 7, 1973	Armstrong's Pt. 1905-06*, Rustler 1906-07*, St. Johns College 1907-08*, Man. Varsity (WSHL) 1909-12*, Wpg. (WpgHL) 1912-13
141	**Savard**	**Serge**	Jan. 22, 1946		Mtl. 1966-81, Wpg. 1981-83
51	**Scanlan**	**Fred**	......	......	Shamrocks (AHA/CAHL) 1898-1901, Wpg. (MSHL) 1902-03
85	**Schmidt**	**Milt**	Mar. 5, 1918		Boston 1936-55
85	**Schriner**	**Sweeney**	Nov. 30, 1911		NYA 1934-39, Tor. 1939-46
86	**Seibert**	**Earl**	Dec. 7, 1911		NYR 1931-36, Chi. 1936-44, Det. 1944-46
52	**Seibert**	**Oliver**	Mar. 18, 1881	May 15, 1944	Berlin (WOHA) 1900-06*, Houghton (IHL)*, Guelph (OPL)*, London (OPL)*
86	**Shore**	**Eddie**	Nov. 25, 1902	Mar. 16, 1985	Regina (WCHL) 1924-25, Edm. (WHL) 1925-26, Bos. 1926-39, NYA 1939-40
87	**Siebert**	**Babe**	Jan. 14, 1904	Aug. 25, 1939	Maroons 1925-32, NYR 1932-34, Bos. 1934-36, Mtl. 1936-39
51	**Simpson**	**Joe**	Aug. 13, 1898	Dec. 26, 1973	Wpg. Victorias (MSHL) 1914-15*, 61st. Battalion (MSHL) 1915-16*, Selkirk 1919-20*, Edm. (WCHL) 1921-25, NYA 1925-31
54	**Smith**	**Alf**	June 3, 1873	Aug. 21, 1953	Ott. (AHA/CAHL/FAHL/ECAHA) 1895-1970, 1908, Kenora (MHL) 1907, Ott. Cliffsides 1909
87	**Smith**	**Hooley**	Jan. 7, 1903	Aug. 24, 1963	Tor. Granites (THL) 1920-24*, Ott. 1924-27, Maroons 1927-36, Bos. 1936-37, NYA 1937-41

	REGULAR SEASON					PLAYOFFS				
GP	G	A	Pts.	PIM	GP	G	A	Pts.	PIM	
542	63	72	142	667	46	5	4	9	70	Rugged, rough and ready are adept terms to describe this fierce competitor.
132	99	*	99	*	18	13	*	13	0	Won his first Cup as part of the "Little Men of Iron" Montreal team.
*	*	*	*	*	*	*	*	*	*	Despite many attempts, pro hockey couldn't steal "Steamer" from Manitoba.
23	71	*	71	*	22	63	*	63	0	He averaged 3 goals per game in regular and playoff games in his career.
0	0	*	0*		7	4	*	4	*	An Ontario native, he put Manitoba and Kenora onto the Stanley Cup map.
121	39	*	39	0	3	2	*	2	*	Teaming with brother Harold, "The Dynamite Twins" were defensive marvels.
1394	541	926	1467	1270	155	59	91	150	169	"Stosh" turned the other cheek to capture 2 Lady Byng awards in the 1960s.
719	261	347	608	652	135	46	64	110	122	This 2-time Art Ross winner was a part of 7 Cup-winners.
550	270	197	467	531	47	21	11	32	68	The outstanding hockey player of the half century.
711	258	282	540	121	22	10	4	14	15	He hit the post or he would have scored four in less than a minute.
438	253	74	327	284	41	16	16	32	33	"Dutch" scored an astonishing 41 goals in 19 games in 1916-17.
534	180	79	259	670	32	2	3	5	37	A Jack-of-all-trades, Reg accepted all challenges with carefree abandon.
509	140	257	397	34	53	15	21	36	6	Canada's athlete of the year in 1948.
603	217	133	350	215	44	12	8	20	26	Harry was known as "Pee-Wee", but his statistics are anything but small.
848	181	421	602	884	115	16	42	58	101	A nifty passer, he twice led the league in assists.
657	270	645	915	953	74	26	66	92	107	Orr won an incredible 16 individual trophies in his short 12-year career.
1113	213	683	896	1429	161	35	90	125	217	A 7-time all-star, Park graced the blueline for 17 seasons.
214	131	63	194	129	6	2	0	2	2	We owe a debt of gratitude to "The Silver Fox", modern hockey's architect.
455	145	190	335	270	44	10	6	16	22	A member of hockey's "Royal Family", Lynn twice led the Rangers in scoring.
33	57	*	57	*	16	27	*	27	*	Played in six Cup series with six different teams. Was on one winner.
890	80	418	498	1251	86	8	53	61	102	Pilote won three consecutive Norris Trophies from 1962 to 1965.
283	239	19	258	71	27	13	2	15	13	"Cannonball" was considered one of the original "Flying Frenchmen".
517	83	209	292	453	63	12	17	29	90	In a 26-year Jr.-to-pro career, Babe played on a total of 15 championship teams.
310	66	177	243	111	38	5	18	23	12	"Gentleman Joe" co-ordinated the "Kid Line" with his smooth passing.
1206	88	257	345	5	134	8	23	31	104	He solidified the blueline for 5 Stanley Cup winning teams.
96	6	*	6	*	22	2	*	2	*	He parlayed his rugby talents to become hockey's first solid body-checker.
774	62	222	284	95	80	2	19	21	12	Won the Lady Byng in 1949 going the entire season without a penalty.
*	*	*	*	*	*	*	*	*	*	Rankin rejected numerous pro offers to remain an amateur.
1281	491	776	1267	276	123	32	66	98	24	Ratelle scored 20 or more goals in 14 consecutive seasons.
341	26	96	122	604	31	2	5	7	62	Reardon displayed a carefree bravado on the ice that became his trademark.
1256	358	688	1046	928	180	49	80	129	181	The "Pocket Rocket" won an amazing 11 Stanley Cup rings in his career.
978	544	421	965	1285	133	82	44	126	188	No superlatives can describe the fierce competitive spirit of the "Rocket".
*	*	*	*	*	*	*	*	*	*	A noted amateur, he led Queen's to the CAHA Allan Cup in 1909.
167	204	16	220	79	8	8	*	8	3	He set the all-time PCHA scoring mark when he netted 43 goals in 23 games.
167	85	*	85	12	16	6	*	6	0	A strong skater and checker, Ross played in 6 Cup series, winning twice.
67	110	*	110	*	2	0	*	0	*	A career amateur, he retired from hockey to avoid turning professional.
98	180	*	180*		11	31	*	31	0	An early sharpshooter, he scored 42 goals in only 9 games in 1907.
*	*	*	*	*	*	*	*	*	0	As an amateur, his teams won 6 championships, including the 1913 Allan Cup.
1040	106	333	439	592	130	19	49	68	88	The "Senator" held office with the Stanley Cup 7 times in his 14-year term.
31	16	*	16	*	17	6	*	6	*	Linemate of Trihey and Farrell, he helped Montreal capture the Cup.
6	229	346	575	466	86	24	25	49	60	Center for the "Kraut Line", the Bruins honored him by retiring his #15.
484	206	204	410	148	60	18	11	29	54	An outstanding winger, he snagged both the Art Ross and Calder trophies.
655	89	187	276	768	66	11	8	19	66	A rock-solid defender, he was named to 10 consecutive all-star squads.
*	*	*	*	*	*	*	*	*	0	A noted speed demon, it was said he skated as fast backwards as forwards.
607	123	181	304	1208	57	6	13	19	193	He is the only defenseman to capture the MVP Hart Trophy four times.
583	140	156	296	1002	52	8	7	15	64	A steady winger, he switched to defense and won the Hart Trophy in 1937.
340	78	61	139	199	6	0	1	1	0	"Bullet Joe" used speed and finesse to be a steady defender for 16 seasons.
65	90	*	90	*	22	36	0	36	*	A bruising forward with a love for rough play, he helped Ottawa win 2 Cups.
719	200	215	415	993	54	11	8	19	101	Right-winger best remembered for his use of the sweep check.

Page	Last Name	First Name	Born	Died	Clubs
53	**Smith**	**Tommy**	Sept. 27, 1885	Aug. 1, 1966	Ott. Vics (FAHL) 1906, Ott. (ECAHA) 1906, Brantford (OPHL) 1909-10, Cobalt (NHA) 1910, Galt (OPHL) 1911, Moncton (MPHL) 1912, Que. NHA) 1913-15, 1916, Onts. (NHA) 1915, Mtl. (NHA) 1916-17, Que. 1919-20
125	**Stanley**	**Allan**	Mar 1, 1926		NYR 1948-55, Chi. 1955-56, Bos. 1956-58, Tor. 1958-68, Phi. 1968-69
55	**Stanley**	**Barney**	June 1, 1893	May 16, 1971	Van. (PCHA) 1914-19, Cgy. (WCHL) 1921-22, Regina (WCHL) 1922-24, Edm. (WCHL/WHL) 1924-26, Chi. 1927-28
125	**Stewart**	**Jack**	May 6, 1917	May 25, 1983	Det. 1938-50, Chi. 1950-52
88	**Stewart**	**Nels**	Dec. 29, 1900	Aug. 3, 1957	Maroons 1925-32, Bos. 1932-35, 1936-37, NYA 1935-36, NYA 1937-40
55	**Stuart**	**Bruce**	1882	Nov. 28, 1961	Ott. (CAHL/ECHA/NHA) 1899-1902, 1909-11, Pitt. (IHL) 1901-02, Houghton (IHL) 1902-03*, Portage Lake (IHL) 1903-06*, Wanderers (ECAHA) 1907-08
55	**Stuart**	**Hod**	1879	June 23, 1907	Ott. (CAHL) 1899-1901, Que. (CAHL) 1901-03, Calumet (IHL) 1903-05*, Pitt. (IHL) 1906*, Wanderers (ECAHA) 1906-07
57	**Taylor**	**Cyclone**	June 23, 1883	June 9, 1979	Ott. (ECAHA/ECHA) 1908-09, Renfrew (NHA) 1910-11, Van. (PCHA) 1912-21, 1922-23
57	**Trihey**	**Harry**	Dec. 25, 1877	Dec. 9, 1942	Shramrocks (AHA/CAHL) 1897-1901
126	**Ullman**	**Norm**	Dec. 26, 1935		Det. 1955-68, Tor. 1968-75, Edm. (WHA) 1975-77
58	**Walker**	**Jack**	Nov. 29, 1888	Feb. 16, 1950	Pt. Arthur 1911, Tor. (NHA) 1913-15, Seattle (PCHA) 1915-24, Vic. (WCHL/WHL) 1924-26, Det. 1926-28
60	**Walsh**	**Marty**	Oct. 16, 1884	Mar. 27, 1915	Queens U. (OHA) 1906, Ott. (ECAHA/ECHA/NHA) 1908-12
58	**Watson**	**Harry**	July 14, 1898	Sept. 11, 1957	St. Andrews (OHA) 1915*, Aura Lee Jrs. (OHA) 1918*, Tor. Dentals (OHA) 1919*, Tor. Granites (OHL) 1920-25*, Tor. Sea Fleas (OHA) 1931*
59	**Weiland**	**Cooney**	Nov. 5, 1904	July 1985	Bos. 1928-32, Ott. 1932-33, Det. 1933-35, Bos. 1935-39
60	**Westwick**	**Harry**	Apr. 23, 1876	Apr. 3, 1957	Ott. (AHA/CAHL/FAHL/ECAHA) 1895-1908, Kenora (MHL) 1907
59	**Whitcroft**	**Fred**	1883	1931	Peterboro (OHA) 1901-04, 1906*, Midland (OHA) 1905*, Kenora (MSHL) 1907, Edm. (ASHL) 1908, 1910*, Renfrew (NHA) 1910
59	**Wilson**	**Gordon**	Dec. 29, 1895	July 26, 1970	Pt. Arthur (OHA) 1918-20*, 1923-33*, Iroquois Falls (NOHA) 1921*

GOALTENDERS

Page	Last Name	First Name	Born	Died	Clubs
15	**Benedict**	**Clint**	Sept. 26, 1894	Nov. 12, 1976	Ott. (NHA) 1912-17, Ott. 1917-24, Maroons 1924-30
96	**Bower**	**Johnny**	Nov. 8, 1924		NYR 1953-55, 1956-57, Tor. 1958-70
67	**Brimsek**	**Frankie**	Sept. 26, 1915		Bos. 1938-49, Chi. 1949-50
96	**Broda**	**Turk**	May 15, 1914	Oct. 17, 1972	Toronto 1936-52
129	**Cheevers**	**Gerry**	Dec. 7, 1940		Tor. 1961-62, Bos. 1965-72, 1976-80, Clev. (WHA) 1972-76
70	**Connell**	**Alex**	Feb. 8, 1900	May 10, 1958	Ott. 1924-31, 1932-33, Det. 1931-32, NYA 1933-34, Maroons 1934-37
131	**Dryden**	**Ken**	Aug. 8, 1947		Montreal 1970-73, 1974-79
99	**Durnan**	**Bill**	Jan. 22, 1915	Oct. 31, 1972	Montreal 1943-50
132	**Esposito**	**Tony**	April 23, 1943		Mtl. 1969, Chi. 1970- 84
74	**Gardiner**	**Chuck**	Dec. 31, 1904	June 13, 1934	Chicago 1927-34
135	**Giacomin**	**Ed**	June 6, 1939		NYR 1965-75, Det. 1976-78
75	**Hainsworth**	**George**	June 26, 1895	Oct. 9, 1950	Sask. (WCHL/WHL) 1923-26, Mtl. 1926-33, 1936-37, Tor. 1933-36
102	**Hall**	**Glenn**	Oct. 3, 1931		Det. 1952-57, Chi. 1957-67, St.L. 1967-71
30	**Hern**	**Riley**	Dec. 5, 1880	June 24, 1929	Stratford (OHA) 1900-01*, London (OHA) 1903-04*, Port. Lake (IHL) 1904-06*, Wanderers (ECAHA/ECHA/NHA) 1907-11
31	**Holmes**	**Harry**	Nov. 24, 1883	1940	Tor. Blueshirts (NHA) 1912-16, Seattle (PCHA) 1916-24, Vic. (WCHL/WHL) 1924-26, Tor. Arenas 1917-19, Det. 1926-28
33	**Hutton**	**J.B.**	Oct. 24, 1877	Oct. 27, 1962	Ottawa (CAHL) 1899-1904
36	**Lehman**	**Hugh**	Oct. 27, 1885	Apr. 8, 1961	Berlin (OPHL) 1909-11, Galt (OPHL) 1910, New West. (PCHA) 1911-14, Van. (PCHA/WCHL/WHL) 1914-26, Chi. 1926-28
37	**LeSueur**	**Percy**	Nov. 18, 1881	Jan. 27, 1962	Smiths Falls (FAHL) 1906, Ott. (ECAHA/ECHA/NHA) 1906-14, Shamrocks (NHA) 1915, Tor. (NHA) 1916
114	**Lumley**	**Harry**	Nov. 11, 1926		Det. 1943, 1944-50, NYR 1944, Chi. 1950-52, Tor. 1952-56, Bos. 1957-60
41	**Moran**	**Paddy**	Mar. 11, 1877	Jan. 14, 1966	Que. (CAHL/ECAHA/ECHA/NHA) 1902-09, 1911-17, Haileybury (NHA) 1910
139	**Parent**	**Bernie**	Apr. 3, 1945		Bos. 1965-67, Phi. 1967-71, 1973-79, Tor. 1971-72, Phi. (WHA) 1972-73
120	**Plante**	**Jacques**	Jan. 17, 1929	Feb. 27, 1986	Mtl. 1952-63, NYR 1963-65, St.L. 1968-70, Tor. 1970-73, Bos. 1973, Edm. (WHA) 1974-75
122	**Rayner**	**Chuck**	Aug. 11, 1920		NYA 1940-42, NYR 1945-53
124	**Sawchuk**	**Terry**	Dec. 28, 1929	May 31, 1970	Det. 1949-55, 1957-64, 1968-69, Bos. 1955-57, Tor. 1964-67, L.A. 1967-68, NYR 1979-70
89	**Thompson**	**Tiny**	May 31, 1905	Feb. 9, 1981	Bos. 1928-39, Det. 1939-40
57	**Vezina**	**George**	Jan. 1887	Mar. 24, 1926	Mtl. (NHA) 1911-17, Mtl. 1917-26
126	**Worsley**	**Gump**	May 14, 1929		NYR 1952-53, 1954-63, Mtl. 1963-70, Minn. 1970-74
90	**Worters**	**Roy**	Oct. 19, 1900	Nov. 7, 1957	Pitt. 1925-27, NYA 1928-29, 1930-37, Mtl. 1929-30

REGULAR SEASON					PLAYOFFS					
GP	G	A	Pts.	PIM	GP	G	A	Pts.	PIM	
159	240	*	240	9	15	15	*	15	*	He twice scored 9 goals in a single game, and scored 5 or more nine times.
1244	100	333	433	792	109	7	36	43	0	Always steady around the net, he quietly helped the Leafs win 4 Cups.
218	143	73	216	183	17	12	0	12	13	A jack-of-all-trades, Barney played every position except goal.
565	31	83	114	757	80	5	14	19	143	"Black Jack" was known for his punishing bodychecks and 5 all-star berths.
654	324	191	515	953	54	15	11	26	65	"Old Poison" was the first man to score more than 300 goals in the NHL.
45	63	*	63	*	7	17	*	17	*	A versatile performer, Stuart was an all-round forward and potent scorer.
33	16	*	16	*	4	0	*	0	*	An early defensive star, Hod led the Wanderers to the Cup in 1907.
180	198	104	312	65	16	17	6	23	18	"Cyclone" was a 6-time all-star who scored 16 hat tricks in his career.
30	46	*	46	*	8	16	*	16	*	He set an early record by netting 10 goals in a single game in 1899.
1554	537	822	1359	752	115	31	59	90	69	he always had the touch around the net, scoring 20 or more goals 17 times.
363	136	81	217	71	46	19	10	29	14	"Hookcheck" made his name with an aggressive but clean playing style.
59	135	*	135	*	8	25	*	25	*	He always had the touch around the net, scoring 20 or more goals 17 times.
*	*	*	*	*	*	*	*	0	*	One of hockey's best amateurs, "Moose" led Canada to Olympic gold in 1924.
509	173	160	333	147	45	12	10	22	12	He established an often overlooked mark with 43 goals in 44 games in 1930.
87	87	*	87	*	24	26	*	26	*	"Rat" was the guiding light of the Silver Seven, shining in 3 Cup victories.
9	5	*	5	*	8	14	*	14	*	Extremely fast and acurate with his shots, Fred scored 49 goals in 1908.
*	*	*	*	*	*	*	*	*	*	"Phat" was a key member of the Port Arthur teams that won 3 Allan Cups.

GP	Mins.	GA	SO	GAPG	GP	Mins.	GA	SO	GAPG	
435	26701	1084	58	2.43	55	3327	121	15	2.18	A 19-year veteran, he was the first goalie to try the mask.
549	32016	1347	37	2.52	74	4350	184	5	2.54	"China Wall" didn't stick in the NHL until he was 35, but stayed till he was 46.
514	31210	1404	40	2.70	68	4365	186	2	2.56	"Mr. Zero" backstopped the Bruins to 2 Cups, winning 2 Vezina Trophies.
629	38167	1609	62	2.56	101	6348	211	13	1.99	The consummate "pressure goalie", Turk played best when the heat was on.
609	35746	1766	40	2.96	107	6547	305	7	2.80	"Cheesey" closed the door for the Bruins in 2 Stanley-Cup-winning performances.
417	26030	830	80	1.91	21	1309	26	4	1.19	"The Fireman" was a clutch goalie, once recording 6 straight shutouts.
397	23352	870	46	2.24	112	6846	274	10	2.40	Ken's name is engraved on 7 individual awards, including 5 Vezinas.
383	22945	9001	34	2.36	45	2851	99	2	2.08	One of the finest, he won the Vezina 6 times in his 7 years.
886	52585	2563	76	2.92	99	6017	308	6	3.07	Tony "0" had 76 shutouts; 6th best in NHL history.
316	19687	664	42	2.02	21	1532	35	5	1.37	He accumulated a remarkable 42 shutouts in his brief 7-year career.
610	35693	1675	54	2.82	65	3834	180	1	2.82	After years in the AHL, Ed thrilled NHL fans for 13 acrobatic years.
553	34797	1149	104	1.98	52	3486	112	8	1.93	He took the NHL by storm, winning the Vezina in each of his first 3 seasons.
906	53464	2239	84	2.51	115	6899	321	6	2.79	"Mr. Goalie" played in every game for 7 consecutive seasons.
60	3600	281	1	4.68	14	840	54	0	3.85	With Riley, the Wanderers won 3 Cups behind his steady goalkeeping.
410	25145	1187	41	2.83	52	3218	128	6	2.38	"Hap" guarded the cage for 7 championship teams, including 4 Cup-winners.
36	2160	106	2	2.94	12	720	28	2	2.33	"Bouse" played a remarkable game of goal despite primitive equipment.
401	24682	1440	20	3.50	48	2899	137	7	2.83	An 11-time all-star, Hughie excelled for 20 professional seasons.
156	718	9360	4	4.60	9	540	40	0	4.44	Perce spent over 50 years connected with hockey in many capacities.
804	48097	2210	71	2.76	76	4759	199	7	2.51	"Apple Cheeks" played for every team except the Habs.
201	12060	1091	2	5.40	7	420	24	1	3.42	A stand-up specialist, Paddy hoisted Quebec to the Stanley Cup twice.
671	38789	1713	57	2.65	72	4372	177	6	2.43	Parent's heroics carried the Flyers to successive Cup victories.
868	51125	2053	83	2.41	112	6651	241	15	2.17	"The Snake" led in goals against a record 8 times, the last in 1971 at age 41.
425	25491	1295	25	3.05	18	1135	46	1	2.43	A 3-time all-star, Chuck grabbed the Hart Trophy as League MVP in 1951.
971	57114	2401	103	2.52	106	6311	267	12	2.54	He holds NHL goaltending marks for games, seasons and shutouts.
553	34174	1183	81	2.08	44	2970	93	7	1.88	"Tiny" in name only, he posted an impressive 81 zeros.
329	19740	1145	15	3.48	39	2340	122	5	3.13	"The Chicoutimi Cucumber" never missed a game in his 15-year career.
862	50232	2432	43	2.90	70	4079	192	5	2.82	One of the last holdouts, Gump didn't wear a mask until his last season.
484	30175	1143	171	2.27	11	690	24	3	2.09	"Shrimp" was the first goalie to win the Hart, adding the Vezina in 1931.

BUILDERS

Page	Last Name	First Name	Born	Died	
62	**Adams**	**Charles**	Oct. 18, 1876	1947	Gave NHL hockey international flavor by establishing the Bruins in 1924.
63	**Adams**	**Weston**	Aug. 9, 1904	Mar. 19, 1973	Took control of a flagging Bruins team, and guided them to Cup success.
63	**Ahearn**	**Frank**	May 10, 1886	Nov. 17, 1962	Ahearn was the guiding force behind Ottawa's NHL success in the 1920s
92	**Ahearne**	**J.F.**	Nov. 19, 1900	Apr. 11, 1985	"Bunny" fostered the growth and prosperity of international hockey.
13	**Allan**	**Montagu**	1860	Sept., 1951	Donated the Allan Cup, symbolic of Senior Hockey supremacy, in 1908.
93	**Ballard**	**Harold**	July 30, 1903		Chief executive of Maple Leaf Gardens and the Leafs.
66	**Bickell**	**J.P.**	Sept. 26, 1884	Aug. 22, 1951	Created the financial foundation that supported Maple Leaf Gardens.
17	**Brown**	**George**	1880	1937	A pioneer of U.S. hockey, Brown helped set the groundwork for the AHL.
68	**Brown**	**Walter**	Feb. 10, 1905	Sept. 7, 1964	Following in his father's footsteps, he boosted school and college hockey.
97	**Buckland**	**Frank**	May 23, 1902		Dedicated amateur hockey coach, manager and executive.
97	**Butterfield**	**Jack**	Aug 1, 1919		Proved his administrative skill as AHL President.
17	**Calder**	**Frank**	Nov. 17, 1877	Feb. 4, 1943	First NHL President, seeing the league through numerous growing pains.
68	**Campbell**	**Angus**	Mar. 19, 1884	1976	Helped establish amateur hockey in Northern Ontario, forming NOHA in 1919.
97	**Campbell**	**Clarence**	July 9, 1905	June 24, 1984	Guided the NHL from its golden years through expansion.
18	**Cattarinich**	**Joseph**	Nov. 13, 1881	Dec. 7, 1938	Played important roles in the development of the NHL and "les Canadiens".
19	**Dandurand**	**Leo**	July 9, 1889	June 26, 1964	A key figure in many sports, best known for rebuilding "Les Canadiens".
99	**Dilio**	**Frank**	Apr. 12, 1912		His insight and care gave birth to amateur hockey in Quebec.
73	**Dudley**	**George**	Apr. 19, 1894	May 8, 1960	Served as President of the CAHA, OHA and IIHF in a 50-year career.
74	**Dunn**	**James**	Mar. 24, 1898	Jan. 1979	Fifty years of service in amateur hockey won Mr. Dunn a place in the Hall.
133	**Francis**	**Emile**	Sept. 13, 1926		"The Cat" helped build the Rangers, Blues and Whalers.
26	**Gibson**	**Jack**	Sept. 10, 1880	Oct. 7, 1955	Organized the first pro league — the International League in 1903-04.
27	**Gorman**	**Tommy**	June 9, 1886	May 15, 1961	Active in many sports, he coached or managed 7 Stanley Cup winners.
103	**Hanley**	**Bill**	Feb. 28, 1915		"Mr. OHA" spent 27 years as a dedicated executive in that organization.
135	**Hay**	**Charles**	1902	Oct. 24, 1973	Prime negotiator of the "Series of the Century", formed Hockey Canada.
77	**Hendy**	**Jim**	May 6, 1905	Jan. 14, 1961	Published the first "Hockey Guide", later became president of the USHL.
76	**Hewitt**	**Foster**	Nov. 21, 1902	Apr. 21, 1985	"The Voice of Hockey" united hockey fans from coast to coast.
31	**Hewitt**	**W.A.**	May 15, 1875	Sept. 8, 1966	A lifetime in hockey as a journalist, manager and executive.
107	**Hume**	**Fred**	May 2, 1892	Feb. 17, 1967	He was a keen hockey observer and a force in the formation of the W
107	**Imlach**	**Punch**	Mar. 15, 1918	Dec. 1, 1987	He brought the Stanley Cup back to Toronto and built the Buffalo Sabres.
108	**Ivan**	**Tommy**	Jan. 31, 1911		Coached 3 Cup winners in Detroit, and went on to rebuild the Blackhawks.
136	**Jennings**	**William**	Dec. 14, 1920	Aug. 17, 1981	An ardent advocator of expansion, he was one of its chief architects.
109	**Juckes**	**Gordon**	June 20, 1914		Recognized for his contributions by the CAHA, IIHF, AHAUS and SAHA.
78	**Kilpatrick**	**John**	June 15, 1889	May 7, 1960	President of MSG for 22 years, he's also a member of NFL Hall of Fame.
79	**Leader**	**Al**	Dec. 4, 1903	May 8, 1982	Spent 25 years of service in the WHL, seeing it from disaster to triumph.
113	**LeBel**	**Robert**	Sept. 21, 1905		Served as president of the ISL, QAHA, CAHA, IIHF and QMJHL.
80	**Lockhart**	**Thomas**	Mar. 21, 1892	May 18, 1979	Spent more than 40 years organizing and promoting US amateur hockey.
80	**Loicq**	**Paul**	1890	1947	International hockey made great strides during his 20 years as IIHF chief.
115	**Mariucci**	**John**	May 8, 1916	Mar. 23, 1987	Devoted his career to developing U.S.-born players.
81	**McLaughlin**	**Frederic**	June 27, 1877	Dec. 17, 1944	Chicago hockey pioneer who named the Blackhawks after his WWI regiment.
138	**Milford**	**Jake**	July 29, 1914	Dec. 24, 1984	After expansion, served as GM of both the Kings and Canucks.
117	**Molson**	**Hartland**	May 29, 1907		His efforts resulted in establishment of the Montreal Forum.
41	**Nelson**	**Francis**	. . . . . .	April 1932	His work enabled the fledgling OHA to survive and prosper.
117	**Norris**	**Bruce**	Feb. 19, 1924	Jan. 1, 1986	Was one of pro sports' youngest owners, taking over the Red Wings at 31